HOW TO
BUILD
STONEHENGE

HOW TO BUILD STONEHENGE

MIKE PITTS

CONTENTS

PREFACE

Stonehenge, simply by its mass, makes us aware of our relative scale and shortness of time. The gesture of removing a rock like the Heelstone from its place of finding, standing it vertical and making a marker in space that then becomes a marker in time and a mean for human individual and collective life, that is the ur-gesture of sculpture. The fact that our ancestors and the early farmers were able to exert these acts of collective imaginative purpose, fills me with joy, admiration and awe, in equal measure.

Sir Antony Gormley

There is, you might think, nothing like it: the simple, graphic genius of three great, arranged blocks. The stones seem to rise from the ground in some antediluvian heave of the Earth: yet an upended pair holds the third high above in joints that look humanly carved. As the day passes the sun casts an elongated frame that ripples across the grass. Beyond the empty, flat space, coconut palms rise above a thicket of hibiscus, frangipani and pandanus. Little clusters of ferns and tropical flowers hang from the megaliths, rooted in their uneven coral hollows.

This trilithon – a word confected from Greek in the 18th century to describe three stones – is in the south Pacific Ocean, on the largest island in the Kingdom of Tonga. Known today as Ha'amonga 'a Maui, it is the other side of the planet from Stonehenge, and, it is safe to say, has no connection with it other than an architectural coincidence. It is the exception that proves the rule: large, unadorned stones assembled in a way seen only in one other place, in Wiltshire, in the centre of southern England – and done there on a larger scale, with a harder rock, sometimes alone and sometimes linked in a massive ring, some stones still standing after 4,500 years, some fallen or missing. There really is nothing like Stonehenge. The most basic of concepts (verticals, horizontals and rings, and nothing else) is despite this simplicity – and perhaps also because of it – unique.

In a children's television programme back in 1987, Tony Hart, the presenter, drew a black vertical shape. 'How long is it going to take you to know what I'm trying to show?', he asked, adding a second parallel shape. 'Not long, I think,' and as soon as he started to block out a line connecting the two shapes at the top, viewers knew. The programme was broadcast in the UK by the BBC, but it could have been shown anywhere in the world, to people of any age, and few would have been unable to answer his question. Stonehenge is among the best known and most visited ancient sites in the world. It is, as *The Sun* newspaper recently put it, 'the famous rocks'.

It is also the most copied monument, its singularity offering instant recognition for the least precise evocation. The modern practice could be said to have begun in the 18th century, when John Wood designed the Circus at Bath – a grand ring of Georgian terraced houses – and William Stukeley his garden in Grantham, Lincolnshire, both based on Stonehenge's layout. Recent tributes are everywhere, according to Nancy Wisser who catalogues them from Pennsylvania in her Clonehenge blog, from Japan to Brazil, from New York to Tasmania, from 'the most realistic replica yet' in the Window of the World theme park in Shenzhen, China, to a curvaceous thing in Taiwan fitted with movement sensors, speakers and mirrors. That simple, iconic π, made in concrete, sparkling pink granite (a faithful full-scale model in Esperance, Australia, on the market as I write for $2.35 million),[1] chocolate biscuits, portable toilets (Glastonbury Festival) or cars (Nebraska – which inspired a more ambitious Carhenge at a sports centre in Kanchanaburi, Thailand, opened in 2020), is unmistakable and needs no translation.

There are really only two big questions we ask about Stonehenge: why, and how? Most commentators address the first, whether it's in books, films or peer-reviewed research, or stapled wads of paper printed in multiple colours of ink with photocopied diagrams and dark photos covered in rings and arrows (after 40 years as a Stonehenge observer, I see no decline in such entertainments). 'Why' might seem the harder question, but it is the easier: imagination is the only limit, and as testing against evidence can rarely be more than superficial, so it is almost impossible to prove a theory wrong. This, of course, is one of the great appeals of Stonehenge. We do not need to be an expert to come up with an explanation – indeed not being constrained by knowledge may be an asset. And when we try to explain we are addressing not just stones, but the nature of human endeavour, the meaning and purpose of our own lives.

This book is about the second question: how it was done. Oddly – not least because you might think its answer a necessary prerequisite for addressing the other question – the previous volume dedicated to the issue in its entirety was published a century ago.[2] How were the stones quarried and transported to the site? How were they shaped, arranged and raised – and then rearranged? And how has the completed monument suffered, decayed and been restored to become what we see today? It feels like the right time for such a book, in a world where people are becoming less interested in unfounded promises about the future and more in the realities of everyday lives. Certainly there is much new to say, not just because the very idea of addressing the question feels new, but also thanks to new research and new scientific techniques. As we journey from quarries to a complete Stonehenge, in every chapter there is new evidence and new thinking, about geology, engineering and archaeology, much of it arising even as I was writing (and frequently rewriting).

The people who made Stonehenge created something that lives on in worlds they couldn't possibly have imagined (see pl. 1). In all likelihood it will survive humanity, in a few billion years, perhaps, its distinctive form encased in new geological strata as the Earth slowly folds the Eurasian land mass back into its arms. In the meantime, while it is still there and we have the skills to do so, we have to ask the question:

How do we build Stonehenge?

CHAPTER 1

THE STONES

If I could choose, I would visit Stonehenge on a May afternoon when the blossom is out and sun-drenched showers roll across the great wilderness of Salisbury Plain. And I would do so in 1805, with William Cunnington.

He had a trick. A local businessman who effectively invented the archaeology of Stonehenge, digging among the stones and in ancient burial mounds, Cunnington (1754–1810) would take guests in a horse-drawn chaise. Before Stonehenge was in sight, he'd stop the carriage and pull up the wooden shutters, obscuring the views. Barrister and poet Richard Fenton (1747–1821) much enjoyed the experience: 'Thus in darkness and durance,' he wrote to a friend, 'we travelled rapidly for a few miles, till our captain, with a most majestic tone, issued the word of command, "Stop, down with the blinds;" when, lo! we found ourselves within the area of the gigantic peristyle of Stonehenge... the effect is wonderful.'

The days of driving into the centre of Stonehenge are long gone, but in one respect the journey two centuries ago has a modern counterpart: the old road we walk on from the visitor centre to the stones today is the road along which Cunnington drove his chaise. This and the busy A303 to the south were created as toll roads in the 1760s, by private trusts known as turnpikes; their milestones still mark the routes. They had a profound effect on how we all see, and imagine, Stonehenge.

Before these roads, people reached the monument by walking or riding over a carpet of downland turf broken by a network of short, braided tracks. Mostly they would come from Salisbury to the south – like the Swiss Herman Folkerzheimer in 1562, the first named Stonehenge tourist, who stayed with the Bishop – and get sight of the stones as they crested a nearby hill. This is a spectacular view,

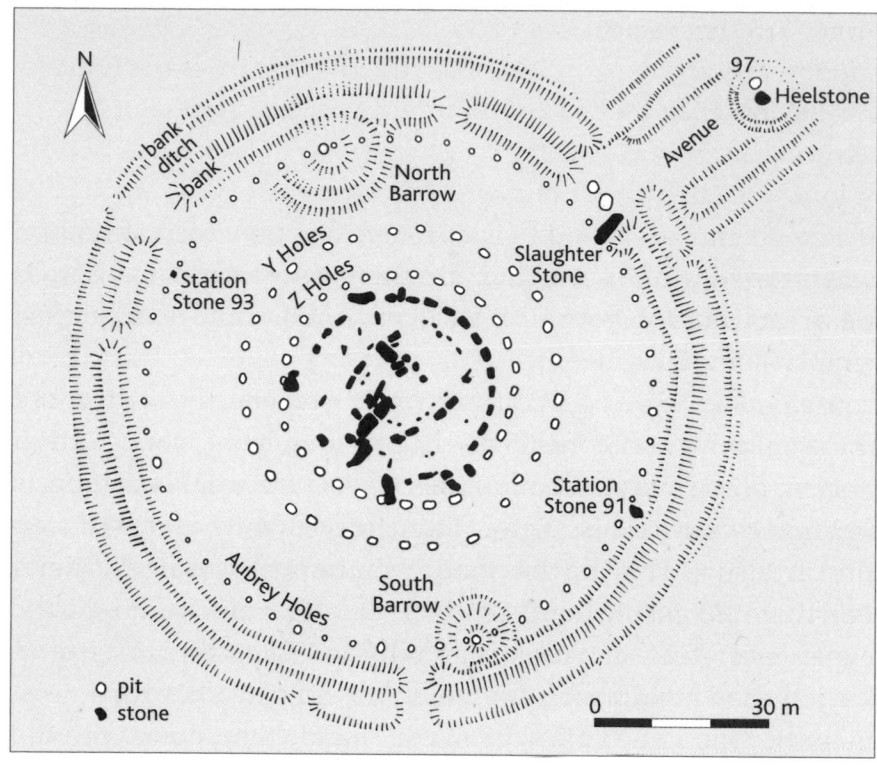

The Stonehenge monument as it is today; pits are either excavated and refilled or unexcavated and identified in surface surveys.

perhaps the best. We can still enjoy it, walking up a quiet wooded valley depicted in V. S. Naipaul's autobiographical novel, *The Enigma of Arrival*.[1] At the end of a winding, grassy way the ground rises, and as we reach the top of the ridge, with Bronze Age burial mounds on either side, Stonehenge comes suddenly into sight, silhouetted against distant hills. With much of the farmland reverting to grass, but for the A303 in the valley below in the short distance between us and the stones, I imagine the panorama is not completely unlike that experienced by Folkerzheimer some 450 years ago.

Today, however, most of us approach Stonehenge differently: like William Cunnington, we see it first from a road as we drive past, and more leisurely as we walk or bus from the visitor centre. The turnpikes we follow were created to exploit a growing demand from traffic between Bath and Bristol and beyond in the west, and London and the home counties in the east. They weren't built to take people to Stonehenge, but almost incidentally they made it accessible to anyone unfortunate enough not to know a local bishop or lord who could show them the way (see pl. IV).

Stonehenge was now on the map. A new market was created for guidebooks, and the stage was set for conjuring a particular way of seeing and imagining the ancient ruin that still shapes our thinking. For many people the first sighting of the stones came on the journey from London, the view we see today looking west from the A303 at the point where the road crests a hill and its two carriageways merge into one. The great English artists Turner and Constable both sketched a view of Stonehenge from the top of this hill early in the 19th century. But it was more distant than the hill to the south, and the prospect, said old hands, inferior. In 1876, Salisbury Museum curator and local guide Edward Stevens (1828–1878) deplored it. 'We scarcely see Stonehenge from the best point of view in going to it by the road from Amesbury,' he told the Wiltshire Archaeological Society who had just taken exactly that route, conveyed by a caravan of charabancs. 'It is seen to far greater advantage if we approach it by way of the Down' – from the south (see pl. v).

You might think that I am suggesting alternative ways for you to visit Stonehenge. Certainly there are opportunities to approach from some special and surprisingly unfrequented directions, and I would encourage you to explore such options. But that is not why I have told this story, of the origins of modern tourism in 18th-century roads. Rather it is to highlight, and explain, that we have today a particular way of seeing Stonehenge and its surroundings, and that this dates back less than three centuries. We pass from east to west and back, in a narrow corridor that both compresses and goes against the grain of the landscape. Importantly, I think, the perspective this gives us is also diametrically opposed to the way the people who built Stonehenge experienced it, and expected it to be seen.

How do I know that? Well of course I can't be dogmatic, but there are several suggestions that support the idea, in the monument itself and in its setting. We'll come to the stones later, but here I want to consider the location through the simple device of standing at Stonehenge, and looking out. For this will help us determine, in this opening chapter in which we are doing no more than scrutinizing the site (just as Herman Folkerzheimer did two years before Shakespeare was born, for it has, it feels, changed little since then), how we will start our journey. What can we see?[2]

Our immediate impression is of open space. Sheep-cropped grassland surrounds us, gently rolling to near horizons marked to north and east by interrupted banks of trees, and to south and west by continuing pasture punctuated by shrubs dotted along chalk tracks, and tree clumps marking ancient burial mounds (there are a lot of these barrows, not least under the trees on the ridge to the east).

Looking again we see that the views are not equal. While the ground sweeps away to north and south, at first falling from the gentle spur on which Stonehenge stands and then climbing again, to the west the slope rises just enough to almost immediately close in, obscuring anything beyond. It's more open to the east, and beyond the ridge of trees across the small valley we can see occasional distant hills. But the overall sense is of a landscape that beckons to north and south, and constrains to east and west. That sense grows the more familiar you become with the downland, walking its slopes and hidden valleys, watching sheep flock and disperse, noticing a tree come into view here and a barrow slip out of sight there. And the feeling is reinforced when you study maps, contours rising to northeast offering unrestricted views, and to southwest creating a succession of ridges that on the ground draw the eye on.

Let us then reverse our position, and approach Stonehenge from the north – the alternative route from the south being blocked by the road. There is an earthwork reaching northeast from Stonehenge, easy to see: a pair of narrow, sheep-tracked parallel hollows some

20 m (65 ft) apart, the ground between seeming flatter and more level than the tussocky grass beyond.

The Avenue, as we call it, heads straight down the slope for 550 m (1,800 ft) with the air of a marked route to or from the stones, that we can now follow (nothing like it is known in any other direction). At the bottom we are in a small bowl, so remote that in summer it almost has a feel of the indoors, the ceiling a skylark's song. With road traffic silenced, we might imagine ourselves in the company of William Stukeley (1687–1765), Stonehenge's greatest observer and antiquary. He published a grand illustrated book about the place in 1740, and spent much time here in preceding years. In our hearts, it is his Stonehenge we would like to experience: endless, unfenced grassland, no tourists, turnpikes or modern ploughing, and ancient earthworks and stones better preserved than they would be for any future recorder.[3]

Stukeley was the first to notice – and name – the Avenue. He saw much else, not least another long earthwork a little further to the north. Two not quite parallel ditches, separated by 100–150 m (325–500 ft) along their length of nearly 3 km (1.7 miles), seem to mark out an east–west way that crosses the valley between two

Stonehenge from the east surrounded by ancient burial mounds, drawn by William Stukeley in the 1720s before maintained roads. At that time the site was reached across open downland and braided tracks.

low ridges – or, as some archaeologists see it, creates a barrier to movement between north and south. Stukeley called it the Cursus, imagining it to be a racecourse for Roman charioteers. Recent excavation shows it was created some 5,500 years ago, centuries before the first identifiable Stonehenge. We now know it to be one of several cursuses across Britain – archaeologists adopted Stukeley's name for them – and the third largest. We can only guess their purpose, though they look ceremonial, and the presence of the Stonehenge Cursus – and a second, smaller one further north again, which Stukeley did not see – are among indications that the area held special meaning from an early stage.

As we start back up the hill – anticipating 'The grand and only access to this work... which makes the building appear really majestic to such as approach it in front,' as architect John Wood (1704–54) wrote 20 years before the turnpike roads were opened – something unexpected strikes us immediately: Stonehenge has disappeared. The two parallel ditches of the Avenue, however, barely visible here, lead us out and up until quite suddenly we see stones. And not just any stones.

As the monument peers over the horizon, it flaunts its most distinctive feature, the part that more than anything says 'Stonehenge': lintels, great horizontal slabs, roughly squared, the grey rock now coloured in subtle lichen greens. There are two bunched together to the left and one to the right, the latter looking more rounded. If we hold still at just the right point, they seem to sink into the ground where it meets the sky.

In the space between is the top of a single vertical megalith, its sharply drawn flat end punctuated in the centre by a bulging plum pudding. The megalith once had a matching partner, and between them they supported a lintel, held in place by the protrusions which fitted into hollows on the lintel's underside, each making a sort of ball and socket joint: in Stonehenge jargon these are traditionally referred to as mortise and tenon (or 'Mortece and Tenant' as antiquary William Lambarde (1536–1601) wrote in the 1570s, 'as

Carpenters call them', in what may be the first Stonehenge use of both the phrase and a woodworking analogy). When newly erected, the three stones – the largest of five free-standing trilithons – might together have weighed 85 tons. Were they still upright and we were to step back a little, all we would see would be that great lintel, like a table or bed, or an altar, perhaps, a threshold, apparently alone on the ground; an invitation, a boastful hint of the wonder that was to come.

Today that marvel, or at least its broken but still potent ruin, soon springs into view. As we proceed, the three surviving high lintels, now seen to be balanced on pairs of great squared pillars to either side, seem held apart by a slightly lower run of three, thinner lintels that form a straight line across the front. Below this, supportive massed uprights merge into a wall that continues to either side with occasional gaps, and what was once a solid horizontal ring is picked up with two lintels to the left, one to the right. Dot, dot, dash, dot: an F in Morse code. Fence? Fort? A bold front? From this distance there is no sense of a ring or an interior, just a wall. It feels more intimidating than welcoming.

As we climb the slope, nearer stones rise against those behind. One in the centre grows fatter and taller than the others, from which it is separated by 60 m (200 ft), until it dominates the view, and we can see it is also differently shaped. Its irregular sides taper towards a rounded top, like a formless cloaked figure. It is one of a handful of isolated stones that over generations have acquired names, invented to suit the times. In the 18th century the antiquary William Stukeley called it the bowing stone, the place where people bowed as they arrived. The term remained in use until the late 19th century, but was soon mostly overtaken by a new one, the Friar's Heel – along with a tale told of the Devil throwing it at a fleeing monk whose foot left an imprint (no longer to be seen). In 1901 an astronomer made much of the way the midsummer sun rises over this megalith, which, with an eye on the ancient Greek sun god Helios, he referred to as the Hele stone – a name that was revived in the 1960s, when astronomy descended again on Stonehenge. Today it is simply the Heelstone.

Only when we walk round this beast of a megalith do we see its character. Relatively flat from the front, behind it swells and crumples in a contorted mass, sometimes smooth, often penetrated by rounded hollows, and marked by a fissure above head height that rises and falls around an angle, giving it the mournful menace of a deep-sea eel. From behind, too, it leans, towards the stone circle from the sides and sideways from the back – its complex shape, which seems to grow as it descends into the turf, is difficult to visualize.

With an estimated weight of 40 tons and some 4.5 m (15 ft) high, it's the largest stone at Stonehenge, and one of very few that is not dressed to shape. The Heelstone is its own monument. And if the grass is cut short and you look carefully, you can just make out the shallow depression of a narrow ditch, now filled, that circled it as if to emphasize its peculiarity and its gravity. I'm not like those fancy, carved stones, it says. I may support nothing. But once I mattered.

The Avenue ditches either side here are clearer, having been excavated by archaeologists in the 20th century and only partly refilled. They lead in just 20 paces to another ditch. This one is different. Wider and deeper, partly so, again, because it has been excavated and its empty form carefully preserved by archaeologists, it maps out before us a perfect circle almost 110 m (360 ft) across. We stand at the only large gap in the circuit, at 12 m (40 ft) across narrower than the 22 m (72 ft) that separate the Avenue ditches, which stop at its presence. The break encourages us to continue towards the stones. As soon as we enter the arena, halfway between the Heelstone behind us and the circle in front, we come to a second large, isolated megalith. It lies flat on the ground, 6.5 m (21 ft) long.

This is the Slaughter Stone. It means what it says. A visitor to Stonehenge in 1871, passing by on their way from London to Land's End, found space to comment only on this stone, on which, 'no doubt, many hundreds of human beings have been put to death, amid the savage rites which once were wont to be celebrated in this desolate spot' (travel in England, they added, avoided 'four hours of solid misery' crossing the Channel, and the consequent bad meals, cold feet and the 'vague feeling' of being swindled). To Stukeley it was simply a great flat stone, but in 1799 barrister Edward King (1735–1807), fresh from reading accounts by Captain Cook of human sacrifice in Tahiti and well versed in the Old Testament and Homer, imagined lintels as flaming Druid altars, and the flat stone at the entrance to be the place of killing – the slaughtering stone.

It is our first dressed – roughly carved – stone. It lies in the grass like a pat of butter dropped into a bowl of flour, the ground lightly mounded around as if it had once been buried in a shallow grave, and is now exposed surrounded by spoil (see pl. vi). Only one face and a little of its straight, parallel sides are revealed, but in good light it's easy to see how these have been more or less smoothed and flattened. Several deeper hollows from the original boulder remain, stained red with blood (or less fancifully by algae combined with iron-rich minerals leached out of the stone by pooled water). Its flat, and presumably top end when erect, points towards the circle, which still has more the air of a broken wall than a ring.

In the distance ahead of us four great serried uprights support three snug-fitting lintels, and to either side further, less regular megaliths seem to bulge and lean, isolated lintels to left and right and glimpses of unidentifiable stones of varied size through the gaps. Now we can make out patterns in the trails of lichen, and imagine shapes and faces in the particular angles and hollows of each stone. More immediate, however, is the surrounding ditch. We can discern a bank either side of it, the low topography emphasized by the mown turf. To our left the inner, larger bank merges into the mound around the flat stone. We turn and follow this earthwork.

Almost immediately, if we have our eyes on the ground, we notice a dinner-plate sized concrete disc in the grass. And then another. They continue every 5 m (16 ft), a ring of markers beneath each of which is a pit, known as an Aubrey Hole. John Aubrey (1626–97), a great, gossipy antiquary who first visited Stonehenge in 1634 when he was only eight, was the first to sketch a plan of the monument, and the pits were named in his honour when they were discovered and excavated in the 1920s.

After 40 paces and 9 discs, we reach a small lump of a stone leaning into the bank. Like the Heelstone and the Slaughter Stone, this too has a name. It's a Station Stone – there are two surviving (of an original four), the second still out of sight beyond the circle on the other side of the monument. The one in front of us is the larger, weighing 4 tons and, like the Heelstone, apparently entirely in its natural state. It looks as if it may once have been standing, and has fallen outwards into the bank, its lichen-splattered curves temporarily shielding plant growth from the mower (see pl. III).

You might wonder if the naming of these two stones had anything to do with the Stations of the Cross, where Christ paused on his way to the crucifixion. But Stonehenge is determinedly Pagan, and in this case the names' origin seems to lie in a vision of the landscape as a great map of the universe in which Stonehenge was Saturn. The idea came to Edward Duke (1779–1852), a local leisured cleric who published a book about 'Druidical temples' in 1846. It was not the stones he called stations (that confusion came later) but two nearby hollows in the ground. We can see the first when we walk a further 30 paces or so. Here there is a small, shallow ditch, a circle similar to that around the Heelstone, and within, in slightly raised ground and less easy to make out, a subtle depression.

In earlier centuries the hollow was more prominent (as is also the case with the corresponding hollow on the other side), an indication, perhaps, that a stone similar in size to the Station Stone had once stood there and not so long before been removed. To Duke, however, the depression was a marker for an astronomer, who would take his station there at the summer solstice (at midsummer, on the year's longest day) and view the sun rise over the adjacent stone. The alignment is parallel to that of the Avenue and the centre of the circle, which Stukeley was the first to note pointed at the midsummer sun. The other Station Stone and its hollow are also on the same alignment: there, however, the positions are reversed, and the astronomer gazed out from his mark to watch the midwinter sun set over the stone to the southwest – rise at midsummer and set at midwinter are dead opposite each other.

Both hollows are inside small, round earthworks, the distant one now bisected by a visitors' pathway, that were identified by early antiquaries as tiny burial mounds. Excavation has since proved that to be wrong, but the names stuck and today they are still known as the South Barrow (where we are) and the North (the other side). Duke observed that part of the North Barrow lay beneath the bank on the inner side of the ditch that surrounds the whole site (this, he thought, represented Saturn's rings), and is thus older. It's difficult to see that now, but detailed modern survey agrees with him. Already we have a hint that not everything we see was built at the same time (later in the book we will need to understand some of that history, which is summarized in the Appendix for easy reference).

Immediately beyond the South Barrow there's a causeway across the main ditch, wide enough for two people to pass at a comfortable distance, the second apparently designed passage into or out of the enclosure. As we continue around, after about 40 paces we approach the hard-surfaced visitor path and the ditch suddenly shallows: this is the point where archaeological excavation a century ago stopped. And we are now more or less on the centre line of the monument, so that if we turn towards it and look back we can squint through the forest of erect and fallen stones before us and make out the Heelstone in the distance.

The view of the stone circle from here is quite different to that from the front – it does feel as if we are at the back. Where before we were confronted with a facade of lintelled megaliths, here we see several large slabs lying in the grass, a great gap in the outer circuit, and within – hidden before – a muddle of gigantic and smaller stones whose layout is impossible to discern. It is as if Stonehenge has been opened up for our inspection, the skin laid back to either side and the guts revealed, an impressive even unsettling sight – more de Chirico than Constable – but one that does little to improve our understanding.

Beyond the path the lone, small but in this case standing Station Stone beckons, rising through a shoreline roll of the turf. But we accept the grander invitation, and cross the grass towards the circle.

Around the edge, you may have noticed, the folk names of the remoter stones – Heel, Slaughter, Station – and the two Barrows were gathered since the 18th-century roads brought visitors wanting stories. Only one of the stones we approach – the Altar Stone, which we will meet later in this chapter – is so singled out: instead we use a numbering system devised in the 1870s by Flinders Petrie (1853–1942), a brilliant and eccentric archaeologist better known for his excavations in Egypt (see pl. II). If these stones have their private secrets, they were told before anyone thought to write them down. We are on our own now.[4]

Nearest as we approach is a fat, upended mattress of a stone, standing alone and streaked with a vertical lichen rainbow, wispy grey-green, deep purple and spattered dark brown. But the one that draws our attention is just beyond: tall, straight-sided, smooth and rising above the megalithic debris with an erect probity, this is the first upright stone we saw from the bottom of the valley. Its sharp, flat top and contrasting rounded tenon – some 30 cm or 1 ft high – are even more striking seen close to. No other stone can match its ruled edges or the soaring monotony of its face, and as we walk round it to the left – our way to the right is blocked by its massive, fallen partner – we note another distinguishing feature: though taller, it looks thinner than the other large stones. Its side too is almost entirely smooth, a slight hint of faceting betraying the enormous labour that must have engineered it. At 6.6 m (21 ft 8 in.) high it's not just the tallest. It's the finest. We know it as Stone 56.[5]

Passing a small megalith that leans away from the front of this proud, polished slab, and the other jumbled boulders that lie flat in the grass or on each other, we find ourselves in an unexpected space. Huge grey stones rise above us, framing a sort of stage onto which a few spectators have impolitely tumbled, and beyond which others huddle in a protective ring. It is suddenly quiet. This arena is created by the stones Stukeley named trilithons. There are (or were) five. Behind us Stone 56 was once part of the largest, with the broken 55 and their fallen lintel 156 – commonly referred to as the Great Trilithon. There are two trilithons to the southeast on our right, both complete, and two to the northwest on our left; of the latter the closer is all in position, while Stone 60 beyond stands alone, its partner 59 and lintel 160 sprawled on the ground, each in three pieces.

These trilithons, with the other great stones around them, are not just carved megaliths. They are sculpture. They are architecture: a unique case of pre-concrete brutalism that deployed a precise vision of scale and design, but allowed for considerable variety in surface execution (a variety, as we shall see, that itself was not entirely accidental). The principle of vertical stones jointed into horizontal lintels is all around us, but here it is executed with the greatest determination. Lintels – another name for them, archi-trave, was popular at Stonehenge with early antiquaries – and posts or pillars are found across the ancient world; they were the standard way of supporting weight over openings or spaces until the development of the arch, and remain common in modern buildings. At Stonehenge, however, the lintels support only themselves. While they contribute some stability to the stones beneath them, through their joints and their mass, their purpose is as much visual as practical.

On the ground the five trilithons are arranged in a U-shape, one at the base behind us and two on either arm, the top opening up for the view towards the surviving run of lintelled circle stones and the Heelstone beyond. Early antiquaries referred to this arrangement as a truncated ellipse or oval. A comparison with a horseshoe came up in the 19th century and it stuck; today we talk of the Trilithon Horseshoe. The lintels in this horseshoe, where in place, are horizontal, but the trilithons grow taller on either side as they approach the greatest represented by Stone 56 behind us.

The lintel on our right (154) is a stylistic match for this stone, the finest carved of its type surviving. All four side faces are exceptionally smooth and flat (as we walk among the stones, we will note a tendency for many of them to be better finished on the inside than the out), meeting at rounded corners. The base is slightly narrower than the top, so that while the ends are more or less vertical, the sides slope out, emphasizing the lintel's mass as we look up from below. And it is curved: while it's not immediately obvious, its long outer face matches the gentle shape of the horseshoe at this point. This lintel, balanced on stones (53 and 54) that rise more than 5 m (17 ft) above the ground, weighs 18 tons.

Half of the lintel beyond (152), having last moved when it was lifted into place over 4,000 years ago, is badly weathered, its faces gouged by vertical grooves. It's thinner than 154, but the better preserved northeastern end shows the same finish and shaping as its neighbour. The other lintels are also in poor condition. On our left 158 shows the same curve as its opposite, and the same smooth faces, rounded corners and sloping sides; but (for reasons we will learn in a later chapter) it has been badly damaged. Worst of all is 160, reduced to rounded lumps spaced out in the grass, which we can identify as parts of a trilithon lintel only from their location.

At our feet, lying on its side, is the lintel (156) from the Great Trilithon. When John Wood surveyed the monument in 1740, he named it the Rocking Stone – at that time it was apparently balanced on another fallen stone – but it no longer rocks, and the name did not catch on. It's so battered that we cannot describe its original finish, though we might imagine a stone at least as fine as the best. We can, however, see the two sockets that would have fitted onto the tenons on top of the uprights, a little over 3 m (10 ft) apart. Curiously, there is another pair of sockets on the other face of this lintel, shallower but in more or less the same position. Unless there was a technical problem with their carving, the implication seems to be that at some point during construction it was decided that it mattered which way up the lintel should go, and that that was the opposite to what had at first been decided.

All the uprights in this horseshoe are extensively dressed, but each is distinct. After Stone 56, the finest, in the sense of the smoothest and flattest, is 53, the closest but one to the southeast: its sides have a slight, symmetric taper, and its faces and edges are all pretty flat, especially on the inside. By contrast its companion (54) is one of the roughest, smooth on the inside but much eaten away by natural hollows down one edge, and on the outer face swollen by prominent ridges with the air of having just been roughed out at the quarry.

One other stone has large, unrefined dressing scars on what we assume is its back, the fallen 59. Its standing companion (60) has a rough back too, though here a pregnant swell over what used to be a cave big enough for three people to squeeze into – a popular challenge before a cautious Ministry of Works filled it with cement in 1959 – was part of the natural boulder. Stone 58 of the adjacent trilithon also has a naturally irregular back, with a diagonal ledge apparently only lightly trimmed, while its companion (57) is smooth but lightly undulating on both faces; both stones look almost dangerously thin seen from the sides. The more you look at these great megaliths, the more you see different textures and tooling, natural holes and fissures, variations in outlines and even colour, so that while they work firmly together holding up their lintels in the horseshoe plan, each has its own personality, its own story.

We can't see the inner face of Stone 55, the fallen partner of the Great Trilithon, though we suspect it to have been especially flat and smooth. We can, however, see something we weren't meant to see: its more or less intact foot, thrown into the air when it fell. It's rounded and swollen, and rises abruptly from the flat back, giving bulk and added stability to the standing stone – albeit not enough – and incidentally revealing the scale of at least some of the dressing to which these stones were subjected.

If the light is right – clear and low – while looking at this great protuberance we will notice on the smooth face beyond a mass of graffiti: WC, ALLEN, ET, DC 1721. Some of it can be read, but more is eroded or overlapping and difficult to make sense of with the eye alone. But once we see it here, we see it elsewhere. On Stone 56 – 1802 (J DAY W LAW) MASONS CAMBERWELL – and on the fallen Stone 59 – HG 1735.

At the very least these engravings demanded planning, as steel tools would have been needed to carve out the often carefully serifed letters. But on the front of Stone 56, on an ultra-smooth panel at around chest height and beneath a prominent line of lettering that looks 17th century, is something different: the shallow but distinct shape of a dagger, tip down, and beside it a sort of mushroom with a triangular stalk that archaeologists recognize as a representation of a Bronze Age axe blade. Around the monument there are many more of these axe shapes (the dagger too is probably Bronze Age – ancient, if not quite as much as the stones themselves), further indication that there is more to Stonehenge than a quick glance reveals.

All of these things – massive slabs variously dressed from differently shaped boulders, carved joints unique to each megalith and lintel, hollows, wrinkles and streaked gardens of lichen – are also characteristic of the other very large stones that act as an immediate backdrop to everything around us, holding it all in. These stones are arranged in a circle. If we look northeast towards the Heelstone, there is a good run of eleven uprights with five lintels, shaped to fit the circle's curve, three of the latter together directly in front of us. Where one lintel meets another there is a new form of carved joint, a vertical ridge on the end of one stone fitting into a channel on its neighbour – a toggle, known here as tongue and groove. Where the lintels are missing, we can sometimes see a pair of rounded tenons on megaliths that supported two lintels rather than just one, as with the trilithons.

Turning round, in the opposite direction along an equivalent arc we can see only three or four stones standing, one of which is oddly small and leans outwards. Several boulders rise from the grass, perhaps more than half-buried, and it's not obvious where most of them might originally have been placed. We imagine the circle as once having been complete, though the amount of visible material seems inadequate to the task. Nonetheless, the surviving 35 uprights and 13 lintels, in place, fallen and fragmentary, amount to a huge weight of rock – the equivalent of eight adult blue whales. And if the circle really had once been continuous, originally there would have been 75 stones in the centre and at least 8 outliers, with a weight, in their complete state, of a dozen whales. Where did it all come from?

One of the things that makes Stonehenge so distinctive is the simple fact that it is made of hard, dark stone: not only does there seem to be no stone like it for miles in any direction, but the ground beneath is only soft, white chalk. It literally looks alien. There was a popular medieval story that Merlin had magicked the stones from Ireland (to where they had been brought from Africa, long before, by giants). Some early antiquaries thought the megaliths might have been moulded from a form of ancient concrete. As an understanding of geological formation processes grew, however, and the curious hammered off samples of rock, it became clear that the stones were not artificial. So there surely had to be outcrops, somewhere, from which they had been hewn and transported. But where were they?

The earliest breakthrough was to recognize that there were, broadly, two types of stone. All the ones we've been looking at so far are a hard, smooth sandstone with the distinctive name of sarsen. Even today sarsen boulders are common on the Marlborough Downs 30 km (20 miles) north of Stonehenge: that, said Stukeley in the early 18th century, was where the great stones came from.

But he also saw, possibly for the first time, that there were other types of stone at the centre of Stonehenge. Not as big as the lintelled sarsens, they are no less strange to be found on Salisbury Plain – more so, perhaps, as nothing like them can be seen even on the Marlborough Downs. They stand and lie all over the place, filling gaps between trilithons and the circle beyond and cluttering up the arena in the middle. If we walk around just inside the great ring of sarsens, we'll find ourselves following fragments of a circle of these smaller stones, 21 of them, standing and fallen. None is as high as a person, and they show a greater variety of colour than the sarsens, in greens, blues and greys, and also texture. Back in the centre are a further dozen, more uniform in shape – taller and rod-like, and more obviously carved, or apparently so – following the inside of the U of the trilithon arc. And alone in pole position in the bowl of the U, though harder to see flat on the ground where it is mostly buried and partly covered by the fallen Great Trilithon, is a long stone with a distinctive feel and colour of its own. Stukeley, and others after him in their own inventive ways, used the name altar for many of the stones at Stonehenge. But only this one clung onto it: it was given by an architect, Inigo Jones (1573–1652), in the 1620s, and the Altar Stone is now the sole named megalith in the centre of the site.

These darker, smaller and more mysterious stones, the Altar Stone among them, came to be known collectively as blue stones, or bluestones: if the sarsens are the crown of Stonehenge, the bluestones are its jewels. It was a popular challenge to come up with a likely source, and geologists soon realized there must have been several. Suggestions included Dartmoor, Snowdon and Leicestershire, and further afield Ireland, Brittany, the Pyrenees or Finland. If you'd gone to Stonehenge in the 1870s, having bought your guidebook in Amesbury and set out in the morning along the dusty turnpike road with the sun behind you, you could have read that they might have come from Africa. Mr Higgins ('author of *Celtic Druids*'), says the writer, had broken off a bit of stone, had it polished up and showed it to a distinguished London geologist. It looks African, said the scientist. Ah, said Mr Higgins, who might have been hoping for a different continent (his book was subtitled, *The Priests of Oriental Colonies who Emigrated from India*), what would you say if I told you it was from Stonehenge? In that case, came the even less helpful reply, it must have come from Anglesey.

I could wander endlessly among these stones, were it possible to do so, and perhaps you could too: speculating about this and that, watching the jackdaws strut along the lintels, noticing little blue flowers growing hidden beneath a fallen sarsen, and marvelling at the great masses and the still fresh-looking scoops of hammered dressing. Where did the stones come from? How were they brought here? How were they carved, and how erected? What inspired the ideas about design and jointing? People have been asking such questions since at least the Middle Ages. 'No one can imagine', wrote Henry of Huntingdon nine centuries ago, 'by what godlike art such great stones were raised so high.'

We will always speculate and wonder. But much evidence about how Stonehenge was built has accumulated to inform our curiosity, especially in recent years. That is what the rest of this book is about, and we start with the raw materials. Where do we have to go to get the rocks to make Stonehenge?

CHAPTER 2

RAW MATERIALS: BLUESTONE

When I was a student in London I was pleased to find a model of Stonehenge which I remembered seeing as a schoolboy. It was in what was then the Geological Museum (since merged with the Natural History Museum), across the road from the V&A. It was made nearly a century ago, and still today there is truly nothing quite like it.

It wasn't large. The great circle was 60 cm (24 in.) across, and it stood on a green, textured board in its own glass case fitted to a custom-made mahogany table. You were meant to look at it from the direction of the Heelstone – as we arrived at Stonehenge in the previous chapter, walking up the Avenue – which was fixed alone near one end of the case. There were three information sheets. One told you about Stonehenge ('erected, presumably as a temple devoted to sun-worship, by a race of late Stone-Age people'). A second displayed the monument's different types of stone, using small polished rectangles of blue and grey rock mounted on card, and looking exactly like something from which we might today expect to choose a new kitchen worktop.

And then there was the title sheet. 'Restoration of Stonehenge', it read in capital letters, 'in the original materials by H. H. Thomas F.R.S. Lapidary work by D. W. Hepple'. On the swatch sheet five of the stone tablets were from named geological locations, and five matching ones were, yes, from Stonehenge. Here, in confident 3D and made out of the actual rocks, was a statement more than a theory of where all the megaliths at Stonehenge had come from. In very broad terms Herbert Thomas (1876–1935) got it right. His interpretation entered Stonehenge folklore as one of the site's key facts, only the second commonly accepted view on the stones' sources since the medieval belief that Merlin had brought them from Ireland. The model vanished from display over 20 years ago when the museum's Earth Galleries were redeveloped, but I was delighted to examine it recently when it was found in storage in Kent and brought back into London. On the face of it, it tells us where we need to go to look for a quarry for every Stonehenge megalith. It represents an extraordinary achievement.

Thomas agreed with everyone else about the sarsens: they were local and had come from somewhere in Wiltshire. We'll look at those in the next chapter, but here we will consider the bluestones, the subject of his breakthrough and the occasion for making the model. As is often the case with scientific advances, luck played a part. Thomas was employed by the government's Geological Survey. Appointed in 1901, his first task there was to map the geology of south Wales. After a decade of fieldwork he was promoted to the Survey's Petrographer, leaving him in London to examine rock

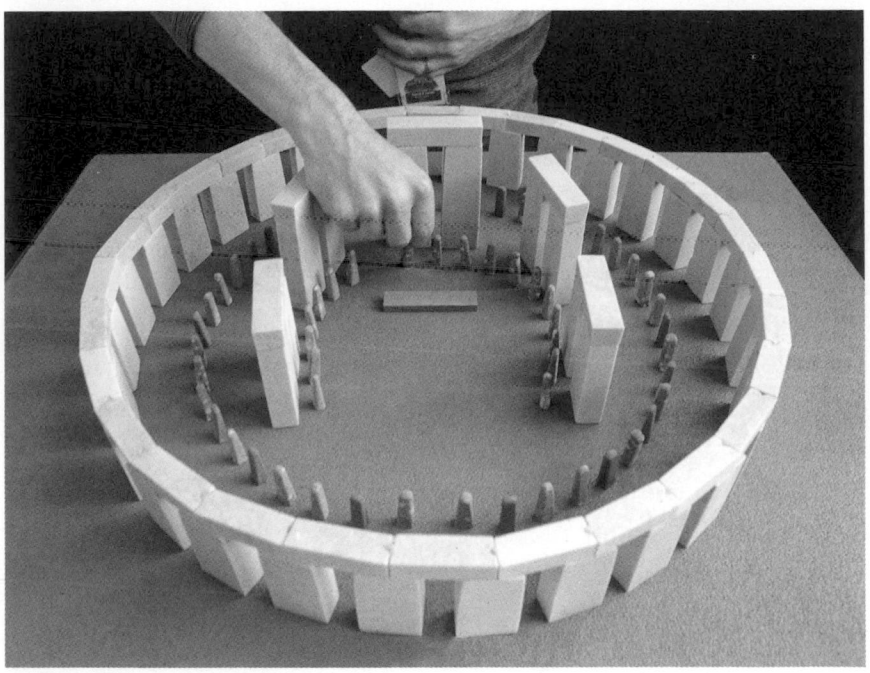

Model of Stonehenge in the Natural History Museum, London, made in the 1920s with stone from appropriate sources identified by Herbert Thomas.

samples collected by his colleagues. He was just 59 when he died, collapsing at Waterloo Station on the way to a fishing trip.

Back in 1906, he'd walked over Pembrokeshire in southwest Wales, exploring its hills, valleys and coastline. At that very time an artist named Edgar Barclay (1842–1913) – who had a nice angle in bucolic paintings of the Stonehenge landscape, in which shepherds tended sheep with an obsessive attraction to megaliths (see pl. vi) – had shown him chips knocked off the standing bluestones. Thomas told Barclay that he'd just recorded the very same types of rock as boulders along the eastern shore of Fishguard Bay and inland towards Haverfordwest – southwards across the peninsula from the north Pembrokeshire coast. The artist jotted the insight down to include in his new guidebook as an addition to the numerous theories then current – eminent geologists had considered the issue since the 1870s, but with no clear result – and Thomas continued with his fieldwork. And so it might have rested, until in 1920 the London Society of Antiquaries sent the geologist a parcel containing some more fragments of stone.

The year before, the Society had started digging at Stonehenge, employing William Hawley (1851–1941) to direct the work; the most important excavations done at the site, they continued until 1926. Hawley found a lot of broken stone – indeed, apart from modern clutter and ancient bones, neither of which anyone took much interest in at the time, it was almost all he found. Here was a chance to solve the long-standing issue of where the megaliths had come from. Thomas was soon able to oblige. Opening his package, he recognized at once what he had been given – but it was something he had not seen in Barclay's chips.

Most of the fragments, he found, had an unexpected character that was so distinctive it did more than confirm his earlier suggestion of Pembrokeshire. They were pieces of what geologists now call dolerite or microgabbro, blue- or grey-green in colour, dotted with unusual white or pinkish spots ranging in size, he said, from a pea to a walnut. Indeed, he now felt certain that almost all the

Lurking among much larger sarsens, the Stonehenge bluestones were last arranged into a horseshoe plan (two pillars, left middle distance) and a circle (foreground and far right).

different types of stone, other than sarsen, had been brought by Stone Age people from a quite specific location: the Preseli Hills.[1]

Out went Cornwall, Scotland and a host of contenders: in came southwest Wales. Everyone knew the bluestones could not have been found in Wiltshire, and the Preselis were closer than the Lake District and easier to reach than Brittany. Nonetheless, even in a straight line they were nearly 250 km (150 miles) from Stonehenge, and significantly further if you took into account the need to negotiate rivers and the rugged landscape. The scientific identification of a real place highlighted the apparently unique ancient challenge, and the achievement, of getting the stones from so far away to Stonehenge. It was such a striking conclusion, Thomas was persuaded to embark on a more detailed study. With one thing and another it took him three years. And, perhaps even to his own surprise, he was able to be yet more precise.

Whatever the original number at the monument (and Hawley's excavations were suggesting that many bluestones had since been removed, leaving the pits they had once stood in for archaeologists to find), 33 of these smaller megaliths could now be seen.[2] Dolerite accounted for 28, almost all of them of the unique spotted variety. They came, said Thomas, from Carn Menyn and Cerrig Marchogion, jagged outcrops in the eastern Preselis, a range of igneous rocks left high and (in my experience) wet and boggy by the erosion of softer sedimentary rocks around them (see pls VII, VIII). Four other megaliths consisted of rhyolitic volcanic rock, and could be distinguished by their dark blue-grey colour, delicate banding and flinty texture (see pls IX, X). These had been taken from Carn Alw, another Preseli outcrop, a bracing 20-minute walk going north and downslope from Carn Menyn, from where it can be seen sticking up like a mound of rubble silhouetted against the lowlands beyond.

The final megalith was altogether different, being not igneous but sedimentary – sandstone. This was the Altar Stone, distinguished by its material as well as its pole position inside the monument. It's

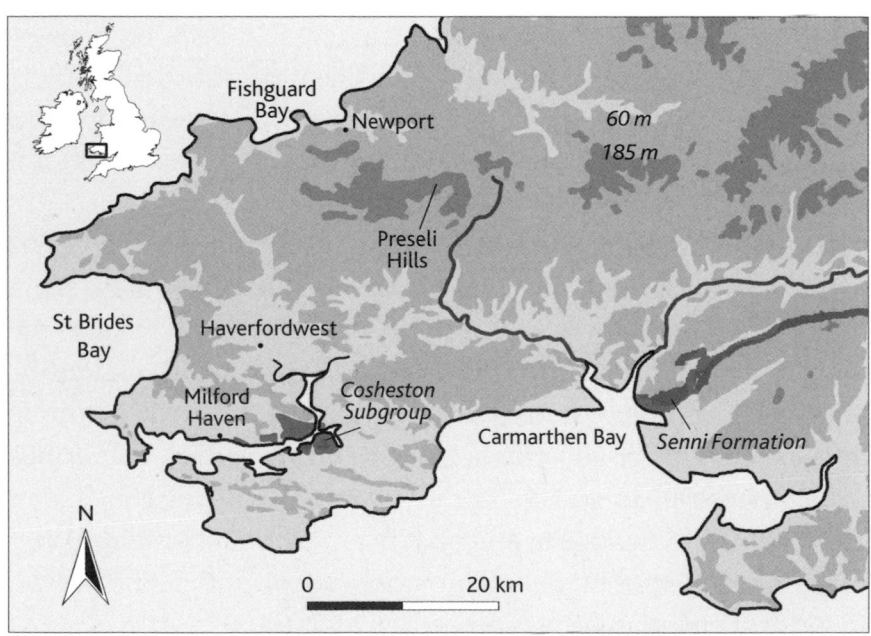

Pembrokeshire, showing Cosheston Subgroup and Senni Formation, identified in the 1920s as possible sources of the Altar Stone at Stonehenge.

a fine, pale-green micaceous stone – mica minerals make it glitter, not an uncommon feature of sandstones. Generally it's much harder to determine a geological source for such stones, but Thomas was undaunted, and steadily zoned in on Pembrokeshire: it's Palaeozoic, he said (formed when complex life was first appearing), probably Old Red Sandstone (rocks found either side of the Atlantic, in the UK at various points from Cornwall to the Shetlands), and it matches rock types in south Wales, in particular in two rock units known as the Senni and the Cosheston Beds. The first is found in a narrow strip reaching across central southern Wales and known today as the Senni Formation, and the other around the inner shores of Milford Haven at Mill Bay, a day's walk south from the Preselis, and the nearest coastline if you travel that way (now called the Cosheston Subgroup).

So Thomas was able to tell his eager audience at the Society of Antiquaries in 1923 that he'd found where all the surviving bluestone megaliths at Stonehenge had come from. But he had another trick up his sleeve. He'd found the source for at least one stone that wasn't even there. It had been once, he said, but it was now represented only by dark grey chips, and possibly a broken and still buried stump that had been found by an antiquary furtling around in the 19th century. And this stone, amazingly, also came from the Preseli Hills: from an outcrop called Foel Trigarn, whose shape is dramatized by the stone ramparts of an Iron Age fort built around three large Bronze Age burial cairns, and which rises above everything in the eastern Preselis a half hour's trudge through the tussocky grass and heather northeast of Carn Menyn.

The museum model is undated, but the design closely follows a drawing of Stonehenge published in 1924 by Herbert Stone (1848–1927), a retired engineer, who imagined how the monument might have looked when complete; the model may have been made soon after.[3] Every little megalith has been lovingly sawn and polished, with tongue-and-groove joints on the lintels. The great circle is made from sarsen (from Salisbury Plain, says the key), 30 uprights and 30 lintels, as are the trilithons, 15 stones around a U, and the Heelstone. Inside the U is the Bluestone Horseshoe, 19 identical little pillars of spotted dolerite from Carn Menyn, and inside the Sarsen Circle is a ring of 44 bluestones made from rhyolite and volcanic tuff (collected from Carn Alw and Foel Trigarn, respectively) and more dolerite. The Altar Stone lies flat, sharply rectangular and perfectly smooth near the centre, looking to me uncannily like a fallen version of the black monolith in the film *2001*.

Every stone is impeccably regular, the Heelstone and the bluestones vertical, a little rounded and tapering, and bluestones all the same height. The sarsens are flat-faced bricks with just a slight taper towards the top in the uprights' edges. The propositions that the Neolithic builders' vision included such identical, perfect stones arranged in perfect, complete rings are both debatable, as we will see. But what concerns us now is how the actual bluestones got to Stonehenge. Do we need to travel to Pembrokeshire and haul them all the way back? Or might they be found closer by, on the edge of Salisbury Plain, perhaps, carried there in an earlier era by glaciers – as some geologists had already proposed?

After all, the normal pattern was for Neolithic megaliths to be very local stones – and if there weren't any, there would be no such monuments. The distance over which the Stonehenge bluestones would have to have been transported was not only exceptional in prehistoric Britain, but also for early societies anywhere in Europe, and, for all anyone knew, around the world. Herbert Thomas had no doubt which it was. The evidence for the necessary glaciers was lacking, he said, and anyway the idea that ice would have selected all those stones from such a small part of Wales and no others, dropping none of them on the journey between Pembrokeshire and Stonehenge, 'was contrary to all sound geological reasoning'. There remained but one option: human agency.

Nonetheless, the glacial theory persists. It's a minority view, it is true, but we all like the underdog, and the idea receives a disproportionate amount of publicity. There has been a good century of geological survey and analysis since Thomas's fieldwork, and it would be reasonable to wonder if new evidence had overturned his confidence that natural transport played no part in carrying boulders eastwards from Pembrokeshire towards Salisbury Plain. It is obviously a matter of interest when we are thinking about the meanings and impacts of Stonehenge at the time it was built, no less than the practicalities of its construction. And we might worry when we discover that today, by and large, archaeologists who have written on the topic are convinced the bluestones were brought from Wales by Neolithic people, and that those who argue for glacial transport are geologists.

Archaeologists eagerly adopted Thomas's explanations, which first entered the official Stonehenge guidebook in 1924 (the 1919 edition had claimed that some bluestones could be found only on the European continent). The case for glaciation, it was said, did not stand up. No small pebbles of the appropriate Welsh stones had been found in Wiltshire gravels, as would be expected if glaciers had reached the county. Neither were there any larger Welsh boulders nearby from which we might now have selected to build our Stonehenge: it would be surprising if Neolithic engineers had scoured Salisbury Plain and removed every one. The glacial argument that there were once more Welsh stones, but they have all since been taken away for millstones, gateposts and road-metal, sounds interesting until it is pointed out that not one quern, post or chip of gravel made from Preseli stone has ever been found outside Wales. Any reference to the glacial theory was dropped from the guidebook in 1953, to resurface in English Heritage's current version in a couple of dismissive sentences.

But one prominent archaeologist did argue against human transport: the doyen of stone circles, the late Aubrey Burl (1926–2020). Neolithic people, he said, would have found it impossible to float the stones along the Welsh coast in their rickety, unsteerable rafts ('a form of seafaring suicide'); they had no reason to go so far when there were decent stones – the sarsens – in Wiltshire, while, by contrast, the bluestones are 'petrological clutter' that include some so soft they would 'weather and crumble'; and 'gullible' archaeologists obtained their 'belief' that some of the stones at Stonehenge came from Wales not from geology, but from the story of Merlin zapping them over from Ireland. Aubrey's case was based on the unspoken premise, in keeping with his view of ancient Britons as a primitive lot eking out their lives in fear of the next disaster, that carrying stones from southwest Wales to Salisbury Plain was contrary to all sound archaeological reasoning.[4]

He did, however, have one geological point to make: there was a bluestone in Wiltshire, he said, which must have been taken there by a glacier. This lump of spotted dolerite, weighing over 600 kg (1,350 lb), is said to have been found early in the 19th century in a Neolithic burial mound on Salisbury Plain known as Boles Barrow, raised a good 500 years before work started at Stonehenge. Glacial believers always cite this stone as a key piece of evidence: if it was there before Stonehenge was built, it can only have travelled with ice. That is false logic (one could counter, with equal sophistry, that as part of a Neolithic monument it must have been brought there by people, ergo, so, at a later date, was all of Stonehenge). In truth we can't be certain whether it came from the barrow or not, or if it did, whether it was put there at the start or when Stonehenge was built – or even later. An alternative and more plausible case is that the stone was in fact taken from Stonehenge itself in recent centuries.[5]

We might expect a better case to come from geologists who favour glaciation, but it doesn't start well. All advocates, who like Aubrey Burl express strong feelings about the issue, deploy his same arguments. Recently, for example, one complained in a reputable peer-reviewed science journal that archaeologists 'unquestioningly accepted... such improbable myths as long-distance transport of heavy blocks of rock by Neolithic humans', implying they were swayed in this 'belief' by 'such absurdities as the "Prophecies of Merlin".' The most vocal proponent, Brian John, has written a book

Archaeologists laser-scanning a fragment of spotted dolerite megalith weighing more than half a ton, known as the Boles stone, in The Salisbury Museum in 2016. It was taken from Stonehenge at an unknown date, and shows extensive damage with metal tools.

on the topic. Most of it is about archaeological 'myths'. Only one chapter describes Welsh glaciers; Brian is a geomorphologist (and a novelist) with a glacier named after him in Antarctica, and the chapter is interesting – but it presents no evidence for a Salisbury Plain glacier, or that any naturally occurring Preseli boulders have been found beyond Pembrokeshire.[6]

Beside rhetoric, what actually is the evidence? The idea of glacial stone transport was first revived by the late Geoff Kellaway (1914–2013), a distinguished geologist who, like Thomas, worked at the British Geological Survey. Much of his research involved mapping the geology of Bristol and Somerset, and in retirement he advised the local council at Bath on thermal springs, saving the famous spa pools, in use since at least Roman times, from permanent closure. Writing in *Nature* in 1971, he argued that new evidence supported the existence of former ice streams that crossed

Pembrokeshire and then the Severn Estuary, continuing eastwards into west Wiltshire (it was the publication of this article that sent me, an undergraduate, across London in search of the Geological Museum's model). That this carried any of the Stonehenge stones, however, remained hypothetical – as did an arrow on his map that passed through Boles Barrow and landed at the monument. None of Thomas's particular rocks appeared among any of the erratics or gravels described by Kellaway.

The geologist returned to the subject at greater length 30 years later, proposing that most of the bluestones were found by Neolithic people close to Stonehenge buried in natural sinkholes, for which there is no evidence – explaining, by a circular route, why Stonehenge is where it is. With still no evidence for a Salisbury Plain glacier, Kellaway suggested the stones had arrived in powerful rivers of melting ice from further west, for which, again, there is no evidence.

Other geologists also considered the issue. In a major study in the 1980s, a team based at the Open University was able to examine new samples (Thomas had examined chips from Hawley's excavations and older collections), some 'taken by an English Heritage stonemason', from 15 of the stones standing at Stonehenge: at the precise moment the drill started to core the first megalith, there was a huge clap of thunder![7] The team compared the chemistry of their new chips with that of samples from the Preselis, which broadly confirmed Thomas's results, though in some cases suggesting other outcrops over a slightly wider area. But most of their discussion was taken up by support for Kellaway's case, without mustering anything new. Further studies, on the other hand, disputed the glacial theory, backing Thomas with new surveys: there was still nothing but local stone in the beds of rivers flowing from Salisbury Plain, there were no deposits to indicate the area had ever seen a glacier, and an ice sheet crossing south Wales would have brought a greater variety of rocks than is seen at Stonehenge.

The case for glacial transport was going round in circles. That ice at some time flowed from southwest and central Wales into the Bath area, 50 km (30 miles) to the west of Stonehenge – but no nearer – seemed to be likely, but no evidence had been shown that it carried the required rocks with it. Though promoted mostly by geologists, the argument relied almost entirely on their gut feelings that Neolithic people would not have gone all the way to Wales to obtain megaliths for use in Wiltshire. A new approach was needed, one that didn't start and end with cultural assumptions about unfamiliar people. As most archaeologists were happy to accept Thomas's case without question, it would have to come from geologists. And it did.

In 1979 and 1980 I directed two small excavations at Stonehenge, one of which was beside and the other just up the road from the Heelstone – literally, since a road then passed close by the megalith, and our trench was on the verge. I've told the story elsewhere,[8] but what matters here is what we found: in 1980 a pile of stone debris. It was the last thing I'd been expecting, and at the time archaeologists had dismissed such fragments lying near the surface (these were just 50–60 cm – less than 2 ft – down) as the unfortunate product of people knocking bits off the megaliths in relatively recent centuries. I thought otherwise, at least in this case, and I was pleased to find that other archaeologists agreed that the pieces seemed to have been put there around the time Stonehenge was built (exactly when is a difficult, and surprisingly significant, question, to which we will return later in the book).

Having decided that the stone fragments were prehistoric, I needed someone to tell me what they were. No one had considered Stonehenge petrology, its geological stories, since Thomas had last looked at it more than half a century before, and I had no money for specialist fees. So I asked the late Hilary Howard (1943–2021), one of the volunteer diggers, for help. She was a PhD student working with prehistoric ceramics, learning about geology so she could understand the minerals they contained. She looked at the stone chips, applying the same techniques she was using with clays, and we both read all we could find that had been written about

From left, in centre: Hilary Howard, Richard Atkinson and the author
at his excavation near the Heelstone in 1979.

Stonehenge geology. I was in the mood for questioning everything,
and in my ignorance I encouraged her to see if she could add to, or
even change, anything that Thomas had said. Most helpfully, we
discovered a young geologist in Cardiff who had just started work
at the National Museum of Wales. He was Richard Bevins.

The year before, Richard had completed his doctoral thesis on
the volcanic rocks of part of the north Pembrokeshire coast, and
he had now turned inland to look at the Preselis. He offered much
useful advice, and backed Hilary's analysis and her proposal that
all the bluestones needed a fresh look, though the main thing I
remember from our meeting was his scepticism – entirely justified – about my theory that perhaps some of the Stonehenge
megaliths had come from Snowdon. He stayed at the National
Museum to become head of its Natural Sciences department,
retiring in 2020 as an honorary research fellow at the museum
and an honorary professor at Aberystwyth University. A decade
before, he co-authored his first article about Stonehenge and the

sources of its megaliths. Many studies followed, to which other geologists and archaeologists contributed, but mostly they were written by just him and one other: Rob Ixer.

Rob too is a geologist, with a different career behind him of teaching at several English universities, mining consultancy, and working with archaeologists to provenance artefacts and metal ores – to determine where the materials had been quarried; he is an honorary research associate at UCL's Institute of Archaeology. He contributed to the Open University study with a detailed comparison between a few samples from one bluestone megalith and from a Preseli outcrop. He found them near identical, as would have been the case if the one came from the other, and his interest was piqued. Aware of the controversy about how the Welsh stones reached Stonehenge, Rob argued that the solution, if there was one, could lie in matching megaliths so closely to outcrops that their origins could be narrowed down to 'within metres or tens of metres' – in other words, a quarry.

Richard Bevins at Craig Rhos-y-felin.

Rob Ixer points to the Altar Stone at Stonehenge, hidden under a fallen lintel.

Richard had also helped the Open University study, by sharing his unpublished research. It was inevitable, if this project was to happen, that he and Rob would work on it together, with the former's exceptional understanding of the local geology, and the latter's petrographical skills and obsessive determination to track down and analyse every last piece of Stonehenge debris – Rob would have sampled all the other bluestone megaliths, too, had he been allowed to. Since their first joint publication in 2010 they have written more than 30 articles, an extraordinary output of highly technical research, all achieved without the grants that usually accompany such work (Rob refers to him and Richard as the Pet Rock Boys – to Richard's horror, they were once so named in *The Times*). What they call the first pass of the project has ended. It has been astonishingly successful. And in its details it has overturned almost everything that Herbert Thomas concluded from what he could see, metaphorically, through his less powerful telescope.

When Richard and Rob began, the idea was to track down every geological and archaeological sample than had been analysed in the past in the quest to solve the bluestone issue, and apply modern, consistent studies. There was already new material as well, such as that from my excavations, and I was delighted to receive questions about precisely where each fragment came from as they progressed through the different rock types. As they worked, a major field project conducted at and around Stonehenge uncovered more pieces of stone, as did a small dig by another team inside the stone circle – the latter contributed most of the more than 4,000 fragments that the project examined.

As well as more rocks from Wiltshire to study, and new samples from potential sources, Richard and Rob had a more sophisticated understanding of Welsh geology and Stonehenge than was available to Thomas. They also had techniques he did not have. And key to their success was what they call 'total petrography', combining complementary information from looking at stone under the microscope, geochemical analysis of the same pieces of rock (over-reliance on hi-tech 1980s geochemistry, they found, had taken the Open University team up a number of false trails) and occasionally radiometric data. As the years passed they experimented successfully with a growing range of new techniques, one, for the first time for the archaeological analysis of stone, being the use of energy dispersive spectrometers (EDS) in university electron microscopes; these allow microscopically thin sections of stone to be analysed in huge detail, and, critically, automatically, generating very precise and accurate data enabling extremely localized potential sources to be sought. Meanwhile, long-lost or overlooked old Stonehenge samples kept surfacing. They even examined pieces of stone they knew probably had nothing to do with Stonehenge – crystals lost or hidden by modern Pagans, roadstone, chips of concrete and so on – so as to eliminate every last possibility.[9]

With all the effort and so much new data, you'd expect there to be a few surprises, and there were. The focus remains on Pembrokeshire, and in that regard Herbert Thomas was on the nail – he was surveying in the right place at the right time, and luck was with him.

The many little details, however, add up to a shift in emphasis that changes the way we think about the bluestones. And it's not over yet.

Thomas claimed to have identified the sources for three different types of Stonehenge megalith, other than the sarsens, and named a fourth from broken chips alone. Richard Bevins and Rob Ixer found that pattern holds – only one of their rock groups has not, as yet, been matched to any known megalith. But two things have changed. First, there are many more types of bluestone – at least 13 of them. Second, the commoner the debris of any one type, the fewer stones now stand at the site; very few of the thousands of pieces seem to have come from any megalith now visible. I have summarized it all in three tables, giving each type a B[luestone] number for the purposes of this book.

So what are the rocks? And where do we have to go to get them?

Let's begin by defining what we mean by 'igneous rocks'. They were all once molten magma deep beneath the Earth's surface, and the different types reflect the magma's chemistry and how and where it cooled and solidified. These processes determine factors

The best preserved section of the Bluestone Circle, at the northeast of the monument, featuring five stones of (from left) rhyolite (B8), spotted dolerite (BU1), rhyolite (fallen, B7), spotted dolerite (B1) and spotted dolerite (BU1).

that might have attracted people to the outcrops for making stone tools or megaliths, such as their hardness, texture and colour, and how they break up, whether naturally or when hammered by a stone worker.

The most prominent igneous rock at Stonehenge is dolerite, known in North America as diabase; both terms are ceding to microgabbro, though at least for now it feels that Stonehenge dolerite and spotted dolerite are here to stay. Microgabbro is an intrusive igneous rock, meaning it solidified beneath the surface. It's tough and relatively coarse grained, often used today in buildings or crushed for road metal. It's found in the Preselis in outcrops that are naturally jointed, so that manageable if often large blocks, sometimes plucked by recent glaciers passing above, lean and tumble against each other. Some Preseli dolerite is riddled with unusual pale spots, which can lend the stone the appearance of agglomerate marble used in the building trade. But spotted dolerite is not a mixed stone: the spots are collections of crystals that formed when the original rock was altered by later geological events.[10]

Thomas described most of the bluestone megaliths as dolerite, and most of those were spotted; this remains the case (Table 1, overleaf). In total there are 27 spotted dolerite stones, and three unspotted. What Thomas couldn't know is that geochemistry would distinguish two spotted groups, and two unspotted. Eighteen of the spotted dolerite megaliths have not yet been sampled, so it's not possible to say which of the two groups they belong to, or, it may be, if some are further differentiated. And one of the unspotted stones does not match either group of that type.

The non-dolerite igneous rocks at Stonehenge are finer grained and extrusive; they formed in volcanic eruptions at the surface, in lava flows or explosions into the air. Rob and Richard have most recently identified them as rhyolite, dacite or andesite, distinguished by their chemical and mineralogical composition and relative grain size. Rhyolites are silica rich, giving them a flinty texture and potentially making them suitable for making stone tools. In some

No.	Rock type	Bevins & Ixer	Where found	Source
B1	Dolerite, spotted	Dolerite Group 1	Accounting for well over half the dolerite fragments from Stonehenge. Stones 33, 37, 49, 65 and 67	Carn Goedog
B2	Dolerite, spotted	Dolerite Group 3	Stones 34, 42, 43, 61 and the Boles Barrow stone	Carn Breseb, near Carn Alw, Carn Gyfrwy or ? Carn Menyn
BU1	Dolerite, spotted	Awaiting study	(Stones 31, 32, 35a/b, 36, 39, 41, 47, 61a, 63, 64, 66, 68, 69, 70, 70a, 70b, 71/72 and 150)	Preselis
B3	Dolerite, unspotted	Dolerite Group 2v	Stone 62	? Carn Ddafad-las or Garn Ddu-fach
B4	Dolerite, unspotted	Dolerite Group 2vi	Stone 45	Cerrig Marchogion
BU2	Dolerite, unspotted	Awaiting allocation	Stone 44	Preselis

Table 1. Dolerite rock types in the Stonehenge area and in their original outcrops. Tables 1–3 reflect research current when this book went to press, with information from Rob Ixer, Richard Bevins and colleagues; stone numbers in brackets are megaliths provisionally attributed to rock types, but not petrographically examined.

parts of the world dacites and andesites were important materials for tools, but the forms present in Wales are less useful.

Thomas was on less certain ground with these, distinguishing two, rhyolite and 'calcareous ash' (the dark grey chips and a buried stump, Stone 32c, found in 1881). Here Rob and Richard can see seven different types – three rhyolites, three dacites and an andesite (Table 2). There are also at least two non-igneous, sedimentary rocks – sandstones – represented by three megaliths, of which the Altar Stone is one, and a lot of chips; we'll come to these later.

Thanks to excavation, the bluestone megalith total at Stonehenge has also risen, from 33 to 44, and to the uninitiated this might now be looking like rather a ragbag collection of rocks. Some might argue that the variety, and in one case a type with no apparent megalith of which all but one piece has been found away from the monument, suggest the sort of debris that might once have been scattered over Salisbury Plain by a glacier. But we're not finished yet.

No.	Rock type	Bevins & Ixer	Where found	Source
B5	Andesite	Andesite Group A (formerly Volcanic A)	The commonest pieces among the igneous debris at Stonehenge, approaching 2,000 fragments. (Stones 33e, 33f, 40c and 41d)	North Pembrokeshire
B6	Rhyolite	Rhyolite Group C	The commonest type among the non-dolerite chips at Stonehenge by weight – well over a thousand are of this type. (Stones 32d and 32e)	Craig Rhos-y-felin
B7	Rhyolite	Rhyolite Group E	Occasionally in the local landscape. Stone 48	North Pembrokeshire
B8	Rhyolite	Rhyolite Group F	Stone 46	North Pembrokeshire
B9	Dacite	Dacite Group B (formerly Volcanic B)	A few chips at Stonehenge. Stone 38	North Pembrokeshire
B10	Dacite	Dacite Group C (formerly Rhyolite G)	Stone 40	North Pembrokeshire
B11	Dacite	Dacite Group D (formerly Rhyolite D)	Rare, small debris only, found near the west end of the Cursus and a single piece at Stonehenge in Aubrey Hole 16, all thought possibly to come from one unidentified or lost megalith	North Pembrokeshire

Table 2. Non-dolerite igneous rock types in the Stonehenge area and in their original outcrops. The Stonehenge B11 piece is sometimes said to come from Aubrey Hole 15, but 16 seems more likely (this matters for reasons we can happily avoid here).

Thomas thought all the igneous bluestones came from a restricted area of the Preseli Hills; he named four outcrops. What does the new research have to say about that?

Rob and Richard, sometimes working with other specialist colleagues, identified their rock types by looking very closely at all the megaliths and debris found at Stonehenge and in the neighbourhood. (A particular area of interest has been near the west end of the Cursus, about 1 km (0.6 miles) northwest of Stonehenge, where 20 chunks of bluestone were recovered in the 1940s: Marcus Stone (1899–1957), a scientist at the government's Biological Defence Establishment on nearby Porton Down who excavated at and around Stonehenge, proposed that a separate 'Blue Stonehenge' had once stood there.[11]) The next stage was to seek matches to these rock types in surface geology. To achieve the precision needed to pin these down to 'within metres or tens of metres' required a huge amount of forensic fieldwork and analysis, and this continues. But

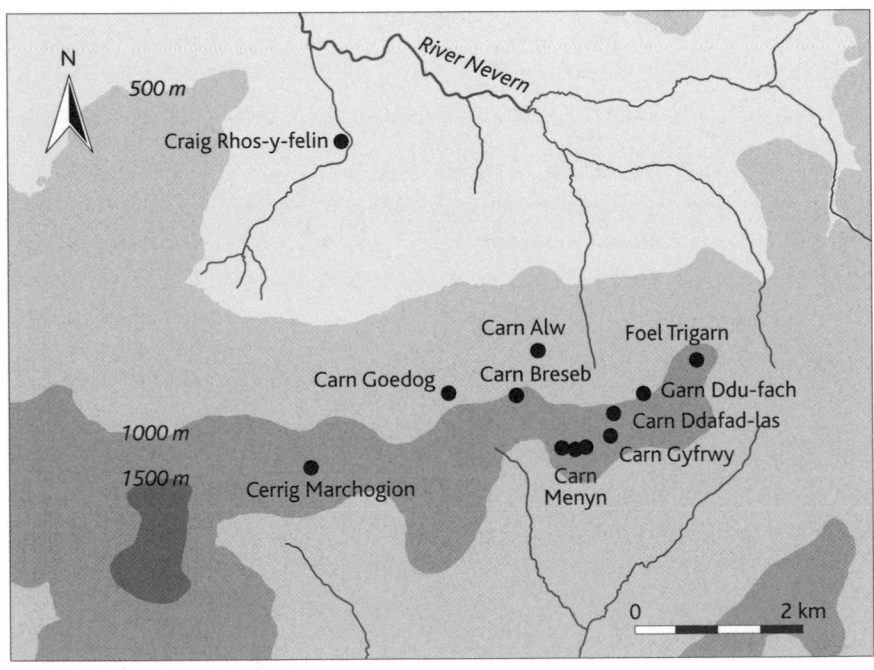

Key outcrops in the Preseli Hills.

the principle has been proven: the researchers have, in effect (a key qualification, which we'll come to), found some quarries.

Each of the four dolerite groups matches distinct geological locations in the Preselis (Table 1, p. 46): Carn Goedog (B1, see pl. VIII); Carn Breseb, an unnamed outcrop near Carn Alw, Carn Gyfrwy or possibly Carn Menyn (B2); in the area of Carn Ddafad-las or Garn Ddu-fach (B3); and Cerrig Marchogion (B4). This is a remarkable number of mostly small outcrops within an area of less than 10 sq. km (4 sq. miles). It's likely that the presently ungrouped dolerite megaliths also came from the Preseli Hills, some perhaps from yet further distinct locations. By contrast, Thomas had proposed just two sources, Cerrig Marchogion and Carn Menyn. The latter – the most prominent of all the dolerite outcrops which had long attracted most interest from archaeologists – is still on the list, but currently only as a possibility.

One of the commonest extrusive rocks at Stonehenge by weight (B6 in Table 2, p. 47) is matched with a small rhyolite outcrop at Craig Rhos-y-felin (see pl. X). This is off the Preselis about 3 km (2 miles) north from the dolerite peaks – and from Carn Alw, which Thomas had thought the source of the rhyolites. None of the other six extrusive groups yet has an exact match. However, the geologists think that all of them probably came from north Pembrokeshire, from rocks belonging to the Fishguard Volcanic Group. These run in a narrow band from west of Fishguard Bay (so Thomas might have been onto something in his early comments to Edgar Barclay) eastwards to Crymych, skirting the northern edge of the Preselis at the eastern end.

To summarize, of Thomas's four locations in the Preseli Hills, only Cerrig Marchogion has so far survived the new research with certainty, and that is as one of at least two possible sources for an apparently less significant type of unspotted dolerite. Carn Menyn had once been thought the key supply. It presents a series of dramatic outcrops around the southern side of the hill, facing south. Now, however, most of the identified quarried Preseli outcrops offer views across the lower land to the north and, on a good clear day, of other rock sources between the hills and the coast and out to sea to Ireland.

Britain's geology is extraordinarily varied and complex, partly accounting for the intense regionalization of modern landscapes within an area that in other parts of the world could be quite uniform, even featureless. That diversity also allows us, when we're lucky, to identify particular rock locations favoured in prehistory – often, by definition, unusual or distinctive, attracting ancient stoneworkers and builders – and to trace their transported products. It has been possible to match Stonehenge bluestones to these very specific locations in Pembrokeshire partly because of the intensive work of Richard Bevins and Rob Ixer. But they would not have got far if the geology had not been so helpful. And by identifying so many different sources in such a small area, they are also excluding many serviceable rock types nearby and beyond. This very localized Neolithic targeting of bluestone occurrences, added to the absence of anything to support the notion that the stones at Stonehenge had been carried even part of the way by glaciers, seems to me to leave no realistic option other than human transport.

There remains the question of the sandstones, including the Altar Stone. Do they challenge the human transport theory? Or confirm it? These were the last significant stone type that Richard and Rob cracked, and while, as I write, further fieldwork and scientific analysis may succeed in achieving a more precise provenance for the two types, their solution further confirms the role of human transport.

Using a battery of scientific techniques, including zircon age dating, automated scanning electron microscopy and X-ray diffraction, they showed that the Altar Stone (B13) definitely didn't come from the Cosheston Subgroup of Mill Bay in Milford Haven – but it might well have come from the other of Thomas's two potential sources, the Senni Formation.

In the 1920s the focus of attention was Pembrokeshire, and the Cosheston Subgroup fitted this narrative. The most westward

No.	Rock type	Bevins & Ixer	Where found	Source
B12	Sandstone	Lower Palaeozoic Sandstone	The third commonest type among the non-dolerite chips at Stonehenge, and occasionally in the local landscape. Stones 40g and 42c	South or central Wales
B13	Sandstone	Devonian Old Red Sandstone	A few chips at Stonehenge. Altar Stone	Eastern Wales or Marches?

Table 3. Sandstone types in the Stonehenge area and in their original outcrops.

extension of the Senni Formation was just outside the county, but like the alternative it was on the coast, in this case where the River Gwendraeth flows into Carmarthen Bay. The location is visible across the water from Dylan Thomas's writing shed on the north shore, a similar distance overland from the Preselis as Mill Bay. For archaeological purposes Senni and Cosheston were almost interchangeable. Stone found a piece of sandstone in the ditch of the Cursus of a type that Thomas had not seen: another geologist identified it as different from the Altar Stone, but also with an origin in Milford Haven, confirming by association, in archaeologists' eyes, the Altar Stone's south Pembrokeshire origins. All the bluestones derived from a corner of southwest Wales.

However, Richard's and Rob's new data for the Altar Stone led them further and further away from Pembrokeshire, to the eastern end of the Senni Formation towards Abergavenny and the Brecon Beacons, close to the border with England. This was a location that had long been overlooked in the story of Stonehenge, though it had once been a contender: in 1811 Richard Fenton noted that some thought the Altar Stone 'a species of porphyry, from the Black Mountain in South Wales', one of four massifs in the Brecon Beacons (a lucky break perhaps – other stones, he said, might have come from the Pyrenees and Finland).[12]

Meanwhile the other, Lower Palaeozoic, sandstone (B12 in Table 3, p. 51) marched off in a different direction: again, as I write, Richard and Rob have not determined precisely where it came from, but it certainly wasn't Milford Haven or the Preselis. Instead its source may lie in Late Ordovician age rocks that extend from east of the Preselis, cropping out intermittently across east and central Wales.

It is clear that the sandstones, the last 2 of the 13 types of bluestone, came from two quite different places; it would have taken at least two different glaciers to have carried all the stones east. There is even a chance that the Altar Stone didn't come from Wales at all, but from northeast Scotland or Orkney – a sensational, if improbable-sounding, notion actually being researched. And there is a final nail in the glacial coffin. One objection to human transport has been the variety of rocks at Stonehenge, and that several of them are just not very tough: why would people bother with soft stones when they could have something harder, more brutal? But the same argument can be used against ice movement. The Altar Stone is currently the largest bluestone at Stonehenge. Any of the other 'soft' megaliths, mostly reduced to weathered slabs and broken stumps, could have been significantly larger than they are now – the quantities of debris at Stonehenge hint at the amount of damage. People could choose what they wanted to build Stonehenge with. But glaciers pick up everything in their path. And as they drag and grind, the softer stones suffer. We'd expect to see the opposite of what we find at Stonehenge: smaller soft stones, without the debris that tells us that, once, they were large.

So now it should be possible to locate actual quarries we need to visit, and then to plot the journeys we need to make with our stones. We will return to these questions in Chapter 5, but first we need to know where to look for sarsens: bluestones are not the only megaliths. This is a quite different story, with a long history, but one that is being properly addressed only as I write. It should come as no surprise that no one had predicted exactly what the scientists would find.

CHAPTER 3

RAW MATERIALS: SARSEN

The bluestones are fine things, distinctive both for their appearance and the now lost stories that must have accompanied them and their journeys. But if we want to build Stonehenge, we need more than that. We need more stones, and we need them to be really big. We need sarsens (see pl. xi).

Sarsen megaliths composed the first ancient monument to enter the protective care of the government, following the passing of an Act in 1882. But they were not at Stonehenge. It would be over 30 years before that site was taken into guardianship, after a new Act that empowered the state to protect monuments in private ownership, and the sale of Stonehenge by an exasperated owner to a philanthropist who gave it to the nation. Instead, the first prehistoric site to benefit from government care was called Kit's Coty House.

Kit's Coty House consists of three sarsen slabs standing close together and a fourth balanced on top. None of the stones is carved and there is no jointing; archaeologists assume that originally they would have been largely hidden within a great Neolithic burial mound, where they made a chamber for the dead, raised centuries before Stonehenge. Turner sketched them a few years before his first visit to Wiltshire. They're in Kent.

Now if you imagine that all the sarsens at Stonehenge were local, taken from the neighbouring downs, it would be fair to ask if the Kit's Coty sarsens had also come from Wiltshire, dragged around 185 km (115 miles) from the west. There are, however, some natural occurrences of the stone in the area of the burial monument, and that is probably where its megaliths were quarried. The question might then be turned around. Could any of the Stonehenge stones have come from Kent?

Until very recently archaeologists and geologists – and guidebook writers – had taken little interest in the sarsens, rarely going beyond a passing comment that they had been brought to the site from the Marlborough Downs, a long day's walk to the north. Sarsen can be found across southeast England and the other side of the English Channel in France. So while early observers looked as far as Africa for bluestones (where they might also have found sarsens), why was it assumed that none of the other stones at Stonehenge had been brought from further afield? Can we go beyond assumption and produce scientific evidence for their origin – and if so, what does that evidence tell us? And anyway, what is sarsen? These are the questions we need to try to answer in this chapter. Where should we go to find large stones fit for megaliths?

Sarsen is a weird rock, and sarsens challenge our idea of how a British landscape should look. Wherever they are found, it feels they shouldn't be there. They don't do what stone is supposed to do: there are no sarsen hills or cliffs, no towering outcrops or rolling sarsen plains. Instead they gather individually on the surface or hide below the turf, great slabs and boulders or cobbles and pebbles scattered across fields and woods as if something has gone wrong with geology (you won't find them on British Geological Survey maps). They look like erratics, aliens dragged into place by ancient glaciers. The word sarsen is thought to derive from a Wiltshire pronunciation of Saracen, once a popular term for a pagan, a foreigner.[1] But they are not erratics: most occur where glaciers have never been.

Sometimes they are rare, sometimes so common 'you may goe upon them all the way', leaping across stepping stones. 'They call that place the Grey-weathers', wrote a miserably wet Richard Symonds (1617–1660), who kept a Civil War diary in 1644 while the troops camped out on the downs near Marlborough, 'because a far off they looke like a flock of sheepe', streaming in thousands off hills and down valleys.[2] Some have been given names, as if they might be megaliths: across southern England are the Toad Stone, the Blowing Stone, the Coronation Stone, the Goldstone and the Three Stones of Titchfield. George Ewart Evans, in his book *Ask the Fellows Who Cut the Hay* (1956), told of the Blaxhall Stone in Suffolk, which grew out of the ground and was still swelling, so that where once a cat had been able to pass under its lip, there was now room for a dog. As I write, Katy Whitaker, an archaeologist who has made a special study of sarsen and its place in people's lives, is tweeting a #DailySarsen photo, each a story in stone.[3] If ever there was a material that needed Stonehenge, it was sarsen.

Sarsen is technically a type of silcrete, formed when silica, dissolved in water, cements sand into a hard stone. As a result sarsen is itself almost pure silica, which has been one of the reasons why the Stonehenge sarsens have until recently attracted relatively little research – without newly developed techniques to study them, there was not much that could be said beyond describing their hardness, fineness and purity. That new work, led in particular

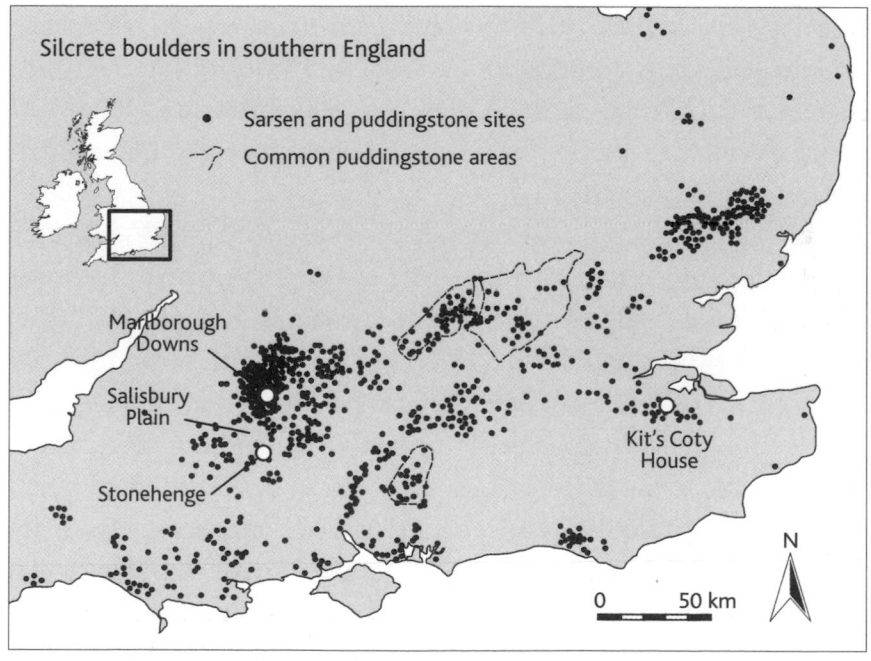

Sarsen fields in southeast England, mapped by Dave Nash.

by Dave Nash and Stewart Ullyott, physical geographers at the University of Brighton, has thrown up fresh ideas about how the English sarsens formed, and, as we shall see later in the chapter, has also brought opportunities to pin down exactly where those at Stonehenge came from.

It used to be said that the sarsen we see today is all that remains of what was once, many millions of years ago, a continuous hard layer near the surface known as duricrust. Sometimes fragments survived, and elsewhere the crust had disappeared. The original layer had formed in a hot, tropical climate, and what look like root casts in the stone were presented as evidence of palm trees – conjuring a strange vision if you were out on the downs in winter, wrapped against the cold and surveying a field of sarsens with pooled ice in their steely hollows. It is now suggested, however, that the English silcretes had more varied origins, growing where sands were saturated with silica-rich water at or near the water table, or where such water rose to the surface or flowed through river beds in a dry climate. Not all are necessarily the same age, and the varied distribution today – isolated scatters in Hampshire, Sussex and Kent, for example, or denser concentrations in parts of Dorset, Wiltshire and Essex – is indicative partly of where sarsen did, and did not, form.

There are three types of English silcrete, which can sometimes be seen to merge into each other. The commonest, and the one out of which Stonehenge's megaliths are made, is a mostly pale grey cemented sand described as 'saccharoid' sarsen – when freshly exposed or broken it can have a sugary texture. It is often seen as slabs of rock, sometimes very large, with parallel, though typically irregular, faces and cliff-like, fissured sides; when weathered it will repel hardened steel tools. 'Hard' sarsen, by contrast, is genuinely hard, formed from finer sand and occurring in small, rounded brown lumps. These too are common at Stonehenge, where they were used as hammers – to shape saccharoid sarsen. Finally 'puddingstone', common especially in parts of Hampshire, Oxfordshire and

Buckinghamshire, is like a saccharoid sarsen packed with flint or quartz pebbles. There is an occasional hint of this at Stonehenge too, where small clusters of broken flints lie trapped in the grey stone.

If we look out from Stonehenge in any direction, the only obvious visible stone that isn't part of the monument is a milestone, marking the way on a road that was opened less than three centuries ago and was removed in 2013. Even before the distinction was made between bluestones and sarsens, the presence of big stones of any kind on Salisbury Plain was the greatest part of the mystery. By contrast, across the plain and the Vale of Pewsey to the north, the Marlborough Downs were littered with stones. The link was made early on.

From at least the late 1500s writers were comparing Marlborough sarsens – 'of unmeasurable bignesse and number', as Elizabethan courtier and poet John Harington (1560–1612) put it – to those at Stonehenge. 'The same kinde of Stone whereof [Stoneheng] consists may be found' near Avebury, wrote Inigo Jones in 1655, 'where not onely are Quarries of the like stone, but also stones of far greater dimensions'. The Stonehenge and Marlborough Downs sarsens, wrote William Stukeley in the 1720s, 'are of the same kind of stone: the same grain, texture, color & composition'. William Cunnington – grandson of the William Cunnington we encountered earlier – in 1852 pictured 'Countless numbers of these enormous stones... winding like a mighty stream'. And so on. The rivers of sarsens, the 'trains' as they are known, entered folklore as the waters into which the builders of Stonehenge sank their copious nets (see pls XIII, XIV).

We can see such trains today between Marlborough and Avebury, and jump from one boulder to another in the Valley of Stones. This is inside Fyfield Down National Nature Reserve, designated in 1955 for its rolling grassland and partly for the stones themselves, which host their own peculiar lichen ecologies among the flowers and scrubby bushes. Elsewhere individual stones are common, scattered across the open downs and hidden in hedges, built into walls and pavements, and continually getting in the way in excavations. And there is Avebury, where hundreds of stones, entirely unshaped by people and often of a size that would have done proud at Stonehenge, were raised into rings and rows around the same time (though dating evidence is poor). And yet what we see is a pale shadow of what was once there.[4]

In a landscape otherwise bereft of hard stone, sarsens were always vulnerable to exploitation. Some of Wiltshire's largest megaliths are within the burial mound of the West Kennet long barrow, constructed near Avebury some five centuries before stones reached Stonehenge (as a general rule, Neolithic barrows are long and Bronze Age ones round). On a smaller scale, for millennia

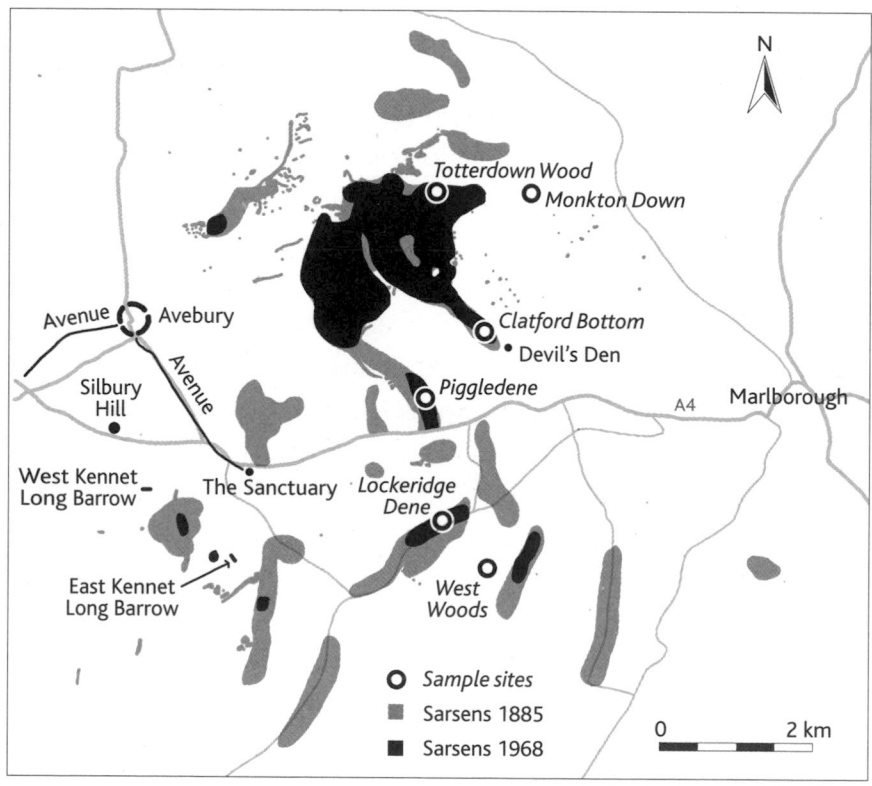

Dave Nash's team sampled six sarsen sites on the Marlborough Downs. By 1968 sarsen fields had shrunk due to use for buildings and road metal, having already been diminished when first mapped in 1885. Neolithic monuments are also marked.

sarsen was broken up and shaped into stones for grinding flour. The ramparts of Iron Age hillforts and the walls of Roman houses have sarsens in them. From the Middle Ages boulders were attacked with gusto by fire and mallet, and later sledgehammer and wedge, and the Marlborough Downs are distinguished by houses built with sarsen. The National Trust bought two valleys in 1908 to preserve their trains, but what remained by then were mostly smaller, more awkward boulders; split slabs marked by steel tools now tell as much of the Victorian industry as of the places once 'so full of grey pibble stones'. In another valley in the 1920s there was a road-metal factory that used explosives (fortunately it soon went bankrupt).

We can study detailed maps made in the 19th century and see great fields of sarsens that have entirely vanished, but it would take fieldwork on a scale not yet contemplated to approach an idea of how these downs really looked in prehistoric times. If the few trains that survive, even these the residues of intensive recent industry, impress us with their strange atmosphere and the incongruity of the massed stones, how in their full glory must the sarsens of north Wiltshire have played on the Neolithic imagination?

However, there is another story. When Herbert Thomas considered Stonehenge a century ago he was more interested in the bluestones, but in passing he noted that the sarsens had probably been collected from the area of the monument. He was not alone in this view. Several other geologists and archaeologists at that time believed that both bluestones and sarsens once lay scattered over Salisbury Plain, perhaps accounting for the very presence of Stonehenge at its particular location. But where was the evidence for these stones? Early antiquaries commonly listed occurrences of individual sarsens in the area, but none was illustrated and it's now impossible to be sure exactly where any of them were supposed to have been. Thomas himself set the scene for land near Stonehenge free of naturally occurring bluestones. Might the same have been the case for sarsens?

Salisbury Plain is not so much level ground as a high, rolling plateau divided by five rivers which flow southward between expansive blocks of chalk downland. Within these islands are no streams or springs, and settlement now and in the historic past has hugged the river valleys. The open plain was a place to avoid, or to pass through at haste in fear of robbery – John Aubrey recorded a local saying: 'Salisbury Plain – never without a thief or twain'.[5]

From 1897 the Ministry of Defence bought up land, first for cavalry training, soon for some of the world's first military flying experiments, and continuing through two world wars to the present when the number of soldiers and their families living in the area has grown hugely. For over a century live ammunition training, and the debris it leaves behind, largely excluded the modern world. Immediately to the north of Stonehenge was a landscape the size of the Isle of Wight – 37,000 hectares or 90,000 acres – with no roads or houses, no buried pipes or cables and no fields (the grassland has never been sprayed with chemicals). It was an ecological and archaeological treasure house known only to soldiers. Then in 1988 the military invited archaeologists to have a look.

There were many discoveries: the number of known ancient monuments doubled, among them some of the best-preserved Roman village earthworks in northern Europe. Archaeologists also found sarsens. They hadn't set out to look for them, but they kept coming across broken rocks. There was a group around Warminster, 25 km (15 miles) west of Stonehenge, where tellingly there were also long barrows that contained sarsen megaliths. Closer sarsens could be found in the area of Bulford and Amesbury, 5 km (3 miles) to the east. At Robin Hood's Ball, an older Neolithic meeting place looking down on the site of Stonehenge from 4 km (2.5 miles) to the northwest, were massive sarsen boulders. The plain had once been full of the stones, it seemed, before they were broken up by early farmers so that now they were hidden in hedges and deep field banks (by contrast, not a single bluestone was found). 'The sarsen used at Stonehenge', the archaeologists concluded, 'need not have come from the Marlborough Downs.'[6]

More recently archaeologists conducted a detailed survey of the land around Stonehenge itself. They wondered if natural hollows in the chalk close to the stones, 10–20 m (30–65 ft) across and up to 2 m (6 ft) deep, might be the tops of filled solution holes reaching deep underground that had once held sarsen boulders that might even now be at Stonehenge.[7] In fact as far back as the 1500s John Leland (1503–1552), a travelling antiquary, told a version of the medieval story of Stonehenge's creation in which Merlin, far from bringing stones from Ireland, sought them on Salisbury Plain, where they were 'enormous and prolific'.

All this was speculation, however. What was needed was scientific analysis of potential sources as Richard Bevins and Rob Ixer had done for the bluestones, ideally to be compared with samples of actual megaliths – an unknown prospect, as by now Stonehenge's guardians were extremely protective of their ward (as Rob knows, to his frustration). Then out of the blue, Historic England got a call from someone who asked if they would like a piece of Stonehenge back. It was in Florida.[8]

In 1958, at a time when you could dig holes at Stonehenge with minor oversight, bring in heavy machinery to move megaliths about and, if you were careless, knock one over (a story told in Chapter 7), the Ministry of Works – the government department responsible for Stonehenge – re-erected a fallen trilithon. One of the three sarsens was Stone 58, an upright among the largest megaliths at the site. While it lay on the ground, engineers were worried about an extensive fissure, and it was investigated – in one of those typical Stonehenge episodes that must have seemed normal at the time – with radioactive sodium.

This material was used in medicine (to track blood flow, for example) and for searching out cracks and defects in metal castings. At Stonehenge, a team of three men and a woman from the Atomic Energy Research Establishment at Harwell, south

Harwell scientists attempt to measure cracks in Stone 58 before its re-erection.

of Oxford, laid sheets of X-ray film across the flat surface of the stone. A small aluminium capsule of sodium buried in a barrel of lead was rushed down from a nuclear reactor pile – radioactive sodium has a half-life of only 15 hours, so if they'd got badly stuck in traffic they'd have had to go back for more. While one of them kept an eye on things with a Geiger counter, the barrel was gently winched down beside the recumbent megalith, the cylinder pulled into a hole dug beneath, and the sodium left there for 36 hours. The radioactivity did its job, penetrating the sarsen and casting shadows on the photographic plates.

The result was that the crack appeared to be safe, and erection went ahead 'with very great care'. However, by the time the stone was upright and set in its new concrete foundation – and a 16-ton lintel balanced on top – the now more easily seen fissures created renewed concern: viewed from the sides it almost looks as if the stone is already in two pieces, like the two layers of a giant contorted Bourbon biscuit. So the plan originally proposed by the Ministry architect was put into place. Three horizontal holes were successfully drilled right through the megalith by L. M. Van Moppes Sons (Diamond Tools) Ltd, to take metal rods tensioned with bolt heads at either end, which were concealed under circular plugs carved from sarsen pieces found in the excavations (if you know where to look, you can see these plugs today).

A by-product of this work was three long cores an inch (25 mm) across, each a complete section through a sarsen trilithon stone – the best samples known not just from Stonehenge, but from any megalith in the UK. Van Moppes was allowed to keep one of them and gave it to the late Robert Phillips (1928–2020), an employee

Men from Van Moppes Ltd drilling Stone 58 in 1958.

who'd been on site during the operation. He hung it in his office in Basingstoke until he left the firm in 1976, taking it with him when he emigrated to the USA. Over the following years Robert and his core moved from Rochester, New York, to Chicago, Illinois; then to Ventura, California; and finally to Aventura, Florida. On the eve of his 90th birthday, Robert told his son Robin, who lived in England, that he was keen for the core to go back home. A packing case was delivered to his house, and his second son, Lewis, collected it and gave it to English Heritage in 2018. Looking like a broom handle in its Perspex tube, the core is just over 1 m (3½ ft) long and in six

Stone 58 today (on left), showing large natural fissures down one side.

sections. Research into its provenance was of a kind that a redis-covered Leonardo might have received. Later, after media publicity, a short length of a second core was identified in The Salisbury Museum – only when details of the first became known was it possible to say exactly what it was. The fates of the third, and the rest of the Salisbury core, remain unknown.

No one was more surprised to hear about the core than Dave Nash. A few years before, he had started work on a pioneering project to find out where the Stonehenge sarsens had come from. He and his team had failed to win the large grant they felt they needed, and had abandoned attempts to drill their own cores at Stonehenge (they had arranged drillers and conservationists, and the next step would have been to get government permission). Instead, armed with £10,000 from the British Academy, they were analysing the sarsen megaliths and debris from excavations using an X-ray technique: it wasn't as good as being able to cut up some rock, but it left the stones unharmed and it kept the project within budget.

They were in the middle of this work when, in late 2017, Dave received an email from English Heritage. Would he be interested in looking at a core – if it could be brought back from America? 'I almost bit their hand off', he told me, and promptly wrote a scientific case for the transport costs. When it arrived they'd more or less finished at Stonehenge, and were working on stone chips from an English Heritage store in Portsmouth. It changed the game.

While little research had been done on the English sarsens, silcretes had generated interest elsewhere, especially in France, Australia and southern Africa. In these regions the flintier-textured stone had been used for making tools in the distant past in ways that would not have been possible with the tougher stone in Britain. This work had challenged ideas about how silcretes formed, and in the 1990s Dave, who had been studying silcretes in the Kalahari Desert in Botswana, proposed with his colleagues that insights gained in Africa could profitably be applied to Wiltshire and Dorset: the revised story of sarsen origins described above came from this.

Dave Nash and Stewart Ullyott then embarked on a study of sarsens closer to home, on the South Downs in East Sussex, before returning to Botswana, this time specifically to consider stone tools made over 50,000 years ago. Their project was a success. They had a theory that trace elements – present in a material in extremely low amounts – could fingerprint different silcrete sources and any tools that might have been made from them. They ground up samples of rock and analysed them with now standard geochemical laboratory kit – inductively coupled plasma mass spectrometry (ICP-MS) and ICP-atomic emission spectrometry (ICP-AES) – which can detect elements in very low concentrations. Not only were they able to distinguish different rock occurrences in this way, but they could match tools to them, sometimes found nearly 325 km (200 miles) from their source. And in 2011, while he was doing this, Dave thought of Stonehenge.

He got in touch with archaeologists and found that they had also been wondering how sources for the sarsen megaliths might be identified. Their interest had come to a head as a result of two excavations which, coincidentally, both took place in 2008. In trenches inside the monument and just to the north outside, university archaeologists Tim Darvill and Mike Parker Pearson respectively had found a lot of sarsen debris. It got them thinking about how the stones had been carved or broken up, and where they came from (as had happened to me nearly 30 years before).

At Stonehenge Dave and his colleague Jake Ciborowski, a petrologist at Brighton University, used portable X-ray fluorescence (pXRF) to characterize the sarsens. A gadget looking like something you might see in a shop in the hands of an assistant sticking on price labels, is aimed at a stone to hit it with X-rays. These cause elements in the megalith to return X-rays, varying in energy according to the element, back to a detector which almost instantly displays the chemistry result on a screen. They took five readings from all 52 sarsens, each one taking a couple of minutes. To keep out of the way of visitors the work had to be done over several days in late shifts, or on one early morning with a mobile scaffold tower so Ciborowski could reach the lintels, wearing a hard hat and a hi-vis jacket. Otherwise, pXRF is quick and easy, and they generated a huge amount of data that was entirely new for Stonehenge. It would never match the precision and range of elements that ICP-MS and ICP-AES could identify and quantify, but that would mean getting deeper into the rock, and grinding it up.

Dave's team were nearly ready to go out and look for potential source areas, when the core suddenly appeared. If they could sample it for spectrometry analyses, they would have the full signature of one of the monument's greatest megaliths to compare with results from sarsen boulders elsewhere. It had worked in Botswana, and there was no obvious reason why it shouldn't in southern England. So Dave asked if they could have a bit of the core, please? 'I don't think it was an easy decision', he told me. English Heritage said yes.

To the 260 pXRF readings from Stonehenge, and a couple of dozen along the core looking for variation within Stone 58 (there was remarkably little), they now added ICP-MS/-AES data from

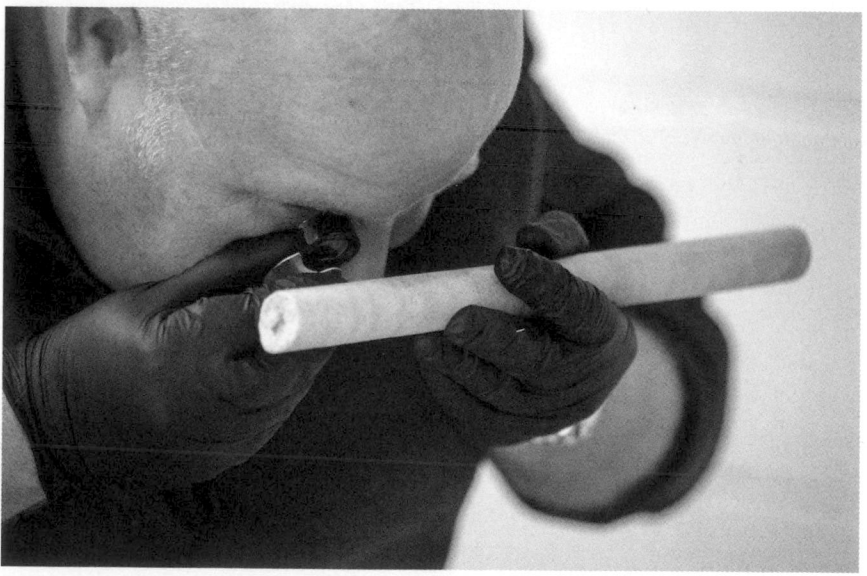

Dave Nash examining a piece of the core from Stone 58.

20 different places across southern England where sarsens are relatively common, sampling boulders at each one with a geological hammer and chisel. They were given the smallest piece from the Phillips core, a stumpy finger-length cylinder like a sandy-coloured candle. They sliced it in half, gave one piece back to English Heritage and carefully cut up the other into 12 parts. Three rock samples went to Spain for ICP-MS/-AES analysis, and the rest were further grilled with a battery of techniques – among them thin sections examined under a microscope, in which Rob Ixer had a hand – making Stone 58 the most comprehensively studied sarsen in the world. Dave Nash claimed that only Moon rock had received more attention!

Natural irregularities on an otherwise finely shaped sarsen at Stonehenge, Stone 54.

The search for sources would now have three stages: an examination of geological variety among the sarsen megaliths at Stonehenge (with the pXRF data); a similar, more detailed study of field samples (with ICP-MS/-AES spectrometry data); and a comparison of Stone 58 with other megaliths (pXRF) and field boulders (ICP-MS/-AES).[9]

One of the appeals of Stonehenge is its endlessly changing effect. As you walk around, a stone's shape defies easy categorization; what looks like a smooth, straight pillar from one side, turns into a leaning boulder from another, and again into a slab penetrated by dark curvaceous hollows or crinkly fissures. Sarsen megaliths range from the UK's tallest, a beautifully crafted, straight, flat column, to the smaller Station Stone, a low amorphous stump. Surfaces are shiny or pockmarked, stained and weathered or seemingly freshly exposed. The colour of sarsen ranges through a palette of greys to satisfy the most pernickety interior designer, breaking into subdued purples and oranges. Tall megaliths are washed with lichens which, in the four decades since daily visitors have been excluded from the central part of the monument, have grown into delicate and fragile gardens, pouring in streaks down faces and painting them with splashes of translucent pale greens. And every sight is different, as rain darkens and emphasizes, sun animates, and times of day and seasons bring their own distinctive light and shade.

The pXRF analyser presented a quite different picture: described by their constituent elements, the Stonehenge sarsens seemed all but identical. The analysis confirmed what geologists had been suggesting for over a century, that sarsen is almost pure silica: the 52 stones typically consist of more than 99% of this one element, quartz sands cemented together by more quartz. A lot of nonsense has been talked about Stonehenge as a computer (it's fun in science fiction, but so are time-travelling rabbits), but in this respect the monument has a profound connection with modern integrated circuits: both are built on silica.

Silica offers little help with distinguishing one sarsen from another. However, the pXRF device can recognize 33 other elements.

Six of these were so rare as to be invisible, and two were omitted from the studies, along with silica, because they might have been affected by weathering; this left 25 elements recorded in trace amounts. Comparing each stone with all the others on this basis showed them to belong to a single group – implying a single source – with just two exceptions: Stone 26, an upright in the circle, and Stone 160, a lintel (and, less distinctly, a second lintel, Stone 156, curiously both of them fallen from trilithons). Stone 58, however, was firmly in the main group, so Dave Nash felt he could treat it as typical of Stonehenge as a whole. That meant that comparing its higher-precision spectrometry signature from the core analysis with the same thing from the field samples, should reveal the location of the great quarry if they happened to have sampled it. Did it match any of these samples – and if so, which?

The Stonehenge stones didn't come from either of the Kent sites, whose field signatures were quite unlike that of Stone 58. Others in Essex, Suffolk and Norfolk, and Sussex, Dorset and Devon, were also dramatically different. Dave's team had sampled six locations on the Marlborough Downs – three hilltops and three valley trains. Five of these were again clearly out of the game. This was a surprise to archaeologists, because it seemed to mean that places that had impressed Inigo Jones and Stukeley, and that many of us had shown to generations of students and tour groups as likely sources of Stonehenge stones – including the two trains owned by the National Trust in Piggledene and Lockeridge Dene, and the Valley of Stones in Clatford Bottom – had not in fact interested the Stonehenge builders.

There was, however, a better fit with the last Marlborough Downs site, the only one of the 20 studied locations with which there was a match for every single element. The earliest maps of sarsens, made before the most recent industry had taken its last great bite out of the old trains, show swathes of stones either side of the A4, the east–west London to Bath road from which the landscape was seen by travellers and tourists, such as Richard Symonds, Samuel Pepys in 1668 ('all along the valleys stones of considerable bigness... thick as to cover the ground') and Daniel Defoe in the 1720s (stones 'of the same kind with those at Stonehenge, and some larger'). What was not seen or mapped was a major spread of sarsens just a little further south. Away from through-roads and hidden by trees, it was once one of the most spectacular groups of sarsens, to be found in an area known today as West Woods. Stone 58, said Dave Nash, and by implication almost all the other stones at Stonehenge, had come from this small chalk plateau crossed by a steep-sided valley.

The Marlborough Downs have long been known to travellers, nature writers and artists as an area of hilly, grassy chalkland rich with ancient earthworks that have survived because of the relative absence of modern ploughing. Even without the dramatic megaliths at Avebury and the great Neolithic mounds at Silbury and West Kennet, it is a landscape immensely attractive to archaeologists, combining an atmospheric aura of peaceful antiquity with highly informative remains; over the past century many of Britain's greatest practitioners have enjoyed and researched the downs. West Woods doesn't fit that story.

There was known to be a small long barrow there and the woods are crossed by Wansdyke, a long Anglo-Saxon boundary earthwork. But the trees and undergrowth otherwise discouraged archaeologists, and until the Forestry Commission took responsibility for the management of West Woods in the 1930s, it remained little explored. With the plantations now open to the public, they are popular with local people, especially in the spring when bluebells carpet the ground in spectacular displays. Local archaeologists have recently conducted the first detailed survey.

For the past 40 years I've lived within 6 km (4 miles) of West Woods, and have often run or walked there, seeking out hidden stones. The failed road-metal business I mentioned earlier had devastated the trains by the time the Forestry Commission took over, but the new planting left industrial remains in place, and in winter, when vegetation is low, you can see a silent snapshot

Sarsens now in West Woods, identified as the source of Stone 58 at Stonehenge, are all that survive from industrial crushing for road gravel in the early 20th century.

of quarrying abandoned overnight: largely buried, undisturbed sarsen boulders at one end of the valley, their mossy snouts poking up through the leaf litter; empty pits at the other; and in between, a marvellous, unsettling scene of rocks still in the ground but excavated and exposed, often split into two or three, and ready to lift out. You get an idea of how much stone lies beneath the soil, and – to my mind – what a Neolithic megalith quarry might have looked like a few years after extraction had ceased; on a number of occasions I've taken TV crews there for that very reason. So I was naturally delighted to hear about Dave Nash's conclusion that this was where the great stones at Stonehenge had come from. We now know where to go for our sarsen, without having to rely solely on historic speculation (see pl. xv).

I do, however, have reservations, and though I'm entirely unqualified to critique the science, I predict that as more fieldwork is conducted, two things will change: first, other locations on the

Marlborough Downs will become potential sources, and second (here I am more confident), we will find that at least one of the Stonehenge stones was raised out of the ground very near to where it now stands. The first point is a simple matter of sampling. Dave's 6 sites (12 samples) show that even over short distances, there is considerable element variation among the Marlborough Downs sarsens, and many fields – not least all those now much reduced – have yet to be characterized. There is a theoretical possibility of finding other sites with signatures as similar to Stone 58 as is West Woods, or possibly even closer (remember that only this one stone has yet been sampled internally, allowing the high-resolution comparisons that pinpointed West Woods). Neither, I think, can the idea that at least some of the Stonehenge sarsens came from Salisbury Plain yet be dismissed (as I write, Dave's sampling has included no stones from this area). In one specific instance, however, I believe that there is already a case for a local Stonehenge sarsen. The argument first struck me when I visited an excavation in 2007.

Mike Parker Pearson's dig in 2008 was one of many trenches opened at and around Stonehenge between 2003 and 2009, as part of a major fieldwork programme called the Stonehenge Riverside Project. Hundreds of students and staff from several universities took part (I played a cameo role myself), and among the project's six leaders was Colin Richards, now an archaeology professor in Orkney. Colin has a particular interest in megaliths, and there were stones in two of his excavations – neither of which was at Stonehenge. Rather they were to the east, either side of the River Avon. The more distant, which he dug in 2005, was near Bulford, where a sarsen he dubbed the Tor Stone lay near a pit from which it seemed to have been taken. The nearer, the Cuckoo Stone, is less than 3 km (2 miles) from Stonehenge, and here too Colin found convincing evidence that it had once lain half buried very close to where it remains today.

Significantly in both cases there were also nearby pits that had been dug to hold the stones standing up. So not only was there a strong suggestion that at least two sarsens had occurred locally, but also that they had been turned into megaliths in the Neolithic. And as I looked at the Cuckoo Stone on a warm, sunny afternoon in September 2007, perched beside its pits, I thought of another, bigger pit, part of which I had excavated myself nearly 30 years before. The two sarsens by the river were different from Stonehenge sarsens, smaller than most, rounded, fissured and misshapen rather than slab-like. There was really only one Stonehenge megalith of this kind, albeit much larger, the massive, bulbous Heelstone. Today it stands immediately beside the pit we found in 1979.

At the time I had thought this hollow was simply where the stone had been standing before being moved to its present position, but its sheer size was difficult to explain: it's big enough to hold the Heelstone lying down. A realistic explanation, it now seems to me, is that like the Cuckoo and Tor stones, the Heelstone once lay half submerged in the ground – its natural presence, perhaps, part of

Site of the Cuckoo Stone under excavation in 2007, revealing both a pit in which it had once stood and a hollow from which it had been extracted.

the origins of the site's early appeal – before being raised more or less on the spot. Dave Nash's pXRF analysis puts the Heelstone into the big group with Stone 58, which he associates with West Woods, but until further work proves otherwise – through analysis of sarsens on Salisbury Plain and demonstration of the comparative validity of surface readings across every megalith – I will continue to think of these three rounded boulders as local.

And there are other reasons for wondering whether almost all the sarsens at Stonehenge came from a single location. The year after our pit discovery, we were back excavating near the Heelstone and found the stone debris I described in Chapter 2. As well as bluestone chips there were many pieces of sarsen. It seemed unrealistic to think we could suddenly discover where the stones had come from, but armed with a pile of rubble from which we could cut samples, it was at least worth a shot at trying out some possibilities. In a pioneering study, Hilary Howard compared quartz grain sizes between samples. There were two different patterns at Stonehenge, and both differed from samples from two locations on the Marlborough Downs. Hilary also found differences in the occurrence of a handful of heavy minerals (minerals in the sarsen that are heavier than its main, silica component, of which she was able to identify eight) across the Stonehenge sarsen samples. No similar work has been done since, but the suggestion of variety contrasts with the uniform impression of the pXRF data.

And then there is colour. Archaeologists have long commented on different hues among some of the large standing sarsens. Most are shades of grey, but some have a light orange cast and others a pinkish purple, and in a few instances – as I noticed on one troubling occasion when spots of bright colours had been revealed by the crumbling away of small spalls from the weathered surfaces – the two colours are paired. In the Sarsen Circle on the west (Stones 4/5 and 6/7) and in the three trilithons where it has been possible to tell (53/54, 55/56 and 57/58), pink and orange stones had apparently been raised side by side. Systematic research is needed, but it seems quite possible that contrastingly coloured stones were deliberately selected. It has further been suggested that these more coloured stones have small iron inclusions, while the grey stones have only flint.[10] Did these come from three different places, grey, pink and orange, even if those might have been close together? And as the pXRF data for Stones 26 and 160 differ, might their source or sources be other than those places?

There are sound geological as well as intuitive reasons for thinking that at least most of the large, dressed sarsens came from the Marlborough Downs. While today nothing as big can be found anywhere beyond Stonehenge, as Dave Nash has patiently explained to me, there are no extensive surface deposits on Salisbury Plain – Paleogene sands, now often represented by the more recent residues of clay-with-flints – of the type needed for sarsen to form; some might well have disappeared, but it would take special pleading to argue for the total erosion of deposits on such a scale. By contrast, much of the Marlborough Downs is covered with Paleogene sediments, consistent with the density of sarsen there.

There do seem to be some sarsens on the plain, however, and archaeological excavation suggests that at least two of those, and I would claim, also the Heelstone, were found and erected close to where they had lain for millions of years. We have, then, a working hypothesis for sarsen origins, and a clear pointer for where to go to obtain at least one. On the one hand the great carved monument is largely, perhaps entirely, a gift of the Marlborough Downs, and one monolith at least came from West Woods. On the other, we have a few stones on the edge of the site – represented today by the two Station Stones, with indications of two now missing, and the Heelstone – which may have a little surface dressing, but are not in any way shaped. The Station Stones are small and lumpy and in the Cuckoo/Tor category: candidates for selection by local convenience. In the case of the Heelstone, we have both the largest and the most irregular megalith at Stonehenge: here we might think, even without the evidence of a source pit, that this is a stone unlikely to have been chosen for hauling any great distance (see pl. xii).

That still leaves most of Stonehenge – over 160 megaliths – needing to be fetched from afar, in journeys adding up to 55,000–65,000 ton-km (35,000–40,000 ton-miles) of bluestone and some 40,000 ton-km (25,000 ton-miles) of sarsen. A lot of research lies behind those apparently simple figures, but that is nothing compared to the challenge of actually making the expeditions. We need to address something that can be summed up in one word that is rarely heard at Stonehenge: logistics.

CHAPTER 4

LOGISTICS

The genius of the builders of Stonehenge, as far as bluestones are concerned, was to choose quarry sites that are mostly near the sea, yet too far inland to allow megaliths to be hauled straight to harbour. As a result, people now argue – I'm tempted to say still argue, it's difficult to believe no one disputed the original decisions – about how we should get our stones to Wiltshire: logistical challenges 5,000 years ago become an analytical hurdle today. In recent years there's been a shift of opinion that transforms the way we think about that problem. If nothing else, the new picture means we should have a lot more fun.

In 1923, with, it seemed, two journeys' end points broadly determined – between Pembrokeshire and Stonehenge for bluestones, and the Marlborough Downs and Stonehenge for sarsens – it became possible to consider routes along which megaliths might have been transported. In his guidebook written a decade or so before, Edgar Barclay, directed already towards Pembrokeshire by Herbert Thomas, had advocated ships. This was partly because a sea voyage avoided the swamps and primeval forests he imagined blanketing a land dissected by unbridged rivers. It was also because a passing Roman fleet, navigating its way around Britain, was in a perfect position to do the job, picking up a few more stones in Scotland as it harried the north.

Barclay's theory about why Stonehenge was built – by native people, he said, ordered by Romans – did not age well (though he was not alone in imagining help from more sophisticated cultures: one 19th-century geologist, who thought the bluestones came from Brittany or Normandy, proposed that Greek ships coming to Britain to trade for tin could have brought stones with them as ballast). But the idea of sea voyaging proved more enduring. And

Thomas wanted to quash that, just as he had done for the theory that glaciers had carried stones from Wales to Wiltshire.

First, up on the Preselis where small outcrops rise above undulating slopes of wild moorland and scattered rocks, he knew the sea was not close: to the north it was around 12–15 km (7–10 miles) away. To the south it was a journey of some 20 km (13 miles) to a navigable stretch of the River Cleddau, which flows west into Milford Haven, a natural harbour (and today site of the UK's third largest port). So however most of the journey was done, at the start a significant land crossing was unavoidable. The people who took stones from the Preselis to Wessex knew how to move them across challenging terrain. And the sarsens, of course, mostly much heavier than the bluestones, could only have been moved entirely overland.

Second, Thomas deployed the exact same argument that glacial theorists have used to refute human transport. The favoured sea route would first have taken the sailors along the south coast of Wales, across the mouth of the River Severn and southwestwards down to Land's End; then back northeastwards past Cornwall and Devon into what is now Christchurch Harbour in Dorset, and north up the River Avon into Wiltshire. Navigating between the tide-swept islands of west Wales and Land's End, said Thomas, would have been too difficult and dangerous for primitive craft burdened with unmanageable boulders. And however close to Stonehenge a boat carrying a 3-ton stone could then make its way upriver, a final push over land was necessary, as at the start. With proof Neolithic people could manoeuvre megaliths on dry land, said Thomas, and the dangers of the long coastal route, why invoke sea travel at all?

Thomas proposed that the Altar Stone played a key part in this debate. It was the only bluestone then known not to have come from the Preselis, so its source was a route marker. Like almost everyone who has addressed the question of where the Stonehenge megaliths came from, he assumed they were all collected and brought to the site at the same time. Thus the Altar Stone was a third fixed point: the journey began at the Preselis and ended at Stonehenge, but on the way passed the sandstone quarry. As we saw, Thomas suggested two options for its location. One, the Senni Formation, stretched across south Wales, where at some point it could intersect with a land route. The other, the more localized occurrence of the Cosheston Subgroup, could be found near Llangwm on the shore approaching a large harbour – Milford Haven.

To Thomas, the Senni Formation suggested a journey by land and the Cosheston Subgroup by sea. In his scientific paper he was undecided geologically about which of the two it might have been, but he favoured land transport on other grounds. The model in the Geological Museum, however, and the official guidebook revised only a year after his study, opted for Milford Haven as the Altar Stone's source. The harbour theory was clinched when a piece of sandstone found at the Cursus was traced to a different outcrop on the same Pembrokeshire estuary, as we saw in Chapter 2. Two sandstone sources on the coast settled it, and it remained only to determine the route. Subsequent guidebooks were undecided between land, sea or half and half, by sea to the Bristol area and then overland. So did the boats find landfall in the Severn, or continue round Land's End?

In 1958 the Ministry of Works hired Richard Atkinson (1920–94), a famous Stonehenge archaeologist who was then halfway through six summers of excavation at the monument, to write a special guidebook. He plumped unequivocally for a part-sea route – and ably helped by an illustrator, effectively sowed the seeds of its demise.

The assistant was Alan Sorrell (1904–74), a one-time drawing instructor at the Royal College of Art and contemporary of better-known artists such as Edward Bawden, John Piper and Eric Ravilious. Richard described the bluestone route, starting at Milford Haven, hugging the Welsh coast and reaching land at Avonmouth, across the Severn Estuary a little downriver from the modern M4 road bridge; the final third of the journey continued inland across Somerset and Wiltshire. Although this was the half and half solution, part sea, part land, in Richard's view almost the entire journey was done on water – by 'rafts or boats' – by continuing along a succession of four rivers, three of them against the current, with only a short land link. This ingeniously avoided Barclay's dilemma of having to cross unbridged waterways, but it left the Stonehenge builders to grapple with Thomas's 'primitive vessels' in treacherous seas. Which must have pleased Alan Sorrell.

There'd been some controversy at the Ministry when Sorrell's name came up as someone who might brighten the experience of visitors to ancient sites in its care. The monuments chief objected that artistic reconstructions of the past were a waste of time, as archaeologists had too many rival theories of what it was like. In the end, however, he agreed to a commission for Stonehenge, on the grounds that there were so many theories it didn't matter (he was a Classical scholar). Sorrell was scrupulous about accuracy. In an era when illustration was much used in archaeological journalism, with results that might send Bronze Age armies out with Roman weapons and 1930s hairstyles, he spent much time with archaeologists checking that a brick was in the right place and people ate the right food. But he was an artist, and the bigger picture was his domain. In particular, he was a historical artist.

Shunning contemporary trends, Sorrell saw himself working in an older tradition of religious and history art. In striking compositions, he portrayed the lives of those swept by the relentless tragedy of momentous times. Stonehenge was even older than history, which made its world both more fateful and more challenging. And few things could have been more death-defying than floating bluestones past Welsh sea cliffs. In his drawings, which bear too many similarities to Théodore Géricault's *Raft of the Medusa* to be coincidental, a dozen naked men with windswept hair cling to a raft of rough-hewn timbers with a makeshift sail, paddling a bluestone between white-sprayed rocks and a roiling sea into which it surely is destined to plunge. In one version, three cloaked figures watch from a nearby cliff like the Fates of ancient Greek mythology.

Alan Sorrell's drawings of Neolithic people rafting bluestones along the Welsh coast, commissioned by the Ministry of Works in 1958, did little to convince a public that the feat would have been possible.

It took a cultural critic to recognize the inherent contradiction. Sorrell's illustrations, wrote Reyner Banham in 1966, with their 'insistent note of expressionist hysteria, gloom and foreboding', portrayed 'a race of woaded oafs' incapable of creating Stonehenge. But Richard Atkinson, like Aubrey Burl, also took a poor view of Neolithic people. On a TV show in 1965 he called them 'howling barbarians... practically savages'. He solved the Stonehenge conundrum by imagining that a Greek architect came north to push the natives into shape. He was not the first to look in that direction to explain the monument: 'The engineer who designed Stonehenge', wrote Herbert Stone in 1924, 'was probably a foreigner – "a wise man from the east".'[1]

Neolithic Brits could, however, make dugout canoes – prehistoric hollowed-out tree trunks tapered at either end are quite common finds – and on another TV film Richard demonstrated how a few schoolboys could punt a bluestone replica on the still waters of the

River Avon ('the operation had much in common', he wrote in 1956, 'with the pleasant pastime of punting agreeable companions (built happily upon less uncompromisingly monolithic lines) upon the quiet waters of the Cherwell'). Out at sea such a craft would have been genuinely treacherous, and between them Richard Atkinson and Alan Sorrell, long before Aubrey Burl or any geologist had thought to question Herbert Thomas's assertion that people had moved the bluestones, made it look all but impossible. Who would now seriously contemplate Neolithic people bringing dozens of bluestones to Stonehenge by sea?

Well, actually, me. In 2012 I took part in a film made for the Discovery Channel in which a crew of 12 paddled a bluestone-sized rock near the coast of south Wales. The boat was extraordinary:

A replica Bronze Age boat (smaller than the original, whose remains were found in Lincolnshire) made for TV in 2012, carrying a 'bluestone' up a river on the south coast of Wales.

a modern replica based on remains dated to around 2000 BC, its fresh, honey-coloured planks stitched together in a distinctive lost technology known in Europe especially from a handful of British finds. At 13 m (43 ft) long the craft was a little shorter than the original and its construction less sophisticated, but there was never any question of it being up to the job of shipping a megalith. The experiment was successfully concluded without any of us having to worry about the risk agreement we all signed, which warned of 'inherently dangerous activities including serious personal injury, death and/or dismemberment'.

The point is that primitive rafts and cowering naked crowds (Sorrell's depictions of stone-moving overland are no less apocalyptic) represent and influenced a way of thinking about Stonehenge that made it hard to see how it could ever have happened – the construction itself was no less believable than the long-distance transport of stones. The problem had been framed as an absence of skills and technology, as if we might be expecting butterflies to make bread. At Stonehenge we have only the end result as evidence for how it was built. But for transport we have boats: three from Ferriby in Lincolnshire (one of which was the model for the TV experiment), and one from Dover, much better preserved – indeed the only one that survives intact today – and now in Dover Museum.[2]

How their boats were made tells us much about the sort of things these people really could do, such as understanding engineering principles of tension and compression and visualizing 3D structures. The stitching was done with long, twisted yew withies, typically looped three times to apply considerable tension and creating what one specialist has described as a mechanical advantage similar to that of a pair of blocks with three pulleys, generating a force six times that of a pulled rope – the classic method of raising heavy weights by hand. These boats are not quite as old as Stonehenge, and their makers had a range of bronze tools unlikely to have been available when Stonehenge was built. But a boat is a complex work developed the hard way, where casual change or minor failure can be fatal. One boat is like one ancient human genome: they show the individual, but also they contain the stories of generations. We know that at least a millennium before stones were taken to Salisbury Plain, people had paddled boats across the Channel with cattle, sheep and pigs, seed corn and everything needed for setting up new lives as farmers in an alien land. Boats, and their rare physical remains, are the best indications we have that Stonehenge's builders lived in a world with sophisticated engineers.

That they had boats, however, does not mean they used them to ferry megaliths out at sea, and the consensus now favours land transport for bluestones. It's debatable how much confirmed sources on the north-facing flanks of the Preselis make sea transport less likely, as some have argued – the point being that to reach Milford Haven the stones would first have to be dragged up to the top of the hill before going down again, and the exposed sea route from the north would have added significant challenges – but other evidence is more compelling. First, the intermediary coastal stops have gone. As we saw in Chapter 2, both of the sandstones said to have marked the start of a journey from Milford Haven are now sourced elsewhere. A second link in that chain had been proposed in the shape of bluestones lost in the Bristol Channel, spotted by divers near Steep Holm island. Like other such claims (none properly published), when examined by a geologist the stones were found not to be of any Stonehenge type, and probably glacial erratics.[3]

On the other hand we now have way-stations inland, one of them yet to be pinned down somewhere northeast of the Preselis, and the other, more significantly – we will go with a Welsh origin, at least for now – near the English border. The simplest theory is that bluestones were taken from their quarries in Pembrokeshire and transported overland by a route that took in the Altar Stone's source in the Brecon Beacons region, and headed towards a Severn crossing. We will consider that route, and also that taken by the sarsens, in the next two chapters, along with what happens when they arrive at the site. But before geography we need to address practicalities. How were these stones moved?

It's a question that has long occupied the minds of people around the world and continues to do so, and if my email inbox is anything to go by, the guessers and experimenters are almost all men. The goal is to come up with a method no one has thought of before, probably impossible given the history of the game, but a claim easy to make. Bonus points are awarded for smaller teams, the ultimate prize going to a scheme with complex engineering that can be operated by one man.

A popular idea is that the stones could have been dragged effortlessly over frozen ground. This can be dismissed easily: the climate at the time was certainly no colder, and perhaps a little warmer than it is today (at least, it must be said, than it was a few years ago). In the coldest winter, the best that could have been hoped for beneath a heavy megalith would have been a semi-frozen sludge. More realistic proposals include wrapping a stone in a bundle of logs to create a cylinder and rolling it; putting a stone on a sledge with a keel that fits into carved wooden rails (when demonstrated in a TV film, grease supposed to facilitate sliding, according to the narrator, 'glued [it] to the track'); and dragging a stone along grooved rails carrying small stone balls to reduce friction. Stone balls exist: the size of an orange and ingeniously carved with knobs or geometric designs, many are thought to date broadly from the Stonehenge era. Unfortunately for the Stonehenge theory, they are found only in Scotland, and when deployed in front of another camera crew (with me on hand for commentary) wooden substitutes sank into the finely shaped but rain-sodden tracks under the weight of the load. Like many ideas, with the right conditions and a great deal of resources it could work. But it felt unduly complicated.

There is a better way to approach the problem: seeing what people actually do when they move megaliths. Around the Indian Ocean over the past century or so, in Madagascar, India, Myanmar and Indonesia, people have been recorded transporting slabs and boulders for very Neolithic-looking monuments – tombs and standing stones – and occasionally it is something they continue to do. Unconstrained by tight television schedules, European labour regulations and health and safety needs, or the budgets of retired engineers, these endeavours have the further advantage of being completed, from quarrying a stone to its use in an important construction. I will draw in particular on research conducted by Ron Adams on the Indonesian island of Sumba, a surprisingly rare case of recent megalithic fieldwork by an archaeologist. This won't tell us what happened in Britain 5,000 years ago. But it does help us think about it.[4]

First, however, we need to consider the stones we are going to move, and their weights. Astonishingly, the size and shape of the Stonehenge megaliths had not been systematically studied until 2012. We will make full use of that project's data in later chapters, but for now we will focus on its estimated weights. These were calculated from the volume and surface area of the stones visible above ground. Drawing on laser-scanned data which reflected

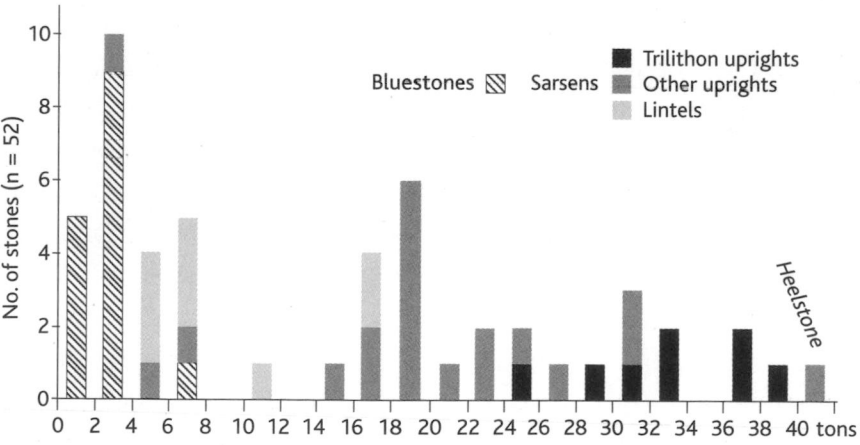

By weight, stones at Stonehenge fall into two groups: up to 8 tons (mostly bluestone, average 2 tons) and 14 tons and above (sarsen, average 20 tons); lintels (ranging from 4 to 17.5 tons) bridge the two groups. Moving sarsens was a much greater challenge than bluestones.

irregularities and hollows, the survey revealed that earlier estimates had mostly been too high. I have combined these new data with my own estimates for stone below ground as recorded in excavations, and occasional allowances for recent damage, and presented them in Table 4. It's not perfect, but it's a good shot.[5]

Looking at the numbers, it's noticeable that the stones, especially if we take only the standing ones (that is excluding the lintels) fall into two distinct groups (see graph on p. 87): below 4 tons (including all the bluestones other than the Altar Stone, which weighs 6 tons) and 15 tons or above (all the sarsens, except for the two small Station Stones and the curious Stone 11, a small megalith in the circle); on average, bluestones weigh 2 tons and sarsens 20 tons. The lintels bridge these two groups, ranging between 4 and 17.5 tons. It's clear that, aside from the different sources and distances involved, transporting bluestones and sarsens demanded their own particular commitments in time and energy – and mile for mile, moving sarsens was a substantially greater challenge.

Weights of most of the stones whose transport has been witnessed in recent times fall at the lower end of the scale. At 25 tomb-construction events recorded by Ron Adams in Indonesia between 2001 and 2005, more than two thirds of the stones weighed 6 tons or less – making them particularly relevant to the bluestone question. The first thing to note is that people seem to have had no difficulty in getting stones from the quarries to the villages where the tombs were built, albeit the distances were mostly small (much of Ron's work was at one village, which had access to a quarry only 500 m – 1,500 ft – away). But moving stones was not the only thing on people's minds.

The operation was expensive – families could save up for a long time before building a tomb, and in one case Ron saw a stone pulled from the quarry to join another which had been waiting for the next construction stage for 27 years! A quarry team had to be negotiated (slabs were carved out of the solid limestone). Large numbers of people could be involved, often many more than could

Table 4. Estimated heights and weights of Stonehenge megaliths, sarsen (left and above) and bluestone (right; for rock types see Tables 1–3).

Circle uprights

Stone no.	Height (m)	Height (ft)	Weight (tons)
1	4.0	13	18
2	4.3	14	26
3	4.2	14	18
4	4.2	14	21
5	4.3	14	18
6	4.2	14	18
7	4.0	13	19
10	4.0	13	23
11	2.7	9	7
16	4.3	14	31
21	4.0	13	15
22			18
23	3.8	12	16
27	4.0	13	17
28	4.0	13	30
29	4.0	13	22
30	4.0	13	25
average exc. Stone 11	4.1	13	21

Trilithon uprights

Stone no.	Height (m)	Height (ft)	Weight (tons)
51	5.0	16	32
52	5.1	17	37
53	5.2	17	24
54	5.2	17	39
56	6.6	22	31
57	5.2	17	37
58	5.2	17	32
60	5.0	16	29
average	5.3	17	33

Station Stones

Stone no.	Height (m)	Height (ft)	Weight (tons)
91	2.8	9	4
93	1.3	4	2

Heelstone

Stone no.	Height (m)	Height (ft)	Weight (tons)
96	4.6	15	40

Circle lintels

Stone no.	Weight (tons)
101	4.5
102	6.5
105	4.0
107	5.0
122	6.5
130	6.0
average	5.5

Trilithon lintels

Stone no.	Weight (tons)
152	11.5
154	17.5
158	16.5
average	15.0

Bluestone Circle

Stone no.	Rock type	Height (m)	Height (ft)	Weight (tons)
31	BU1	1.9	6	3.5
33	B1	1.7	6	1.0
34	B2	1.0	3	0.5
37	B1	1.3	4	1.5
46	B8	1.0	3	0.5
47	BU1	1.5	5	2.0
49	B1	1.8	6	2.0
average		1.5	5	1.5

Bluestone Horseshoe

Stone no.	Rock type	Height (m)	Height (ft)	Weight (tons)
61	B2	1.8	6	1.5
62	B3	2.0	7	2.0
63	BU1	2.1	7	2.0
67	B1			2.5
68	BU1	2.5	8	3.5
69	BU1	2.6	9	3.5
70	BU1	2.3	8	2.0
average		2.2	7	2.5

Altar Stone

Stone no.	Rock type	Height (m)	Height (ft)	Weight (tons)
80	B13			6.0

be found in the local community and were actually needed to shift a stone. For one tomb Ron reckoned there were around a thousand men present – they might be aged 10 to 60 and occasionally joined by women, though it was very much a man's job – but at any one time 200 men were pulling a 6-ton stone, and 100 one of two stones weighing 2 and 1.5 tons. Across cases for which Ron was able to calculate the number of person days consumed in building a tomb, by and large, as you would expect, the more stone was moved, the more men were needed; to pull stones weighing a total of 5 tons, for example, took around 2,000 person days, while 28 tons of stone demanded nearly 30,000 days.[6] But the relationship was not always consistent (in another example, 13 tons also took 30,000 person days), and the size of the gangs was also affected by social and political factors. There was a lot of dancing, music and socializing, local politics, debt settling and joshing for status, and, especially, slaughtering of pigs and water buffaloes, cooking and feasting – accounting for much of the bill.

But the actual transport, the engineering required to move a stone weighing anything from 1 to 14 tons, was simple. There were five ingredients: timber, rope, labour, time and organization. Slabs at the quarries were tied with ropes or vines to wooden sledges some 3 m (10 ft) long and 2 m (6 ft) wide (see pl. XVI). Long ropes were attached to the sledges, which were pulled by hundreds of men along temporary wooden trackways – logs and poles scattered about in sufficient numbers to keep the sledge off the ground and provide a less resistant surface for the runners (see pl. XVII). A large stone can be seen underway in a recent video made by the Government Tourism Office of West Sumba. It's an extraordinary sight.

A rectangular slab perhaps 3 m (10 ft) across and twice as long, with a carved superstructure and said to weigh 12 tons, is encased in a timber raft. This rests on two great round beams fixed together with jointed crossbars, parallel to the stone's long sides and its direction of movement, and spaced so that each is approximately beneath one side of the stone. Long ropes as thick as a man's wrist are attached to the beams through holes at front and back, held by a crowd of well-dressed men who pull and steer the sledge over quantities of long, thin and roughly trimmed sleeper poles lying perpendicular to the sledge and around 1 m (3 ft) apart. The size of the stone is exaggerated not just by the raft, but also by a wooden and bamboo framework and a mass of flags rising above it. Three men stand on the front and one on the back, guiding the activity and adding to the weight.

The hard part is getting the sledge started, with short, heavy bursts of energy, but once free it slides forward at a good walking, even running pace, as it slips, yaws and leans like a ship at sea. Poles snap and writhe on the ground as the stone passes, and are collected by boys like firewood to carry forward for re-use. At the start, while it is still dark, costumed women sing and dance and musicians play. During the pulling a drone of chanting and shouting men rises and falls – imagine a football crowd meeting a country fete tug o'war competition – and at the end amid congratulations and celebrations there is much food. Pigs and water buffaloes are roughly handled and sacrificed for the feast. Even in a 14-minute, pixelated film, the occasion is quite extraordinary to behold, theatre of a grand kind involving thousands. And this is a short, simple journey, over flat, dry ground.[7]

Mention of buffaloes prompts the question, could draught animals have been used to pull megaliths in Neolithic Britain? The short answer is that we can't say; it's possible, perhaps, but unlikely. While evidence for the presence of domestic horses at the time remains unconvincing, people certainly reared cattle, often the commonest animal represented by their bones at excavations. It's debatable whether any were trained as draught animals (oxen). There is no evidence for wheeled vehicles this early in Britain, and no draught paraphernalia such as yokes or collars have been found (though being made of perishable materials, they would rarely survive); marks in the soil made by simple ploughs could imply human effort as much as animal.

A case has been made for Neolithic oxen on the grounds of the ages at which cows and bulls died and their relative occurrence, supported by occasional bones showing pathologies – growth changes or injuries – but such data can be variously interpreted. Historically, oxen were important in Britain: in one spectacular event in 1797, 86 beasts yoked 6 abreast hauled a windmill uphill out of Brighton, East Sussex! My archaeological instinct, however, given current evidence, is that in the Neolithic the situation would have been more akin to that observed by Ron Adams and other researchers around the Indian Ocean. Here buffaloes and oxen are important draught animals, but they also have significant social value – herds are displays of wealth and status. At megalith construction events, cattle are more likely to be sacrificed than put to work, not least because the opportunity for people to do the labouring is also of great social significance.[8]

On Sumba, Ron notes a clear discrepancy at the stone-pulling events between numbers of people and needs: there are just too many men. It's not accidental. A tomb owner's aim is to make an impressive spectacle, and stones might deliberately be moved slowly, the better to show off their wealth. Everyone wants to be associated with the achievement, and contributing to the effort sets up a debt to be repaid; it banks a future obligation. It seems quite reasonable to imagine something similar in Neolithic Britain, if only for parts of the journeys. We can learn from Sumba. But we also need to address the particular circumstances of Stonehenge.

Alan Sorrell did exactly that in his illustrations, as we saw, depicting a savage view of the past. Yet superficially, at least, when he shows a large sarsen being dragged up a downland slope – as we must imagine, though it looks more like a blasted heath in which bent, leafless trees play the Fates – we see just what we might expect from our visit to Sumba. The stone lies flat, tied to a sledge with two runners and dragged over wooden poles by what seem like hundreds of men (albeit almost naked) straining on two long ropes; a man stands on the megalith urging them on.

For many years the images featured in souvenir guides, and were copied and redrawn for books and magazines, acquiring a sort of reality that allowed them to shape ideas, not just show them. But, we can see now, they are misleading. They demean the people who built Stonehenge – and, as far as the sarsens are concerned, underestimate the Herculean nature of the task.

We can safely assume Neolithic people had good clothes (they could weave as well as work leather). To pull a 20-ton sarsen would have required more ropes and more people, even for the minimal challenge of moving it forward. But it's less about scale, important though that is, than the details of the technology. The sledge that features in the Sumba video is well crafted. The great pair of runners protrude for some distance at front and back to allow for free movement of the ropes. The rest of the sledge has been built around the stone. The latter lies on six transverse poles, fixed to the runners, which in turn support a rectangular frame two timbers high which wraps around and conceals the lower third of the stone's thickness (at front and back, both timbers are carpentered into rectangular sections; the upper, thicker sides are round poles). These eight timbers are jointed at the four corners like a log house, using technically what is known as a full scribe or a Scandinavian saddle notch, and all the joints are also tied. A fence of bamboo poles rises vertically from this, but it is to create a decorative framework and is not holding the stone. That job is done by the boxlike timber frame. It's strong. As the sledge moves forward across the sleepers, it creaks and shivers but nothing comes loose.

Sorrell's sledge is in another class. The stone is tied to five cross-bars attached to two runners, but that's it – no jointing, no frame to hold the stone in place, not even attachments for ropes. A few years before Sorrell drew this vision, Richard Atkinson took part in an experiment for a BBC TV film, as I noted above. As well as floating a concrete replica bluestone weighing one and a half tons along a river, boys pulled it on a sledge in front of Stonehenge. Made of oak, the sledge looks much like a smaller version of Sorrell's, with five bars on two runners, but there is a significant difference: the timbers are roughly squared and jointed in similar fashion to those in Sumba, reinforced by wooden pegs, and ropes pass through holes in the runners. Richard's specifications – for they were his – were inspired. Sophisticated jointing has a long history in Europe, in houses and other structures. Recent excavations in Germany recovered the wooden linings of four Neolithic wells, made between 5500 and 5000 BC and preserved by waterlogging. Planks had been shaped to create square frames that gave the wells continuous side-walls, jointed at the corners either by mortise and tenon with pegs, or an interlocking structure comparable to a dovetail. Some 2,000 years before Stonehenge was thought of, farmers in Europe were using stone tools for carpentry every bit as sophisticated as that in the great Sumba sledge – or a modern furniture outlet. Stonehenge was built by a Neolithic culture with deep roots, not by the Flintstones.

Yet at the same time, Richard's experiment reinforced an idea that took archaeologists up a false trail. The concrete megalith was dragged over wooden poles that turned in the grass as the sledge passed – rollers. Sorrell drew rollers, and as Barney Harris has pointed out, the idea 'is probably one of archaeology's longest-held beliefs', based on the view that rollers would allow fewer people to move large stones. John Aubrey thought this was how it was done ('brought hither upon Rowlers', he wrote of the sarsens at Stonehenge in the later 17th century) and so did William Stukeley in the 1720s. The latter envisioned a frame 'laid on rollers, which are to slide on another timber work upon the ground & made rough at the bottom with snags, so that it won't slip'. Rollers feature in everything from a BBC children's educational animation to a full-scale test-your-strength device at the Stonehenge Visitor Centre. But Barney, a doctoral archaeology student at UCL, could fairly claim to have debunked this much-loved theory.[9]

The difficulty is that rollers don't work. Away from the television studio, Richard Atkinson confessed that their advantage was not as great as it looked: you could cut the size of the pulling team,

A replica sarsen rests on rollers at the Stonehenge Visitor Centre in 2020, reflecting the traditional view of how the stones were moved; in fact rollers are unlikely to have been used.

but you needed extra people to move the rollers about, and more on ropes to counter the stone's tendency to slip off. In yet another Stonehenge television project, in 2005 I advised on the creation of a full-scale replica of a newly built Stonehenge.[10] Sadly this was not in stone but in polystyrene (the effect was wonderful, though it would make a shorter book), but we did have one very heavy concrete megalith. I introduced Gordon Pipes to the production company. He was a carpenter, and was determined to move the stone without rollers. First, he explained, they would have taken a lot of work to make: they would all have to be the same diameter and parallel-sided, not tapering like natural-growth timbers. The ground beneath would need to be firm and flat, and great care would be needed to place the rollers at precisely the right angle in front of the stone or it would run sideways. Other experimenters have noted how rollers bunch up and jam, and distort and stick under the heaviest weights; on slopes, trying to manoeuvre stones on rolling timbers too easily results in complete loss of control.

Gordon was not joking when he put a disclaimer at the front of the book he later wrote about his research: 'Moving heavy stones can be extremely dangerous, any accidents might prove fatal.'[11]

A key piece of evidence for Barney Harris was a dramatic photo taken on the Indonesian island of Nias before 1917. It shows a seemingly endless crowd of men pulling a large stone with six long ropes. Timbers on the ground, which other ethnographers had described as rollers, disappear into the distance ahead of the stone. In fact rollers seem to have been everywhere, and Ron Adams himself used the word in his research on Sumba. But looking closely at the photo, Barney noticed that the poles had been staked to the ground: the stone was being dragged up a slope along a fixed trackway. Like archaeologists, anthropologists had got into the habit of writing about rollers – and in this case there was proof that they had not been used. Ron told Barney that he had followed traditional nomenclature, but the timbers under the stones he watched did not in fact roll.

We know there were permanent wooden walkways in Neolithic Britain, as several have been found, especially on the Somerset Levels, preserved by the bogs which they had been made to traverse. One, known as the Sweet Track and laid in 3807 or 3806 BC (wood can sometimes be precisely dated by counting tree rings – this is one of the oldest known such tracks in the world), consisted of a line of planks supported on cross-pegs hammered into the peat and underlying clay. Another on Hatfield Moor, South Yorkshire, was formed of poles lying perpendicular to the route in a continuous surface which archaeologists call corduroyed. This was laid around 2900–2500 BC, the age of Stonehenge, and is equivalent to the loose poles beneath a moving sledge, but fixed and amplified. Which raises the question: were there permanent megalithic tracks?

Ted Garfitt (1914–2003), a forestry consultant, suggested just that, remembering how he had transported lumber in tropical forests in Malaysia.[12] But is it necessary? A moving trackway – the poles are really a form of open caterpillar track, the return loop made by

I Snow highlights key features at Stonehenge. A circular ditch with low banks on either side opens to the parallel banks of the Avenue leading away northeast, framing the Heelstone. Two small Station Stones lie near the bank ring to left and right, with most of the stones at the centre. A visitor footpath arcs across from the left.

II The centre of Stonehenge today, with stone numbers and key rock types.

Sarsen, standing
Sarsen, lying
Sarsen, lintel
Dolerite
Other bluestone

0   5   10 m

III One of two surviving Station Stones, among the few sarsens at Stonehenge not substantially shaped in the Neolithic.

IV Stonehenge from the east; the ring of visitors is just outside the Neolithic circular ditch; note Heelstone alone on right.

V Stonehenge from the southwest.

VI Edgar Barclay, *Heel Stone*, 1881. The Heelstone and (flat in the foreground) the Slaughter Stone, looking northeast.

VII Carn Menyn, a large outcrop in the Preselis thought by Herbert Thomas to be the source of spotted dolerite at Stonehenge but revealed by new research to have been a minor quarry, at most (Stonehenge rock type B2).

VIII Spotted dolerite at Carn Goedog, Preseli Hills (B1).

IX A much battered Stone 46 at Stonehenge, a rhyolite of uncertain origin but probably from the Fishguard Volcanic Group in north Pembrokeshire (B8).

X Rhyolite at Craig Rhos-y-felin (B6).

XI Dressed sarsen trilithons at Stonehenge, the very large stones in the middle ground, from left: Stone 56, with lintel on ground at foot; Stones 57 and 58 supporting lintel; Stone 59 and lintel on ground, each in three pieces; Stone 60.

XII The Heelstone is a large, fissured sarsen boulder largely in its natural state.

XIII Small areas of formerly large sarsen fields have been preserved on the Marlborough Downs, such as this on Fyfield Down.

XIV A sarsen train at Lockeridge Dene.

XV A sarsen in West Woods, identified as a source of the largest stones at Stonehenge.

A megalith is dragged uphill along a slipway of fixed logs on Nias, an Indonesian island near Sumatra, in photos taken in around 1915. Held in a well-carpentered sledge, the stone is moved over poles that were once described as rollers, but are held in place by vertical stakes.

Neolithic footway across
the Somerset Levels,
excavated in 1972.

Excavation of trackway on
Hatfield Moor in 2004.

portering – is as easy to operate, more adaptable to difficult terrain and errant sledges, and not vulnerable to breakage, disturbance by animals, theft and landslide. For the lengthy bluestone journeys, at least, solid timber tracks seem to be a possibility for particular situations, but improbable for the entire route.

There is another use for poles: as levers. This was Gordon Pipes's alternative to rollers. In his 2005 TV experiment people stood on either side of the stone, holding onto poles whose far ends were stuck beneath it. As the two teams rowed in unison, the stone moved forward in the direction they were facing. In the 18th century Stukeley called this 'stone rowing', and he drew a sledge with poles that projected sideways to engage the 'leavers in the nature of a galley oars'. Gordon's experiment worked well, but compared to the sledges on Sumba progress was slow, and pole length, and the need to accommodate the rowers in the spaces beside the stone, will put a limit on the maximum number of people who can be brought to the job – in theory, no such restriction exists with ropes, which will matter more the larger the stone to be pulled. There are, however, clear roles for levers, manoeuvring a stone onto a sledge

Filmed for TV in 2005 in front of a polystyrene Stonehenge, a concrete megalith is moved with levers, as first proposed by William Stukeley; relying only on levers limits the number of people who can take part.

(quarry scenes on Sumba bristle with long levers), handling it when it snags and helping to move and restrain it on slopes.

We are nearly there, but one trick remains: carrying. With blue-stones now thought to weigh half what had once been envisaged, as Mike Parker Pearson has pointed out they fall into the higher end of the range of what it is possible for a gang of men to lift and carry forward. If that seems far-fetched, carrying small megaliths, like sledges, has been recorded. John Hutton (1885–1968), who began his career in 1909 as a civil servant in Assam, on the border between India and Burma (as Myanmar was known then), described how members of a Naga tribe built a great wooden frame to this end, some three times as long and twice as wide as the stone to be carried; 60 men stood inside the frame and grasped the poles. This is a technique particularly favoured over rough, broken or very steep ground, and, notes Hutton, is only possible with smaller stones.[13]

Another British observer of megalith carrying, Ursula Graham Bower (1914–88), spent nearly a decade among Naga people in the late 1930s and early 1940s. A pioneering anthropologist, she left an extraordinary record: her book is as revealing, and honest, about

A small megalith ready for carrying in northeastern India in the 1920s.

Naga crew and observers rest while carrying a small megalith in northeastern India, photographed by Ursula Graham Bower in 1941.

herself as it is about the people with whom she was living.[14] Stone moving made a big impression on her.

'Only manpower was used,' she wrote, 'but until one has seen what can be done by it, properly handled, one can have no real conception of its efficiency. Once one has seen it, Stonehenge and Avebury are comprehensible. I always wished I could hear Namkia, who had dragged, and superintended the dragging of, many stones in his time, give his expert opinion on those two monuments.'

The general rule, she said, was to carry uphill with around 100 men, and pull down downhill, but in the event she describes, rough ground made dragging impossible even on a downslope, so steep that most of the men were too busy trying to keep upright to lift. When they could move, it was at a fast walking pace. It could be as dangerous as it sounds. On one occasion when a stone was being pulled downhill, the last man on the rope slipped and fell in front of the sledge; cries to stop were drowned out by chanting, and the man was killed. They destroyed the stone. A fire was burned around it for a day, then water was poured over and the would-be megalith shattered into fragments.

Moving stones takes skill and experience, and a great number of willing helpers and supporters, but it can be done without complex processes. The key machinery is a sledge, which to survive the strains imposed by heavy loads and the competing forces of ropes and gravity, will need to be well carpentered. Our word, 'carpentry', derives ultimately from the Latin for a maker of carts, and if for lighter stones a less sophisticated structure will suffice, for the heaviest the sledge will be like a ship, in the Neolithic probably made by boatbuilders or housebuilders. We will need hundreds of levers and piles of long thin timbers for laying on the ground, to stop the sledge from sinking into the soil and to reduce friction – fresh poles will be self-lubricating, releasing sap as they are crushed. Occasionally we will need further wood for carrying bluestones through awkward corners and over steep, rocky ground. And we will need a great deal of strong rope, for holding the stone to the sledge or portering frame, and for pulling the sledge and strengthening its joints.

Neolithic rope of that size and quality has not been found in Britain, but there is no reason to doubt that it could have been made. Short lengths of withy are known from the Dover boat (in yew, around 1550 BC) and Seahenge, the curious Bronze Age ring of oak posts found on the Norfolk shore (honeysuckle, 2049 BC). Large numbers of withy fragments were found near Stonehenge in the 1960s at the bottom of a deep chalk well, at least some of which may have been hazel. In addition there were a few short lengths of a three-strand reverse-twist cord, with a breaking load of 250 kg (550 lb), possibly made from bast fibre (from the inner bark or skin of flowering plants or trees). Such cord could readily have been braided into substantial rope capable of pulling tons. Its age is debated, but it's probably Bronze Age, around 1400 BC.[15]

As well as sledges, poles and rails, I further suggest, as we will see, that at one point we will need a boat. We might reasonably ask, where would all this timber come from? There's not a lot of old forest today on either the Preselis or Salisbury Plain, so would there have been more in the Neolithic? The simple answer is yes, though most of our evidence is indirect, and it's rarely possible to say of any one particular place exactly how it looked. The best indication, perhaps, comes from the tools used to cut the trees down: stone axe blades. They are everywhere (I drew thousands for my doctoral research), skilfully flaked and ground into beautiful cutting tools whose efficacy has been demonstrated in many experiments. These blades incidentally throw light on another aspect of Neolithic life, revealing, in the choice of materials, that people knew their land and were prepared to go to great lengths to find the right stone – excavating deep mines into the chalk of southeast England for flint, for example, or climbing high in the Lake District to reach perilous outcrops of fine-grained green tuff. Debris from making axeheads from a distinctive rhyolite has been found at the eastern end of the Preselis – and a few fragments of axes from there have been discovered by archaeologists in Wiltshire.

Ecological evidence – from soils, pollen, hollows left by falling trees and so on – suggests there was never a dense thicket of continuous forest, but rather a changing mix of ancient woodland and regrowth, scrubby or grassy clearings and sometimes, as on Salisbury Plain at the time Stonehenge was built, quite extensive open areas. There seems to have been no shortage of wood, however: holes in the ground for large posts are especially common in the Neolithic, for great timber halls and a range of ceremonial structures, including equivalents to Stonehenge. And occasionally we see the wood itself: remnants of submerged trees on the Pembrokeshire coast; oak, ash and lime planks from split trunks in the Sweet Track, or pinewood poles on Hatfield Moor; and, importantly, evidence for a knowledge of woodland management – the pegs in the Sweet Track were cut from coppiced hazel and alder poles.

A good sledge; ropes at front, back and sides as long as are needed to provide holds for the required hands; poles on the ground, levers in waiting and the labour to operate those too. We have the stones, we have the kit and we have the know-how. We may not roll, but we are ready to rock.

CONSTRUCTION: BLUEHENGE

In a sunny September in 2015 I rented a car and drove from Wiltshire to Pembrokeshire in search of an outcrop. It should have taken me three hours, passing the Brecon Beacons to the south on the M4 and following the coast before cutting inland on small roads, circling the Preseli Hills and reaching Craig Rhos-y-felin. So concealed was the outcrop, however, deep in a thickly wooded, narrow valley, that I spent half an hour trying to find it. The reverse journey in the Neolithic, from Craig Rhos-y-felin to Stonehenge, would have taken – using the route I am about to describe, some 350 km (220 miles) with a 2-ton boulder – more than a month. Used as we are to travelling at speed with no effort, half an hour lost in country lanes feels like an eternity. By comparison, a few weeks of drama moving a megalith in the Neolithic might have seemed to have ended too soon.

Stonehenge has a long, complex history, and the more we know the longer and more involved (and debatable) it becomes. We can escape the details here, but we do need to have an outline idea of what it is we are about to build, and what goes up when. For this purpose I have simplified the story into two eras (the key elements are listed in the Appendix). I call them Bluehenge (the subject of this chapter) and Stonehenge (of the next). The former, under construction from around 3200 BC, is characterized above all by bluestones, and was a focus of cremation burial throughout its time. The latter, begun around 2500 BC and dominated by huge sarsens, is the wonder whose ruin is what we know today as Stonehenge. But it started with bluestones and these were born in Wales, which is why we are at Craig Rhos-y-felin.

Approached from the southeast, the Craig looks like a low cliff flanking higher ground, blanketed with bracken, gorse, heather and ivy through which streaky grey blocks of stone occasionally

The rock at Craig Rhos-y-felin breaks naturally into blocks suitable for megaliths.

rise to breathe. It drops to the north, however, and when you walk round you find it's not a cliff at all, but a rock, a small Uluru, rising suddenly from the hillside like the fin of a giant fish, breaching the surface and gripped there for eternity, the sea's ripples and spray caught in a scatter of boulders and rubble (see pl. XVIII). And on this occasion, the reason for my visit, the ground has been filleted by archaeologists.

As we saw in Chapter 2, 13 bluestone types have been identified at Stonehenge, most of them relatively rare and matched to localized geology in the eastern Preselis or nearby, or the Brecon Beacons. The commonest rocks are dolerite, andesite and rhyolite, and among them one of each dominates the fragments, which I have labelled B1, B5 and B6. For us, it seems remarkable luck that so far two of the Stonehenge rocks that Richard Bevins and Rob

Ixer have been able to track down confidently to lone outcrops are two of these, so well represented at Stonehenge: B6, from Craig Rhos-y-felin, is the commonest rhyolite at Stonehenge, including two identified megaliths; B1's Carn Goedog accounts for more than half of Stonehenge's dolerite fragments, and at least five megaliths.

But perhaps it's not luck. Perhaps in the Neolithic it was the very distinction of these small, unexpected protrusions in the landscape that attracted attention, that had accumulated histories and that gave them something special. And such was the detail of Richard's fieldwork, he and Rob were able to say that it was only part of Craig Rhos-y-felin that had been quarried for megaliths, the extreme northeast end – 'an almost impossible provenance of ten square metres' as Rob Ixer has described it – which is where the archaeologists are digging on my visit.

This is the last of five seasons at the site. Mike Parker Pearson, wearing heavy boots, a faded red T-shirt and baggy green trousers, and leading a team reunited from the earlier project that spent seven years excavating on the downs around Stonehenge, wants to show me their prize catch: a megalith. On this northwestern side the outcrop has a near vertical face, emphasized by the archaeologists who have stripped away vegetation and soil to expose the clean, fissured rock and a tumble of blocky boulders and debris at the base. The largest stone rests on its own, 4 m (13 ft) out from the face, propped up on stumpy horizontal pillars that hold it expectantly, as if at any moment it will be pulled forward onto a waiting sledge. Scenes like this – apparently abandoned megaliths on stone trestles and rails – have been described in Orkney by Mike's colleague Colin Richards, whose experience at megalithic quarries in Scotland proved invaluable at these Welsh excavations. Elsewhere three small stones have been set in pits, two of them crushed on top as if they had once been under heavy weights, and a recess in the rock face – at the precise location of the closest geological samples to Stonehenge pieces – is the right size and shape for an extracted bluestone megalith.

It would be easy to dismiss this as evidence for Neolithic quarrying, as indeed Brian John, who thinks the bluestones were carried out of Wales by glaciers, has done. Stone – except in special circumstances that do not apply here – cannot be dated to show when it was worked. For that we rely on radiocarbon dating of associated organic material. Over the centuries, soil and debris accumulated beside the outcrop, burying the stone on its platform and everything around it. At the very bottom of these silts were burnt hazelnut shells, leftovers from meals eaten by hunter-gatherers over 9,000 years ago – the outcrop's presence in the human imagination may have a very long antiquity. Higher up were remains dated to the Neolithic and above these to the Iron Age and early medieval times. Through the gate at the bottom of the field, where the narrow lane dips beneath the waters of the wooded stream that flows from the Preselis above, two stone posts that almost certainly came from the rhyolite outcrop frame the start of a footpath. When were *they* quarried? There is no time limit to working stone.

A large slab at Craig Rhos-y-felin, thought to be an unfinished megalith.

The prone 'megalith' at Rhos-y-felin is bigger than the known igneous bluestones, the closest in scale at Stonehenge being the Altar Stone (5 m or 16 ft long, compared to the Craig's 4 m or 13 ft); Mike Parker Pearson thinks it was selected for local use, centuries after Stonehenge was built. Nonetheless, there is a precise geological correspondence between the outcrop and stones in Wiltshire, people were there doing things at around the right time, and stone was being worked. As I clamber over the site, I feel confident that I am looking at one of the places that gave megaliths to Stonehenge.

We leave Rhos-y-felin, drive northwards out of the wood to the edge of the open moor, and climb to another outcrop. This is Carn Goedog, on the Preselis' north-facing slopes (see pl. XIX). There are good views, across lowland Pembrokeshire and out to sea, and inland along the hills where further dolerite outcrops spatter the turf like giant wormcasts. From the north – the only direction with a flat approach – Goedog has a similar profile to Rhos-y-felin, an outburst of rock that rises and falls against the sky like a fin. Without trees it's easier to see, and in the nature of the dolerite it's more broken, a jumble of angular blocks and slabs. As at Stonehenge,

Looking northeast across the Preselis from Carn Goedog towards Carn Alw on the near horizon (left) and Carn Breseb (right).

The outcrop at Carn Goedog has been heavily quarried.

clumps of pale crystals are often visible, slightly raised above the more weathered, green stone. This is Stonehenge's famous spotted dolerite in its natural habitat.

Mike, Colin and their colleagues are having similar success here, excavating where readymade megaliths seem to fall from the rock. Marks of steel tools can be seen among the debris, but they have also found what they think is older evidence for quarrying: stone hammers and wedges, scars of simple stone-splitting, and a pair of large slabs set on edge about 1 m (3 ft) apart – a stone trestle. From the previous year's dig they obtained Neolithic radiocarbon dates similar to those from Craig Rhos-y-felin, the older apparently pre-dating bluestones at Stonehenge (albeit that date is itself contentious, as we shall see) and fuelling the team's theory that the Wiltshire stones' journeys began not at the quarries, but at stones already arranged into circles nearby – an idea first proposed in the 1920s by the geologist Herbert Thomas.

Mike and I stride out across the hill, climbing to the more extensive outcrops on Carn Menyn. Here there is rock everywhere, from a wide, low scatter that makes walking tricky on the approach, to great masses of angular blocks on the ridge, leaning, toppling and piled on one another where glacial ice tipped them over and carried them south, ready to trap ankles. There is clear, flat ground right up to the small outcrops at Goedog and Rhos-y-felin (and, apart from Carn Menyn, the other outcrops proposed by Richard and Rob as possible dolerite sources are also small), but here, we agree, it would have been harder to manoeuvre a sledge close to a chosen slab. Perhaps that was one reason to favour Goedog and Rhos-y-felin, their fins rising and dipping in stories no longer told.

It was ten years since I'd last been there among the rubble and tumble of Carn Menyn, when I'd come to see another excavation. This one was run by Tim Darvill and the late Geoff Wainwright (1937–2017), who, after a distinguished career as an excavator and chief archaeologist at English Heritage, had recently retired and returned to live near Pembrokeshire, the county of his birth. They were soon to dig together at Stonehenge, but now they were looking for the source of the monument's dolerite pillars. They were convinced they'd find it at Carn Menyn.

As Tim and I crawled and slipped over the Preseli outcrop in driving rain, he showed me slabs that might have been destined

Geoff Wainwright excavating at Carn Menyn in 2005, a possible bluestone quarry site.

for Wiltshire. In one case there was no question that someone had shaped it: a flat stone like a small megalith lay on the turf, chipped around its edges to an even shape and apparently abandoned when it had broken in half. It looked convincing, but the difficulty was that there are dolerite gateposts in the area, as there are rhyolite posts at Craig Rhos-y-felin; their almost-megalith could have been relatively modern. And over the years, as Richard Bevins and Rob Ixer analysed more and more Welsh outcrops and Stonehenge rock, nothing seemed to link Stonehenge and Carn Menyn. But then things changed.

First, further excavation by Tim and Geoff led to them finding what they believed to be a dolerite quarrying and working area, with stone debris and hammers and a small megalith that had once been standing up. Like Mike's team, they obtained Neolithic radiocarbon dates, ranging from around 2300 BC to 2000 BC. That evidence, tentative as it is, is not enough to prove a Stonehenge connection. They needed geological support, and for long that failed to come, as Richard and Rob's work consistently surprised us all by finding no match for Carn Menyn. Though thin-section microscopy, which Herbert Thomas used, does not rule out a Carn Menyn source, geochemistry seems to do so. At least it did, until 2021, when new study tentatively restored Carn Menyn – as a possibility among four different outcrops for rock type B2. Research continues.[1]

The Pembrokeshire quarries lie between 300 and 1,000 m (1,000 and 3,300 ft) above sea level. Stonehenge is only 100 m (330 ft) above sea level, but of course there are many ups and downs and hazards on the way, and I propose six principles to keep in mind when we consider routes from there, and, in the next chapter, from the Marlborough Downs:

1. Moving a stone involves more than engineering.
2. Other things being equal, river valleys make good routes…
3. …but frequent river crossings are better avoided.

4. Moving stones over flat ground is easy...
5. ...and steep slopes are especially challenging.
6. Sarsens are much bigger than bluestones.

No less than with flying a plane from Pembrokeshire to Stonehenge (there were once military airfields near the Preselis and at Stonehenge itself), moving a stone is about more than contrivances. Planning, people and infrastructure are critical, and in the Neolithic we can safely assume that the project goal was not to get a stone from Wales to Wiltshire at the minimum cost: if expense was a driving factor, Stonehenge would not have been built in the first place. There is nothing practical about a megalith, in Indonesia today or in Britain 5,000 years ago.

Taking our cue from Sumba and elsewhere, and considering the ambitious, glorious futility of Stonehenge, there surely would have been ceremonies and celebrations to accompany stone pulling. However, moving 80 or 90 megaliths across Wales and part of southern England, with the continuous intensity of munificence that characterizes a 500 m (1,650 ft) trip in Sumba, would bankrupt everyone. We might expect dance, music, feasting and superfluous crowds, but only at key junctures: where sponsors live (over such a long journey, it's likely several communities would contribute); across difficult terrain, perhaps, where a stone has to be carried, with more labour and greater danger; and especially at the finish. At other times the crew might be no more than is needed to haul, to collect and carry sleepers, to mend sledges, cables and bindings, and to attend to food, water and necessities.

Some 5,000 years ago when this happened, people in Britain had been growing food and rearing animals for a millennium. The land was settled and places marked, by homes and monuments, by communal meeting and burial sites, and by sources for precious supplies such as clay for potting, wood for fires or stone for making knives. There were places for growing and places for browsing stock, and all would have been connected by tracks and paths,

A stone is pulled along a forest track in northeastern India in the 1920s.

some wide and clear enough for small herds, others no more than a sigh under the soles of nimble feet. The more frequented trails would have connected villages – clusters of rectangular, thatched wooden homes, stores and animal pens, some perhaps housing no more than an extended family – to each other and their resources. These would often have been close to streams and rivers, where food and water are abundant and, down from the hills, shelter from storms is more easily found. This is where much of a stone's journey would have occurred, following old tracks on relatively level ground along intermittently peopled valleys.

Arriving at a village would be a moment for celebration: leaving the next morning, a frenzy of noise and excitement, shouting crowds and easy pulling, and, perhaps, with a local leader, priest or official wanting to make a mark and many less experienced with the process, of occasional accidents. There could be a core team who travel the entire journey, who know the route and the ropes and who will be able to share stories reaching back to the mountain source. Ron Adams's research can help us imagine that team, which need be no larger than 25 or 30 to pull a 2-ton stone, with a few others picked up on the way to help, at most, say, a total of 40. Among dispersed Neolithic communities that is still quite a group. It would not have passed unnoticed, and food and accommodation would have challenged smaller villages. At various points en route the numbers could rise to two or three hundred, falling away as progress continues into remoter territory until only yapping dogs and a few laughing, running children remain, and then they too are gone, so that all that sounds is the steady, rhythmic chant, the swoosh and crunch of runners sliding over poles, the rattle of dislodged stones, the creak of ropes and wooden joints and the occasional startled bird. The stone moves on.

All of this could have happened, and none of it might. I'm guessing, but these are informed guesses. From Carn Goedog we can look south downslope to where the Craig Rhos-y-felin quarry is, though the outcrop itself is hidden in the valley. Turning to the right, beyond Goedog's heathered, fractured slabs we can see carns Alw and Breseb, and Foel Trigarn rising between them on the horizon. It is probably late summer, when wheat and barley – staple foods – have been cut, threshed and stored, the days are still long and relatively warm and uncultivated autumn foods are starting to appear, such as berries and wild apples; hazelnuts, whose popularity is attested by copious amounts of burnt shells at places where people lived, are ripe for picking from late September. Today there is a stark contrast between the open moor around us and the greener pastures with patches of woodland lower down; the walls of distant white houses catch the sun. In the Neolithic the difference would have been less marked, with more trees, no hedgerows, and buildings, gardens and small clearings that merge into a landscape decorated with rising threads of smoke.

Perhaps there is a gathering place below Goedog where stones from both quarries await the long journey, prised out of the fractured rock and selected for their shape and size but not carved. Initially the pile might grow faster than it falls, and some stones have probably been collected the previous year if not earlier; certainly rope will

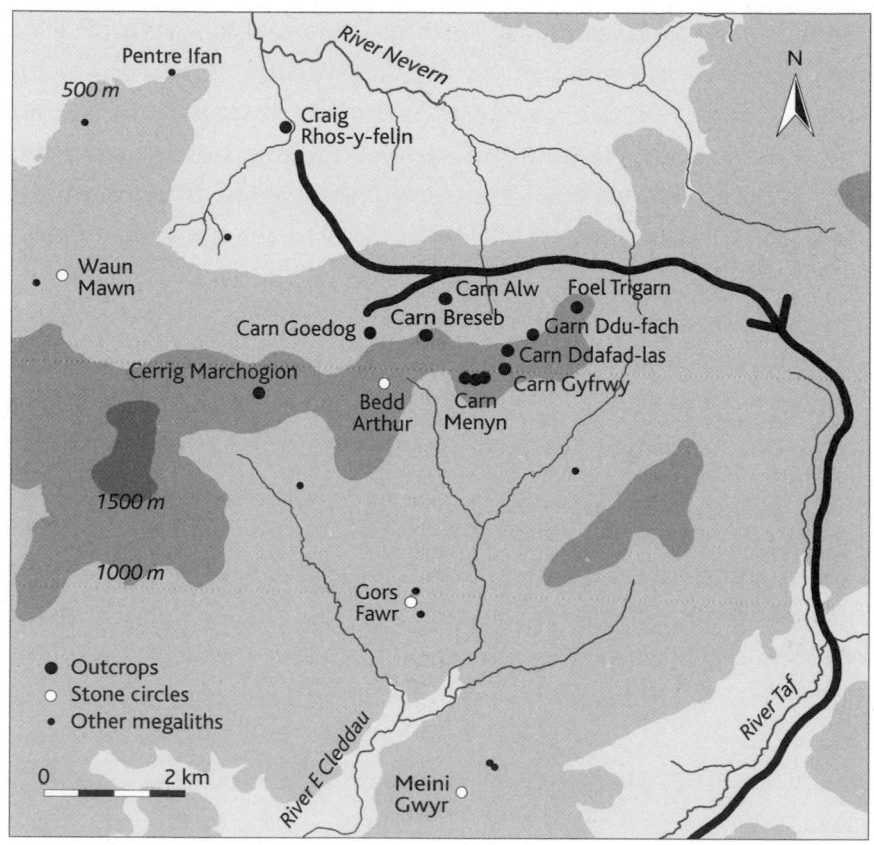

Proposed route out of the Preselis at the start of journeys to Stonehenge; note that outcrops identified as sources of megaliths are mostly along the hills' northern slopes.

have been made over many months. The route from here is east, following close to the contour below the carns and avoiding the spreads of stone clitter, heading towards a col between the end of the Preselis and rising ground further east. We turn south at the top, following the stream down to the River Taf, crossing to its east side while this is relatively easy, and continuing south and east down the valley until the Taf turns towards the sea and we keep going east, now along the Tywi valley.

What follows is the greatest climb of the journey, from near sea level to the watershed of the rivers Tywi and Usk between

Mynydd Du (the Black Mountain) and Mynydd Epynt (Welsh for the horse-path mountain). It's relatively gentle at first, rising 60 m (200 ft) over 65 km (40 miles), then turning southwards along the Gwydderig valley, clinging to the riverside in a narrow, twisting gorge and climbing a further 150 m (500 ft) over 15 km (10 miles) until we join the River Usk near what is now Trecastle. From here it's downhill back to the sea, a fall of 230 m (750 ft) over 95 km (60 miles) beside the winding, ever widening Usk until it reaches the Bristol Channel. And the first, most challenging leg is over.

How long has it taken from the hills overlooking the Irish Sea to the tide washing up the mudflats at Newport? There can be no definitive answer, and it's likely one stone's voyage is different from another's. There is the pulling and lifting to do, of course, but so much more too: greeting and socializing, catching up on news, swapping stories and jokes, resting and attending to injuries, collecting poles, repairing ropes and sledges, eating, sleeping and occasionally getting caught up in local incidents such as a death

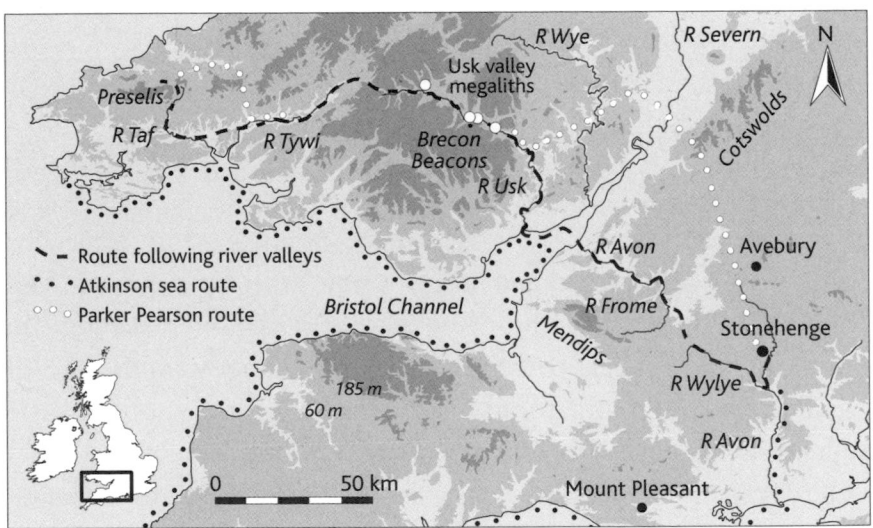

Proposed route for bluestones to reach Stonehenge from the Preselis, with earlier suggestions by Richard Atkinson and Mike Parker Pearson. Four unusually large, lone sandstone megaliths on the Usk are in the area of a possible source for the Altar Stone at Stonehenge.

or the completion of a new house. Yet the stone draws the team on, offering independence from the endless rounds of obligations, promising new places and encounters and ultimately recognition and anticipated gratitude.

From a variety of experiments and observations a stone and sledge together weighing 4 or 5 tons can be moved 4 or 5 km (2.5–3 miles) over flat ground in an hour – walking speed – but that distance drops dramatically climbing steep slopes.[2] Overall this Welsh journey is mostly on gentle slopes and most of those are downhill, but there are significant ascents and terrain is varied. There will be many awkward moments where, perhaps, fixed wooden tracks will aid the movement of a sledge or the stone will be carried. If we imagine an average speed of 5 km per day, the whole route – 220 km (135 miles) – could be covered in 45 days, arriving at the end of September.

There are interesting things on the way, not least where the Usk flows between the Brecon Beacons and the Black Mountains and the valley sometimes widens into a flat plain. Four enormous megaliths mark the route from Brecon to Crickhowell. Lone standing stones are common in Wales, but these are exceptional. Like the outliers at Stonehenge, they have names: the Battle Stone, Cwrt-y-Gollen and Llwyn-y-Fedwen (all 4 m or 13 ft high), and Maen Pyscodyn (4.5 m or 15 ft). They are the size of typical sarsens in the circle at Stonehenge, and made from Old Red Sandstone: it's possible that some are the same rock as the Altar Stone. Perhaps, even, that stone was once a fifth in this extended row of waymarkers, all on the river's east bank, where we take our stone to avoid a crossing near its mouth.

Richard Warner (1763–1857), a priest and writer based in Bath, came this way in 1797.[3] He saw Cwrt-y-Gollen, the 'growing stone' at Crickhowell ('a Druidical remain connected with the religious worship of the ancient Britons'), while his 'progress was frequently retarded by numerous droves of black cattle'. The animals were heading for a Severn crossing and markets and better pasture in Bristol and beyond, and were manifestations of a once common

Cwrt-y-Gollen
megalith, a little over
4 m (13½ ft) high, is one
of four large standing
stones in the Usk valley
along the proposed
bluestone route to
Stonehenge.

sight across Wales and England, targeting especially London. Moving
10–15 km (6–10 miles) a day, herds, not just of cattle, but also pigs,
sheep and more exotic creatures like geese and turkeys, were taken
along well-tried routes or droves that might begin even in Ireland
or Scotland. Warner's cattle had set out from Pembrokeshire and
Carmarthenshire; some might have grazed the Preselis, following,
like our stone, a route that avoided numerous river crossings along
the coast.

Many people around the world move their herds into high pastures in summer and low in winter – that may have happened in
Neolithic Britain – but this droving was different; the cattle had
no return. The idea also may have considerable antiquity. In 2019
a study was published that argued that pigs had been driven from
Scotland to Durrington Walls, a great henge earthwork, to provide
for feasting associated with the construction of nearby Stonehenge.

The evidence for this lay in isotopic varieties of elements in the bone, which would vary in proportion to each other depending on where the pigs grew up: strontium ratios suggested to the researchers that the nearest such location was in a region of distinctive geology in Aberdeenshire. However, more localized candidates have also been suggested: most of these lie across central southern Wales in a band west of the River Severn above Gloucester, and in the Malvern Hills in western England, 100 km (65 miles) northwest from Stonehenge.[4] A similar study of remains of people buried at Stonehenge also identified many individuals who might have grown up in south Wales. Megaliths, moved on routes already well travelled, may have been only part of the links between Pembrokeshire, Wiltshire and regions in between in the Neolithic.

Much of our stone's journey through Wales matches that proposed recently by Mike Parker Pearson. However, while the latter heads northwest after leaving the Brecon Beacons to cross the Wye and then the Severn above Gloucester, we are taking the shorter option of staying with the Usk to its source. Traditionally that poses a problem in the form of a sea crossing. It can equally be seen as an opportunity: a challenge easily met with boats of the time led by people familiar with the channel, to be celebrated and exaggerated as a triumph of power over nature – and, perhaps, mythical forces – and bravery over danger.

If the sledge is pulled across the low land to face the mouth of the River Avon in England, the crossing there today is no more than 9 km (5.5 miles) – an hour or two's paddling, but enough to create legends. In modern times, further out to sea from the Severn estuary and in journeys of several times the length, a windsurfer in Swansea Bay found himself so far out that he decided to continue to Devon (the worst part, he said, was having to ring his wife and ask for a lift home). That was in April. On another occasion, in November, a kayaker crossed from Wales to Devon in three and a quarter hours (the return journey, when the wind got up, the cloud came down and darkness set in, took a good five hours). And in Wales at the narrower crossing point opposite the Avon, in the muds and peats of the relatively sheltered channel shore, archaeologists have found prehistoric wooden trackways, boat planks and footprints – none of exactly the right age for the bluestone journeys, but people were there. While dragging the stone so far, why would they pass up the chance to create a momentous memory at the junction of the two quite different parts of its journey (and incidentally shorten the land passage)?

And so we arrive in England. Here we adopt another archaeologist's route: Richard Atkinson's. There's no escaping the fact that his idea of following rivers from the Bristol Channel to Stonehenge offers the simplest, gentlest way to achieve the goal. The Bristol Avon invites us to continue up its meandering course between the Cotswolds to the northeast, avoiding substantial climbs necessitated by a higher Severn crossing, and the Mendip Hills to the southwest. Whether we raft our stone on the river or drag it alongside is a secondary question: the Avon valley is the only way to avoid these hills. We arrive in a boat, however, and at least while the river is wide it might almost seem perverse not to continue on the water.

As we do this, we might well ask why we didn't take to a boat long before, up in the Brecon Beacons where the Usk first becomes deep enough to raise a craft clear of its stony bed – around Brecon, perhaps, at a point which happens to be marked by the first of the great sandstone megaliths. Splitting the voyage that way results in around 130 km (80 miles) overland and 80 km (50 miles) by river, and with a speed of 5 km (3 miles) per hour paddling with the flow down the Usk, the theoretical overall journey time falls to 30 days. River or bankside, both are possible.

From the Bristol Avon, Richard Atkinson's route joins the Frome above Bath, to the Wylye at Warminster, the Nadder just above Salisbury and then the Wiltshire Avon, following north upstream to what is now Amesbury and close to Stonehenge. Apart from the final haul, there is only one unavoidable overland section, a brief 10 km (6 miles) between the town of Frome and the upper reaches of the Wylye, with a steady climb of 50 m (165 ft). Another, shorter dry option might be to cut across from the Wylye to the Avon above Salisbury, heading up a valley from Great Wishford and down the other side to Middle Woodford, rising and falling 40 m (130 ft) over 4 km (2.5 miles). This avoids 20 km (12 miles) of looping south and immediately back north again, more attractive, perhaps, if the stone is already on a sledge; a boat might continue to follow the rivers.

The whole trip from the Bristol Channel takes 10 to 25 days, depending on how much the stone is floated along the way. With a day to cross the Severn estuary, and if we assume stones were floated down the Usk from Brecon, we now have an estimated total journey time of 41 to 56 days. Allowing for days on which the stone did not move at all, we can hazard at around two months to reach Stonehenge from Carn Goedog, arriving, perhaps, in mid-October. Alternatively the journey could be split into two at the Severn, arriving at the Welsh shore at the end of September and picking up again (perhaps in the hands of different people) in mid-August the following year, reaching Stonehenge in a couple of weeks.

That's one megalith. If we could say precisely when each bluestone was first raised at Stonehenge – at this stage there are at least 56 – we could make an informed speculation about the transport programme. Did it take as many years as there are stones, one every autumn? Was the departure of a stone from Carn Goedog followed by another the next day, and another and another, moved, perhaps, by local gangs pulling in relay (logistically and socially unlikely)? Unfortunately we don't have precise dates for early bluestone works in Wiltshire, and such calculations are hopeless. It's archaeologically possible, to take an extreme position, that no more than two or three stones arrived from Wales every generation. So as we approach the site up the Avon near Amesbury, I will assume simply that some stones are already there and others will be arriving, in time enough to support their arrangement in a planned design.

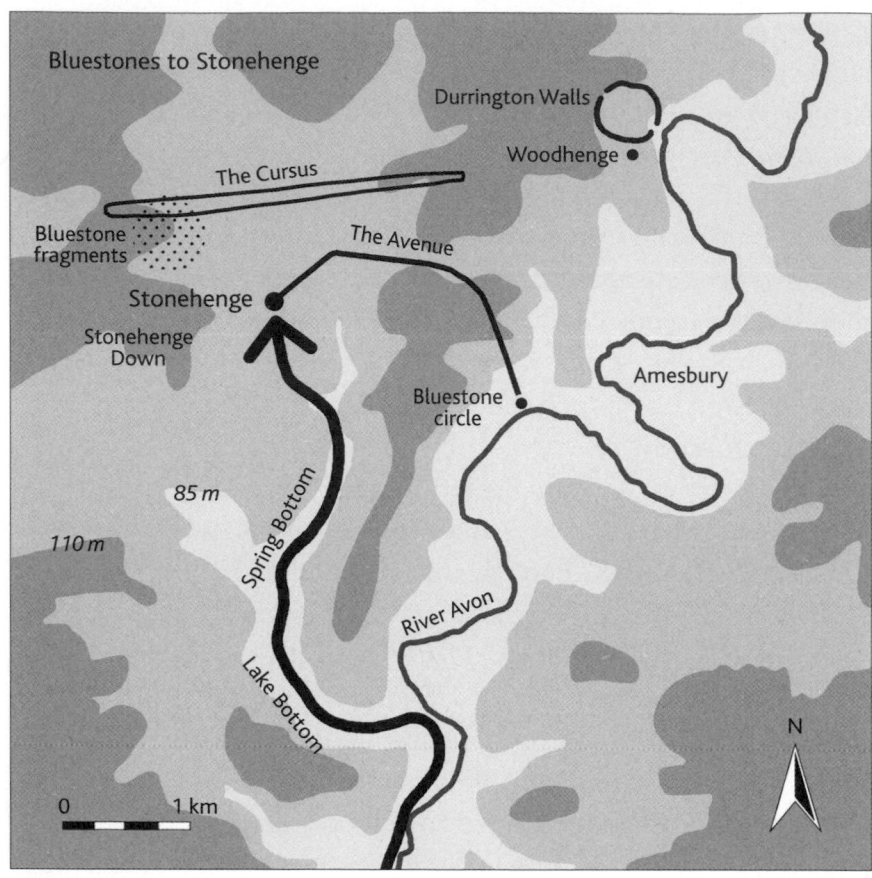

Proposed route for bluestones at the end of the Stonehenge journey.

And here we face a small dilemma. Which way to go? For the first time there is a marked route, a wide passageway across the downland framed by parallel ditches and banks that connect the river to Stonehenge – the Avenue. Climbing northwest, then turning west and again southwest (the final stretch we walked in Chapter 1), the Avenue reaches the entrance to the monument after 2.7 km (1.7 miles). Current evidence suggests it was not dug until centuries after the bluestones arrived, but the earthwork could have been a late marking of a long-used track; the Avenue has often been proposed as channelling the stones' final approach. Following our transport principles, however, it's not the best way.

The Avenue climbs nearly 40 m (130 ft) out of the river valley to a ridge, then falls down into a hollow and climbs back again to Stonehenge; neither is it a direct route. We can leave the river earlier, turning west up Lake Bottom, a long, gentle dry valley that curls to the north as Spring Bottom, bringing us to below Stonehenge where there is a smaller climb of 15 m (50 ft). This amounts to 4.5 km (2.8 miles; from the same starting point via the Avenue, it's 6 km or 3.7 miles), and if the Avenue leads us to the site's northeast entrance, this route takes us to the other one at the south. We have arrived.

Π

What do we see as we ascend Stonehenge Down?

When I set out to write this book, I had no intention of getting into the archaeology of Stonehenge – the details of what has been found in the many excavations, and what they tell us about what was built when. It's surely fascinating only to a small group of people, and there is a newly researched and quasi-official construction history which would be easy to adopt. However, as we crest the hill with our sledge, what comes into sight is not quite what we might have expected, and I must briefly explain why.

Stonehenge is a circular monument, but there are only two perfect circles, which share the same centre point: the Sarsen Circle and the Aubrey Holes, a larger ring of pits (today there's general agreement that these pits were probably dug to take the first bluestones, which is why this matters here). On the edge of the site, the Aubrey ring must have been set out when there was nothing much standing in the middle to get in the way of a rope, suggesting it appeared early on. There is otherwise little to tell us when the pits were dug, but for one thing. A cremation burial in one of them is radiocarbon dated to around 3000–2900 BC. Unfortunately how much time passed between the digging of the pit and the burial of the remains in its fill is now hard to say, but the original excavation must have occurred at least 5,000 years ago.

However, this ring of pits is enclosed by a ditch, excavated from the chalk in a slightly irregular circle with approximately the same centre point and a diameter of 110 m (360 ft), and this *is* dated. Many red deer antler picks, a popular Neolithic digging tool, were discarded in this ditch. They are ideal for radiocarbon dating, which tells us people used them around 2950 BC, give or take 50 years. It looks as if the Aubrey Holes and the ditch were dug out at the same time, so in the traditional view what we should see is the gleaming white chalk of the ditch and low banks of spoil on either side marking out a great arena, in which the most prominent feature is a slightly smaller ring of pits and their spoil, some of which perhaps already contain upright bluestones.

Instead, what we actually see is the emerging circle of pits and standing stones, surrounded not by a ditch but another circle – perhaps a perfect circle – of discrete, larger pits. This somewhat nerdy distinction matters, because it implies that instead of being dug in 2950 BC, the Aubrey Holes would have been made some two

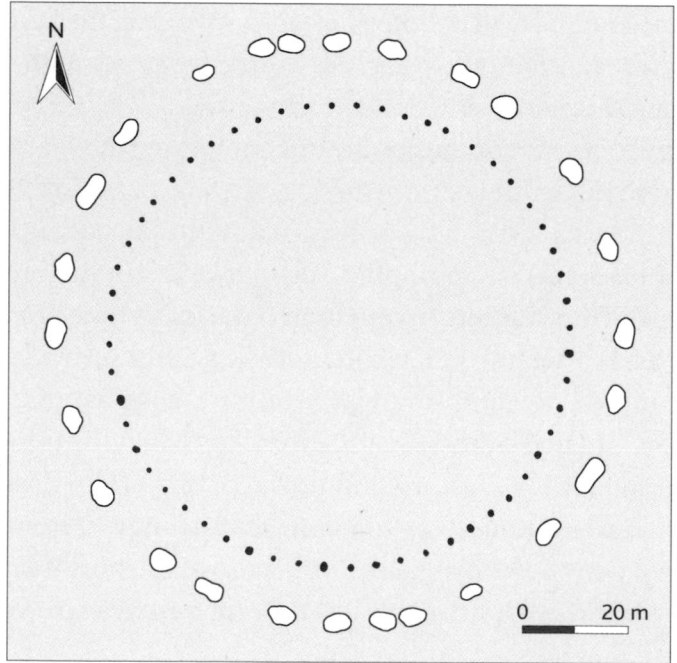

Bluehenge, the first Stonehenge monument: a circle of 56 stones inside a – now largely disappeared – ring of chalk pits.

centuries earlier. Not only would this mean Stonehenge is even older than we thought (we are looking at the oldest known part of the monument), but the bluestones would then have been brought to the site and erected around 3200 BC – which happens to be roughly the time the two excavated quarries were being worked in Wales.

How does this work? First, although the ditch, as we know it now, almost certainly *was* dug around 2950 BC, four bones – a cattle skull and two jaws, and a red deer leg bone – gave much older radiocarbon dates. The conundrum was originally solved by assuming that the bones were ancient relics (large cattle bones are found in burial mounds raised in the area by earlier generations) that had been placed carefully in the ditch when it was dug. But an alternative explanation, frankly more likely, is that the bones had been buried when they were fresh in pits that centuries later were joined up to make the ditch – which is exactly how the present ditch looks, a string of straightish sections connecting pits. These older bones are evidence for an older ditch ring. This highlights the significance of a really distinctive feature of Stonehenge and the next link in this story: cremation burials.

Early in the history of the site the cremated remains of many people – women, fewer men and even fewer children, among them an infant – were buried in little pockets on the edge of the site, apparently unmarked, in and around the enclosing ditch and the Aubrey Holes. No funeral pyres have been found, and it's possible some of the individuals at least, like the bluestones, were not local – isotopic study of charcoals within the cremated remains points to fires having been set in landscapes more wooded than that around Stonehenge at the time. Mourners scraped bone fragments out of the ashes and put them into portable bags or boxes before burial, and these too reinforce the impression that right from the start Stonehenge had more than local recognition: here isotopes suggest that two in five of the people who ended up with the Welsh stones on Salisbury Plain had spent the last decade of their lives somewhere else.

The practice seems to have continued for as many as 20 generations, but some of the cremations occurred a century or so before the continuous ditch was dug. A reasonable theory is that the focus for the cemetery was the circle of bluestones, which becomes possible from the start if we picture the stones to have been raised around 3200 BC. The simplest explanation, then, is that cremation burial began then, at the same time as the creation of the Aubrey circle and the enclosing broken ditch ring.

I left open the choice of our final approach between Lake Bottom and the longer and harder Avenue route, which I suspect would have been determined by immediate factors invisible to us (what else was happening where, what should or should not have been seen by who, land use and so on). If we arrive by the gentler southern route, however, we will notice as we pass between two pits that there is a large cattle jaw in each one: a symbolic link, perhaps, to the ancestors buried in the old barrows of the plain. Even now, five millennia later, we can see that gap between the pits, preserved as a grassy bridge across an otherwise continuous ditch around the south side of the site.

Fortunately we do not have to build a pyre, but we do have a stone to erect. What do we do with it?

I've imagined that a site for our stone has already been marked out, and we should briefly consider how that was done. Though it would be easy to define a circle with a post and a length of rope, this is the first time we see it happen in Britain on the ground, here (at 87 m or 285 ft across) and at a handful of other ritual earthworks of comparable size across the country: perfect circularity was a choice and it meant something, even if we can never know what. It's less clear whether the number of stones, 56, was arrived at by design or accident. Either is possible, though as the stones had to be brought from so far, we might think this too was planned. If that were the case the challenge would have been to arrange them evenly around the ring – done precisely, centre to centre, they would be around 5 m (16 ft) apart, which is, more or less, how the pits were dug, give or take half a metre (with gaps of between 14 and 18 ft). Much modern ingenuity has gone into guessing how such a layout – 56 evenly spaced pits – might have been achieved with a geometric design that was then executed. It would be equally possible that laying out was trial and error, first dividing the circle into two, then into quarters and then eighths, leaving seven stones to be spread along each of eight arcs. Any or every part of this, from 56 to 7, from half the circle to an eighth segment and so on, could have carried symbolic meaning – and probably did.

First we dig a pit. Below the soil at Stonehenge is a creamy coloured mix of silt and broken chalk. The triangular scoops of cattle shoulder blades seem to offer ready-made hand shovels, and they are often found in Neolithic excavations along with the more common antler picks. How they might have been used, however, is an open question; most likely is that they served not to dig or to throw spoil as we might do with a modern spade or shovel, but to move loose material, perhaps by spooning it back between the legs to someone else doing the same thing in a human chain.

More useful to start would be a wooden spade and a digging stick. Though none have been found of this age in Britain – wood rarely survives – an oak shovel used in a copper mine around 1800 BC has been identified, and digging sticks, long wooden rods driven into the ground with two hands, are almost universal among communities using non-industrial tools (and in their iron manifestation as a crowbar are still in use in Britain).

Our pit needs to be around 1 m (3 ft) across and the same deep. When the turf is at around knee height as we stand on the bottom we hit white chalk, a relatively soft but firm rock that needs a different approach. Now we reach for an antler pick, the prehistoric digging tool bar none. When soil conditions are right for their preservation (chalk is good) we find them anywhere Neolithic people dug holes in the ground, sometimes in their hundreds. The antlers would have been collected, perhaps by children foraging in woodland, in the spring or early summer after the annual shed. The beam makes a

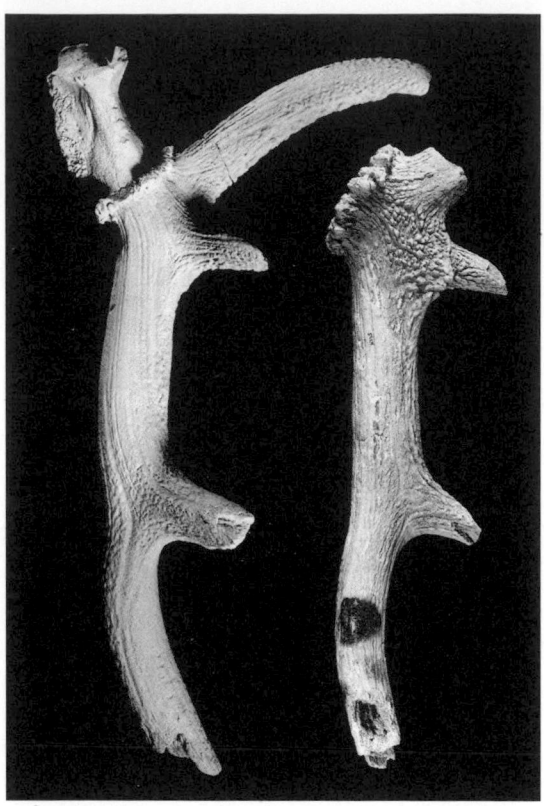

Red deer antler used as digging picks at Stonehenge, cut from the skull of a dead animal (left) and collected shed (right). Bez and trez tines (lower protrusions) have been cut off, leaving the brow tine at the top as the working end (this tine has broken off the antler on the right). Charring on the handle (dark patch lower right) is not uncommon, but how or why it occurred is not known.

natural handle, the brow tine the pick's working end, and the rest is cut away with a sharp flint blade – it's as simple as that. And like the deer that shed them in the spring and grew new ones in the autumn, when they were done people threw them into their completed excavations, knowing they could trim fresh ones the following year. Occasionally we see fingerprints preserved in chalk mud encrusted on a handle. They are immediate, intimate reminders that ordinary people, blistering their palms in back-breaking work, used simple, familiar tools to make extraordinary things.

We don't swing our pick, but hammer and coerce its pointed tine into cracks, and lever out the white rubble, until we are ready to stand our stone. Fist-sized lumps of flint, of which many have been found at Stonehenge, battered and discarded, may also have played a part here, held in the hand or fixed into wooden hafts.

In 1921 John Hutton watched a megalith being erected in northeast India, close to the border with Burma, which was the same size as ours – 2 m (6 ft) long and weighing nearly 2 tons. Then working for the Indian Civil Service and later to become a celebrated Cambridge University anthropologist, Hutton left a superb description of a stone-raising event.[5] As we would expect, it began with a ceremony. This involved herbs, leaves, beer and a chicken, and a 'performer' who threw four heads of wild oats into the air and told the stone it was time to go (lying on a sledge, it had a journey of 350 m or 1,100 ft ahead of it to the site). As on Sumba, many more men and boys came to help than were needed, often 'young bucks... too beautifully adorned with elaborated head-gear to pull very much'. Once arrived the stone was given some cooked rice, and the next day was left alone.

Come erection time, with the sledge positioned so the intended base of the stone was in the right place, a hole was dug at its foot. Ropes tying the stone were cut while several men wielded long poles to keep it on the sledge, and its top end was slowly raised with levers, at each lift a progressively longer wooden wedge being inserted to prevent it falling back. Once in the air, the top end could be harnessed with a creeper. On one side men pulled this rope, bracing their feet against the bottom of the stone to help keep it on the sledge, while others continued to lift and insert wedges at the top until it reached an angle of about 45 degrees.

Now it was time to release the base, and pull on the creeper to bring the stone to a fully upright position, as the top crew, dropping their levers, pushed with their hands. A great cry went up. 'Romance', said Hutton as he recalled concentrating on his note-taking and photography, 'was never further from my mind.' Yet he was caught up in the event. 'I experienced on hearing that shout a most extraordinary, inexplicable and disconcerting thrill,' he wrote. 'It was as though it had touched in me some obliterated memory of a similar triumph handed down through uncomprehending generations from some Neolithic progenitor of the remote past.'

While a scrum steadied the megalith, it was wedged underneath so it could stand on its own, and the pit was filled, the earth rammed down, filled in and rammed again. Thin creepers were ritually tied around the stone, cups of liquor were offered and bull's blood poured, the sledge was taken away and the site tidied up as the sun set behind a distant mountain. That, apart from the chicken and the mountain, is *exactly* how we will erect our bluestone. And we will do the same another 55 times.

Our perfect circle, each stone around 5 m (16 ft) from the next, no longer exists: almost certainly some of its stones stand on the site now, but in different locations. Those sites are not where the bluestones went next, however, for there is a *second* absent Bluehenge,

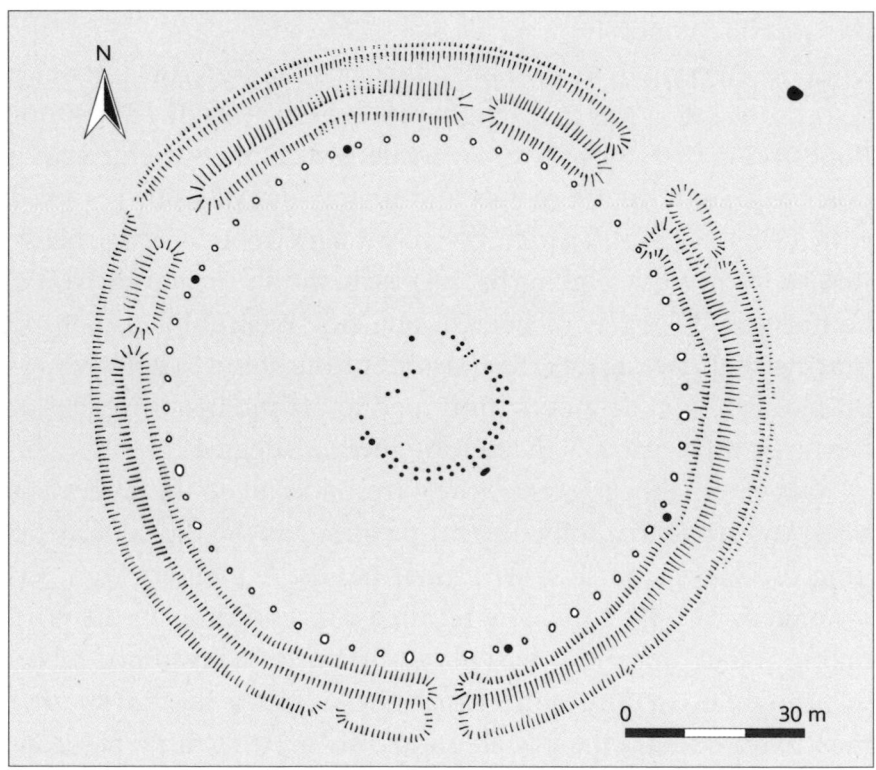

The second Bluehenge, with bluestones rearranged into a double arc in the centre of the site, and four sarsen Station Stones in place of the original circle; the pit ring has been converted into a continuous ditch.

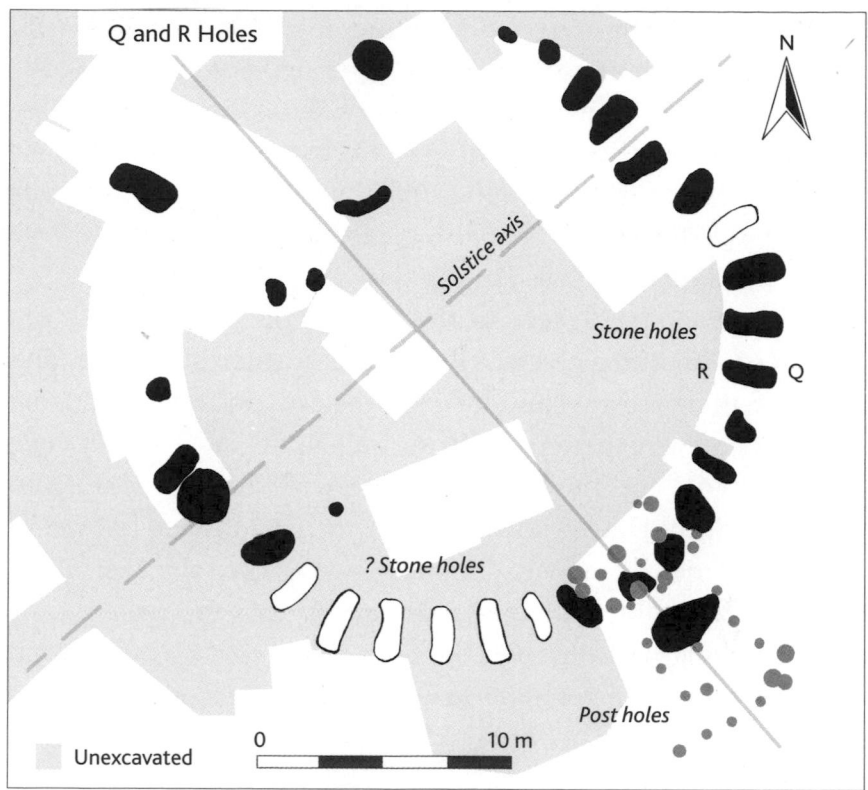

The second proposed major bluestone structure stood in pits known as
the Q and R Holes, in a double U-arrangement (a stone at the end of each pit)
open to the northwest; grey areas are unexcavated, with hypothetical pits
white. Lines indicate the Station Stone rectangle alignment, the dashed
northeast/southwest line being on the solstice axis.

this one both less well understood, and more complex than the
first. In the guidebook you will see its pits described as the Q and
R Holes, which with a few others once held a double ring of stones
in two close concentric circles. Archaeologists dispute whether this
ring was complete or not, and I'm going to take that debate further:
not only was it not complete (the evidence seems pretty clear on
that point), but it wasn't circular. Its plan was U-shaped.

At some time before 2500 BC, the bluestones were moved into
the central area and re-erected. Most of them were raised in pairs,
at either end of single, elongated pits, of which there were perhaps

24, laid out in a northwest-facing arc 20 m (65 ft) across with straight extensions to form the U.[6] Other scattered pits bring the total number of stones now at the centre of the site to more or less match the quantity removed from the Aubrey Holes. The largest is at the back and just outside the U: perhaps it was the Altar Stone, newly arrived. Here there is also a box-like arrangement of the deepest postholes recorded at the site.

Were we to stand there, at the back of the stone U with the large megalith and a cluster of tall posts further behind us, and look out along the axis and through the open side, we'd see that near horizon we experienced in our walk in the first chapter. Over four millennia ago, the stones smeared with dirt but bearing no lichen, we would have known that beyond that brow, a few weeks of hauling and river navigation away, was the sea channel where they had crossed from Wales; and beyond that the river and its valley snaking back through the mountains to the source. That view also roughly corresponds to where the sun sets at midsummer, and every 18 or 19 years we would see the full moon set at its most northerly point – next up, as I write, in spring 2025.

There is another arrangement of stones on the same alignment that may have been erected at this time: the sarsen Station Stones. Two now survive of four that were set up on a perfect rectangle that frames the bluestone structure, whose long sides, like the latter's, lie on a northwest/southeast axis. They are perpendicular to the axis of the rising midsummer sun in one direction and the setting midwinter sun in the other. The sunrise line passes through the Heelstone, the monument's other locally sourced sarsen as I suggested in the previous chapter, which raises the interesting possibility of a sort of alliance of symbols. The Welsh stones are arranged to face their source in Wales and the setting midsummer sun, while the sarsens hold a contrasting (and more precise) alignment on the rising midsummer sun. The two come together in a solar dance, as if, perhaps, to celebrate an alliance of peoples from distant parts of southern Britain.

This arrangement of megaliths and posts, a ghost in the story whose detailed form will always elude us – even though many of its stones are now surely standing at the site in other pits – was unparalleled. If we cannot see the monument, we can feel its presence and its ingenuity. Over generations, something unique had been created on the soft chalk downland with a blend of local sarsens and stones from the hard country hundreds of miles away. The journeys the bluestones had undertaken, the stories they had accumulated as they moved across landscapes and through communities, and later as worlds and lives had changed around them, were like none told anywhere else.

Or were they? One of many achievements of the Riverside Project that would be notable on their own was the discovery, in 2009 in West Amesbury, of an entirely unpredicted stone circle (illustrated overleaf). Appropriately, it was beside the River Avon – at the end of the Avenue earthwork (which was what the dig had innocently set out to investigate). There were nine close-packed pits, of a size and shape suitable for the taller, thinner type of bluestone, on the line of a ring of what might once have been 25 stones. The obvious question was what had happened to them? And to everyone at the dig, looking uphill along the Avenue (and on my visit, watching the pits pool with water in the rain, some of them lined with flint cobbles to stop the megaliths sinking into the soft ground) the obvious answer was that they were now at Stonehenge.[7]

Meanwhile in Wales, Mike Parker Pearson had been determined to find a circle there that might have been transported for rebuilding in Wiltshire. One of several possible sites was Waun Mawn, on the southern slopes of the Preselis. There were four dolerite stones: could they have been all that survived of a circle comparable to the first one at Stonehenge, such as Herbert Thomas had predicted nearly a century before?

Determined fieldwork – geophysical surveys failed to show anything, but in 2017 and 2018 the archaeologists went ahead and excavated anyway – revealed enough pits to show there had indeed

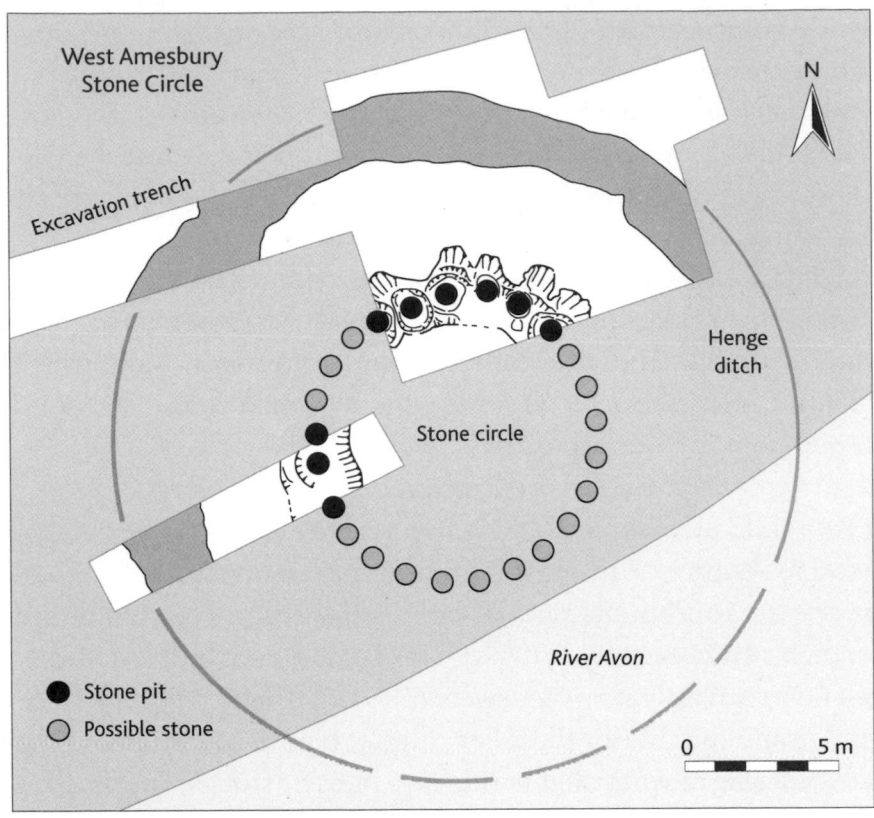

Arcs of stone pits were discovered by the River Avon in 2009, imagined here as a circle of 25 stones. The henge ditch and outer bank (of which little survives) seem to have been eroded by the river.

once been a stone circle at Waun Mawn. It was unusually large, and slightly bigger than the first at Stonehenge (110 m across and 87 m respectively, or 360 and 285 ft). The stones, and in one pit a single chip, are of unspotted dolerite. Originally, there might have been anything between 25 and 50 small megaliths.

This clinched it for Mike: the Aubrey circle was not made from newly quarried stones, but from one, and probably more, older Welsh stone circles. Critics noted that unspotted dolerite is rare at Stonehenge, where the stone pits are larger than those in Wales. But Mike's enthusiasm impressed the BBC and presenter Alice Roberts, and a film about the Welsh dig made strident claims for Waun

Mawn being moved to Wiltshire: Stonehenge was 'second-hand'. There were predictable headlines around the world.[8]

So now we have three bluestone circles, at Waun Mawn and West Amesbury, and at Stonehenge – or four, if we include the Aubrey circle and the later Q and R structure. Or perhaps even five, remembering the bluestone fragments near the Cursus. How might these be related to each other?

The short answer is that we really don't know. Megaliths are notoriously hard to age, and notwithstanding some optimistic claims, none of these sites is at all well dated. I have put the Aubrey circle at around 3200 BC. Waun Mawn could be as old. So could the West Amesbury circle. All we can say with reasonable confidence is that the Q and R structure is younger than the Aubrey circle – noting that Waun Mawn, West Amesbury, or both, could also be contemporary with the Q and R stones. If, and this remains completely hypothetical, the missing Waun Mawn stones were uprooted and moved to Wiltshire (perhaps those that remain were left because they were not spotted?), West Amesbury seems as likely a destination as Stonehenge. We can at least ignore the putative Cursus circle, which recent fieldwork has failed to locate (there may be another explanation for the scatter of stone fragments there, as we will see in Chapter 7).

Something has changed, however, in the way we think about Stonehenge origins. To imagine another bluestone circle nearby, and a third in the distant land where the stones came from, is to put the early monument into a different light. Not as unique as we once assumed, it now stands as part of a wider world, the focus of a grander megalithic cosmology of belief, ritual and creativity – and the only one where, on current evidence, people buried their cremated dead.

It is what happens next that transforms all this into something utterly extraordinary.

CHAPTER 6

CONSTRUCTION: STONEHENGE

Sarsen is hard. And it's heavy.

Easter Island (Rapa Nui) statues, so elegantly and massively carved and smoothed, are made from a soft volcanic tuff that weathers into a substance more like Weetabix than rock. And just as the stone is relatively easy to work, so most of the figures have since lost much of their detailed finish, eroded by rainfall empowered by industrial acidification.

The trilithon in Tonga that we encountered in the Preface is made of coral limestone. If you look along beaches on the islands where old limestone is exposed, raised out of the sea as submarine volcanic activity grows and tilts the land, you can find megalithic quarries (what else should an archaeologist do on a Pacific beach once the books have run out?). Waves curl around rectangular hollows where slabs, carved out with stone and shell tools, have been taken away, half concrete, half expanded polystyrene, soft, firm and relatively light. The hewn limestone megaliths on Sumba leave the quarries like slices from a loaf of white bread.

Sarsen, by contrast, is one of the hardest stones found anywhere. Wiltshire farmers and builders will tell you it can't be broken, and when they come across a boulder in the wrong place they drag it to the edge of the site or bury it deeper. Before coring the mega-lith at Stonehenge, Van Moppes experimented with rock samples. They found that a diamond drill could penetrate sarsen at a rate of 7.5–10 cm (3–4 in.) a minute. Our task, however, is not to drill a few narrow holes with industrial tools, but to carve an entire megalith with Stone Age technology, reduce it to 32 tons, shape it and create joints. Before we have to think of moving it over steep, hilly downland to Stonehenge, a distance of 28 km (17 miles), and once there contrive to raise it into the air so that it will stand for millennia, we face what seems to be the greatest challenge in this challenging enterprise. How do we carve sarsen?

First we find our stone.

I wrote this book in 2020. For several months the UK was in lockdown because of the COVID-19 pandemic, and for most of the year normal travel and work were curtailed. Deprived of my usual meetings and events at the end of train or car journeys, I spent more time walking. My favourite local site is West Woods, and over the year I became more aware than ever that it is alive.

One day in late October the wood was absolutely still, the only sound a barely audible white murmur from air moving across the tops of trees. The temperature was mild and the colours were bright, an exceptional autumn display of orange and green: but the light was cold and grey, as if a moose might suddenly rush across the path. For a moment it seemed I was in northern Scandinavia, or in Britain long ago. I looked for wolf scats.

I followed a path down a steep, narrow crevice through trees, crunching flints on bare white chalk where rain had washed away leaves, and the track became wide and deep enough to take a cart, or a trail of sheep, bleating and slipping. Ahead of me on a rising wooded slope I saw my first sarsen of the day. It was small, a rounded lump almost entirely smothered in emerald green moss, alone. I walked into this new part of the forest, tall straight trees and brown leaves on the ground, and saw a scatter of boulders. These were not sheep, not greywethers muzzling turf, but deer or cattle, lying down together asleep. Sarsens as beasts.

I saw no people, but with reports of rising infections in the area I was nervous of suddenly bumping into another woodland explorer, unmasked. I imagined this other, over 4,000 years ago, looking for sarsens with greater purpose. What would have been their experience?

The present woodland is new: the serried trees are the same size and age, planted less than a century ago after the explosions and banging crushing machinery of the road-metal industry had gone silent. There was older woodland before that, but archaeological survey has shown that at various times in the past the ground was more open. There are banks marking out field boundaries, perhaps of Iron Age or Roman date, when two millennia or so ago crops were cultivated or animals grazed. That needn't mean, however, that when people came to the valley in search of great sarsens to take south to Stonehenge another two millennia further back, it was not then wooded.

There is no evidence yet from West Woods, but locally, especially in and around Avebury (where long ago in a small excavation I uncovered a preserved soil, the turf on which the people who erected the stone circle would have walked), there is much ecological data to indicate that forest was once more extensive than today, probably more so than around Stonehenge. Ancient chalk soils, and hollows left by falling trees, preserve the shells of snails, creatures which are surprisingly fussy about where they live and whose different species thus tell stories about light, vegetation and humidity. These suggest woodland was widespread in the region until at least 3500 BC, and during the following centuries was being cut down, succumbing to grassland.

People were in West Woods before Stonehenge was built, making and visiting the long barrow, and there must have been small clearings from an early date. But archaeologists imagine that areas with heavy covers of clay-with-flints, never popular with farmers or gardeners and including West Woods and much of the eastern Marlborough Downs, were the last to be fully opened up. While to the west at Avebury and Silbury Hill woodland with grassy clearings ranged from young hazel regrowth to more mature oak and elm forest, at West Woods this forest was older and denser.

Long barrows, where the living could meet the dead, may have marked landscape boundaries too: to look beyond the barrow at West Woods would have been to gaze into a dark, ancient forest of lime, oak, ash and elm, trunks tall and straight fighting for light, the soft ground thick with leaves and rotting timber. This would not look like any woodland we see in Britain today. Many of the trees would be centuries old, and the twisted and split trunks and branches of fallen giants, their stumps sometimes rising into the air for two or three times the height of a person, would divert the paths of deer and wild cattle. Browsing herds would keep the forest open, by eating undergrowth and saplings. Wild pigs, foxes and badgers, grubbing in the soil and tunnelling into the decayed chalk, would expose the earth that grew food and took the dead, as did those trees whose fall ripped out their roots, revealing stone and clay to those who looked. Where animals make tracks, people fear to go, and not just because of the wolves. But it is in this forbidden gloom that they must search for sarsens, and though easier than today in that there are so many more, that search is also harder as generations of accumulated forest litter have buried the tops of even the largest beasts.

Entering that forest then, happy for dogs to follow us in, we would have needed our digging sticks, our picks and our axe, and a stone hammer of the kind we have seen at Stonehenge, a hard sarsen cobble. Before we can begin to find and choose the right stone, we have to poke around among vegetation and debris, sweeping up leaf mould and hauling away branches so that we can dig, exposing the edges of slabs that grow and change shape as we go deeper until we can rate the scale and the quality, peeling away moss, banging a stone for the sound it makes, peering underneath, stroking the cold damp surfaces, testing, judging, exploring.

The only record we have of people working sarsen is of the men who made road setts and wall stones. The industry petered out in the 1930s (one of the last jobs was to supply four wagon-loads for the repair of Windsor Castle, in 1939). Yet despite its interest – the last mason died in 1976 – only one archaeologist, an amateur, seems to have noticed it at the time, other than to complain about it: Herbert Stone, Chief Engineer for Construction of the East Indian Railway, who by 1911 had retired to Bath. Not only did he observe and photograph sarsen workers on the Marlborough Downs, he used the knowledge so gained in experiments, and he could also draw on his visits to granite quarries in India. The unexpected result of his studies (though he didn't entirely see it this way himself) is that modern sarsen working has little directly to tell us about Stonehenge. What might seem like a less than helpful insight, however, is the opposite, and holds the key to what we are about to do.

Richard Atkinson, the most influential Stonehenge archaeologist of the last century, emphasized the near impossibility of dressing sarsen. The chief method, he wrote, in the absence of modern steel tools, was laborious surface pounding with a heavy stone hammer, releasing small amounts of silica dust. Basing his vision on Stone's research, he suggested fire might have been used for coarser shaping and blocking out (as had been done in early modern times in Avebury to break up megaliths) or lines of wooden wedges hammered into cracks. However, all this sees the problem through relatively modern eyes. In the 1850s masons who had been working sarsen in Buckinghamshire, looking for new sources and markets, discovered the Marlborough Downs. They brought with them steel tools – specialist chisels and hammers to pummel out lines of small holes, into which they could insert steel wedges which in turn they could hit with massive, 14-lb (6-kg) hammers to split boulders. A great slab was split and split again until it was reduced to a pile of small, square blocks.

It requires a different mentality to make a megalith. Here the goal is not to undo a boulder, but to shape it by reduction; the boulder *is* the megalith. Trying to carve sarsen with steel, in the manner of sculpting limestone, is doomed because of the hardness of cemented silica. But Neolithic people were masters of the silica universe, making tools and arrow tips from flint, and stones from sarsen for grinding cereal grains, with an understanding of the technologies required that reached back hundreds of thousands of years. Herbert Stone, in a flash of brilliance, described the dressed bluestones as 'enormous flint implements', by which he meant that to shape a megalith people applied the tricks that they would use to make a fine arrowhead. What he missed is that you could describe the dressed sarsens in the same way.

The hard, intractable reputation that sarsen had acquired by the 20th century was built on the frustrations of recent masons. The absence of steel tools in the Neolithic was not a hindrance, because you didn't need them. You needed stone tools. You needed the imagination to look at a boulder weighing many tons, and to see it as a piece of flint you could hold in the palm of your hand. And when you could do that, you'd know what to do to make Stone 58.

The key distinctions to help us understand this are the differences between splitting, sculpting and – to use a technical word – flaking. Splitting is what recent masons did, defeating the best intentions of a sarsen slab by creating an artificial crack with wedges, then extending the crack with mallets. Sculpting is what people think we should be able to do with sarsen if only it behaved like normal stone, when we could chisel away at the surface and shape it to our heart's content, knocking off chips and powder where it suited us. Flaking is in another class. It requires an understanding of sarsen and fracture mechanics, and considerable skill, and unlike splitting and sculpting, which effectively succeed by over-riding the stone's natural properties, it works with and exploits them.

The only tools needed are stone hammers, rounded boulders and cobbles of the extra-hard sarsen variety, which are brought down near the edge of a slab (see pl. XXIV). Hammer weight, angle of blow, energy applied and precise location of the strike are all critical to success. On impact, other things being equal, force waves will expand in a cone shape as they penetrate the stone. It is the inequalities that the worker exploits. Near the edge of a slab, only part of the cone has the chance to develop, and if the blow is successful a chunk of rock will fall away where that part shears the slab. Force waves will respond to ridges and hollows in particular ways, which the stoneworker uses to gain some control of the shape and scale of the removal. With good flint, the break is perfect and you can see a seashell-like effect, giving it its name of a conchoidal

fracture; it will be less so with sarsen, which has different properties to flint, but the principle is the same. Were we to come across
a megalithic mason while we searched for our stone, we would
notice that much of their time was taken up with examining their
slab, especially underneath where they had excavated the ground,
walking around it, pondering and muttering, as a bowls player
might scrutinize the turf before gently releasing a ball.

We have a good idea of what we are looking for. To jump ahead
to what we will discover when we arrive at the construction site,
every part of the new monument has been designed in advance.
The vision is not, as it might have been with earlier arrangements, a
megalith or two to which others will be added at some future date
until perhaps one day there will be a ring or who knows what? There
is not one stone that is not, in some way, dependent on another.
This will make it difficult to change – perhaps one of the things its
designers had in mind. At the point of creation, it means a relatively
brief timetable, which means a large and probably unprecedented
labour force and all the support and families that come with that.
A lot hangs on us getting our stone right.

Our mission is to find a sarsen of a certain size and shape. In
fact, it is to find two stones, and it's a fair bet that the lintel that will
join them is also on our shopping list. Stones 57 and 58, re-erected
in 1958, were flat on the ground when Stonehenge was surveyed
early in the last century, so we have a record of their entire form,
and they are distinctive and almost identical, below as well as
above ground.

It's unlikely we will find any slabs big enough today, but if we
could we'd need two of approximately the right length and width.
They'll weigh at least 40 tons each, possibly significantly more, and
measure no more than 1.5 m (5 ft) thick (the Stonehenge uprights
are little more than 1 m/3 ft 3 in. across, unusually thin). Whether
or not Neolithic people had a system of measurement (there have
been many attempts to show they did, but I find none convincing),
we also know that, in modern terms, the stones need to be in the

order of 8 m (26 ft) long and 3.5 m (11 ft) wide. As we search, almost all of that bulk will be underground.

When we have finally found and exposed our rocks, having excavated large pits, the first working begins. Small cobbles sufficed for sounding out the slabs' strength and purity, but this is something different: now we need rounded lumps of hard sarsen of around 20–30 kg (45–65 lb – we are, of course, strong and fit, and mostly adult men). Whether or not we might find these in West Woods, we will not have to go far; many such small boulders have been found around Avebury, crammed unshaped into pits to support standing megaliths.

Using skills we have acquired making stone axe blades, we feel our way around the first slab, dropping hammers near the edges to remove great irregular chunks, hewing away to achieve roughly straight and parallel sides. The finer shaping will happen at the destination, but what we do here is critical. It will set the character and determine the limits of our finished stone, and it will expose flaws, if there are any, that could prove fatal to the project. Accidents that could break the stone in two are most likely to happen now. We can only guess at the rituals and precautions we need to respect, but these will be no less forceful than a 30-kg hammer.

If we have chosen well and all goes to plan, we will create a roughed-out megalith whose soundness has been proved. We will pare off a substantial amount of surplus weight – and thinking ahead, we will leave a large pit full of sarsen debris and antler picks that one day will allow archaeologists to discover exactly what we were doing and when we did it, if only they can find it. Then we will be ready for the real challenge: transporting Stone 58. There are two key issues here (apart from the rituals and the partying, surely on a scale people would have talked about for generations, but now entirely unknowable): the route, and the method.

We need to set the satnav before we start the car, so we will begin with the itinerary. If again we look at what has been suggested in the past, as we did for bluestones, we similarly find Richard

Atkinson's route and more recent modifications. The former began in Avebury, on the assumption that the sarsens would have been gathered together at this 'revered sanctuary' to be blessed by 'the presiding arch-priest' before embarking on the big journey. From there a straight line towards Stonehenge would involve a climb of 100 m (325 ft) over 7 km (4.5 miles) to the top of the chalk ridge overlooking the Vale of Pewsey, which cuts an east–west swathe between the Marlborough Downs and Salisbury Plain. After a precipitous decline into the valley, there would follow a steep climb out, back up to a similar height.

Richard went southwest, taking a valley across the western end of the downs for a gentler fall into the vale near Devizes, and climbing back onto the chalk along a route followed by a modern road up Redhorn Hill. Today that road, its barely maintained tarmac hairpinning up the dramatic scarp on the northern plain's edge, stops abruptly at a shed. If you go there you are likely to see a red flag flying from a tall pole: you are looking into the army's live-firing zone. The old track continues, however, isolated for over a century, and bar a few bends to avoid the steepest slopes it makes a beeline for the visitor centre, from where there is a short, gentle downhill stretch to Stonehenge. Nonetheless, there is still that climb up Redhorn Hill to navigate, 75 m (250 ft) above the vale floor, followed by an undulating passage as the route makes a net fall to the site of 45 m (150 ft).

Mike Parker Pearson revisited this after a colleague found an old drawing by William Stukeley that seemed to show sarsens lying about at Clatford, ready-dressed for Stonehenge (a search failed to locate them). As it happens, Clatford is just north of West Woods, so a route starting there is a serious contender for Stone 58. Looking for a less challenging climb up onto the plain from the Vale of Pewsey – and unconcerned with the perils of an earlier steep descent – Mike alighted on a chalk spur south of Marden, where there is a large henge earthwork comparable to those around the stone circles at Avebury and at Durrington Walls, an alternative,

XVI A freshly cut stone is dragged from a quarry over sleeper logs on a makeshift sledge, in Sumba, eastern Indonesia.

XVII Pulling a large capstone for a tomb in Sumba along a track of loose sleepers.

XVIII The small outcrop at Craig Rhos-y-felin, source of the commonest rhyolite at Stonehenge (B6), after excavation by archaeologists.

XIX Excavation in progress at Carn Goedog, a source for spotted dolerite megaliths at Stonehenge (B1), looking northwest towards the Irish Sea.

XX Stones 32 (left) and 150 in the Bluestone Circle, showing the latter's two mortise holes from use in an earlier arrangement as a lintel. Immediately behind, looking southwest, stand sarsen trilithon Stone 51 and to its right Bluestone Horseshoe Stone 61. All three bluestones are spotted dolerite (BU1, BU1 and B2 respectively).

XXI Trilithon Stone 52, looking northwest into the centre of the site; the fine longitudinally dressed surface on the side continues from the top to below the modern turf.

XXII Northwest face of Stone 16 in the Sarsen Circle. Fine pick-dressing overlies fine longitudinal dressing, with a small area of stone polish near the centre.

XXIII South face of Stone 10 in the southwest of the Sarsen Circle, where a rough finish characterizes stones. Hugo Anderson-Whymark points at a band of coarse longitudinal dressing that runs from bottom left to top right; the stone has been finely pick-dressed above this to top left.

XXIV The Salisbury Museum has over 250 stone-dressing hammers from excavations at Stonehenge, mostly of a very hard type of sarsen (scale 10 cm).

XXV Lintel 158, supported by Stones 57 and 58 (above right), was on the ground between 1797, when the trilithon fell, and 1958, when it was re-erected. Compared to William Stukeley's drawing in the 1720s (above left) the lintel today shows damage caused by visitors hammering off souvenirs. Lintel 154 (left) has never fallen and remains undamaged.

XXVI 18th- and 19th-century graffiti on sarsen Stone 55, fallen as long as historic records go back.

XXVII Stone 61, a spotted dolerite stone in the Bluestone Horseshoe (B2), shows a large ancient damage scar on the side and more recent damage to the top.

XXVIII The broken foot of spotted dolerite Stone 35a (BU1) revealed in excavation by Tim Darvill and Geoff Wainwright in 2008. Stone 34, another Bluestone Circle stone, is wrapped for protection.

perhaps, to Richard's assembly point in Avebury. There remains, however, a climb of 75 m (250 ft) over a short distance, and this seems to me – following the principles I set out in Chapter 5, valleys good, steep slopes bad – a problem we can't ignore. Especially when there is an alternative, first suggested, I think, by a Canadian geologist called Patrick Arthur Hill (1922–1998).[1]

Born in Calcutta to tea-planter parents and working as a coal miner while seeing himself through university in England, Hill is described in his obituary as an 'actor, rebel and iconoclast'. He was not to be cowed by archaeological authority, listing six objections to Richard's route, among them that it was unnecessarily long and that the Redhorn Hill climb was 'unnatural' – moving the sarsens, the archaeologist had said, would have taken 1,500 men an improbable ten years. Instead, after exploring the landscape in 1958, Hill proposed a solution in which more than three quarters of the journey was downslope. One of his preferred starting points was in West Woods in Hursley Bottom, where remains of the stone-crushing plant can be seen today. He too was not bothered about the steep fall from the ridge to the south, proposing that sarsens could have been pushed over the edge to slide down and pile up at the bottom. There are other aspects of his study which are less than convincing, such as the suggestion that 25 men could have pulled a 50-ton sarsen on a sledge by working at night on packed snow, his inspiration being an Inuit sled designed for Arctic sea ice. But his idea of following valleys, especially that of the River Avon, seems eminently sensible – not to float the stones, which would have been more than the shallow water could have achieved, but as a way of avoiding the climb up onto the high plain.

Now, there may have been locations en route that needed to be visited – Marden perhaps, or any number of unknowable sacred or politically important sites, Avebury even – and these may be added at will. However, as an opening gambit I'm going to describe the simplest route to Stonehenge. One of the appealing aspects of West Woods is that it is closer to the destination than previously

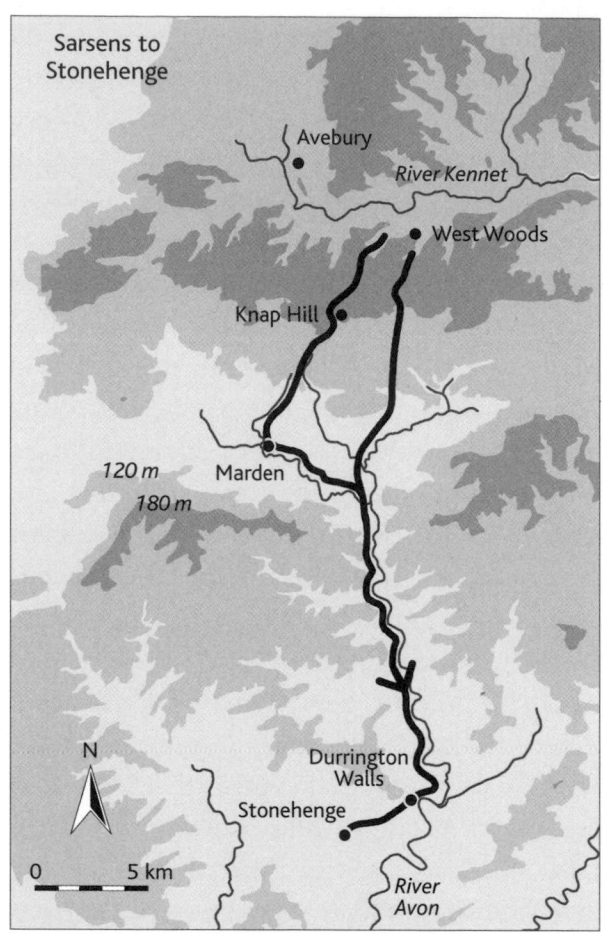

Proposed route
for moving
sarsens from the
Marlborough Downs
to Stonehenge, with
an alternative past
an Early Neolithic
enclosure on Knap
Hill and a henge
at Marden.

suggested sources (and, unlike them, south of the River Kennet so
that no crossing is needed). As we head southwest along a gently
rising valley we reach the ridge in no more than 2 km (less than 1.5
miles); we have climbed under 20 m (65 ft). We then pass between
Draycott Hill and Huish Hill, drop down into the vale and continue
more or less due south until we arrive at Rushall. Like the Bristol
Avon carving a pass between the hills either side, here the Wiltshire
Avon opens a significant flat route through the forbidding northern
edge of Salisbury Plain.

Hill continued until he reached the Avenue south of Amesbury,
but from a purely practical perspective – and bearing in mind that

at this point, as we have seen, the Avenue does not yet exist – it makes more sense to cut across towards Stonehenge a little earlier, by rising out of the valley at Durrington. This necessitates the second climb of the journey, of 30 m (100 ft), the easiest option being to skirt immediately north of the Durrington Walls henge and turn southwest to face Stonehenge across the valley, where the final climb (15 m or 50 ft) will be along that walk we made in Chapter 1. We have avoided the longer, steeper ascents of the other routes, without travelling any further, and we have stayed closer to water and the places where most people are likely to have lived, offering rest, food and support, and witnesses for the grand expedition. It remains only to consider exactly how we do it.

We need a sledge. A major construction in its own right, if it survived the journey to Stonehenge it's likely it would be used again, though it would need repairing and adjusting. As we survey our stone there may be other people in the wood, working to take their own megaliths out, and sledges returning as well as leaving. We have no ancient examples from Britain to guide us, but as we saw in Chapter 4 we do know that carpenters had a good understanding of tension, compression, jointing and binding, and in the absence of other evidence we can reasonably use a Sumba sledge as a model – if turning to heavier oak trees rather than coconut palms. We can also expect a specialist team to do the job for us, perhaps boat or house builders as I suggested earlier.

The key part of the sledge is a pair of oak poles to serve as runners. As the stone is 8 m (26 ft) long, the two trimmed and de-barked trunks will need to be at least 10 m (33 ft) so that they extend beyond the stone, spreading its weight, allowing ropes to be attached and accessed, and giving the sledge extra leverage to aid manoeuvrability. They will need to be joined firmly with mortise-and-tenoned cross-timbers, 3.5 m (11 ft) long. Above the runners will rest further cross-timbers, a little longer and sunk in with half-lap joints, on which the stone will rest, its irregular form sometimes cutting into the wood, sometimes held with tied wedges.

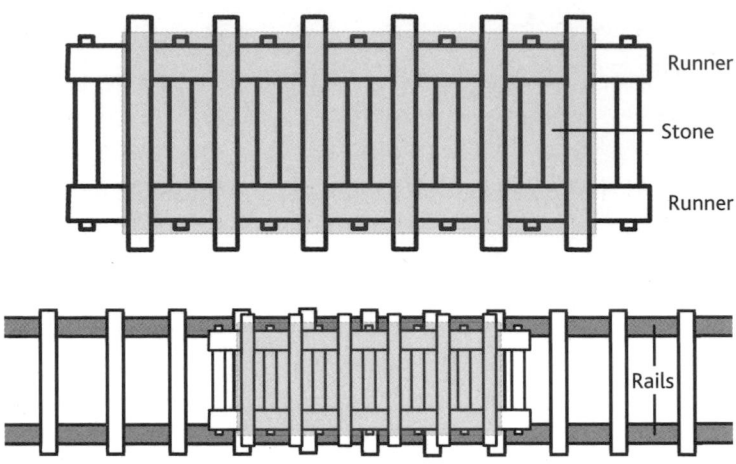

Schematic sledge for carrying a slab for Stone 58. Two 10-m (33-ft) long runners are joined by seven crossbars and support six bars to take the stone.

If the runners are 60 cm (2 ft) in diameter, each will weigh 3 tons. With 40 cm (16 in.) diameter cross-poles, these will add a further 7 tons to give a total of 13. There will be much rope, to tie joints and hold the stone, adding to what is the minimum construction, so that sledge and stone together will weigh over 45 tons. Skill and effort applied to reducing the stone as much as possible while leaving scope for the final shaping on site will not be wasted. As alternatives to oak, beech would weigh the same and ash more. We may lose some mass by squaring timbers – the narrowed bases of dressed runners, split and cut with flint blades, would slide with less friction – but this remains a huge load. How on earth are we to move it?[2]

Here, it seems to me, a fixed trackway is unavoidable. On Sumba, sledges, mostly of significantly less weight, are pulled over flat, even ground, sometimes on surfaced roads. Our sarsen has to be taken out of a wood and across downland turf, gardens and meadows, up and down slopes, through freshly disturbed ground and thickets of shrubs and brambles, its weight displacing old paths and crushing steps and banks. In late summer or autumn, after crops are safely taken in, there will be times when the ground is very wet, and there will be small streams and marsh to cross. A journey through such varied, soft surfaces would be an endless trial of losing control, getting stuck and trying to free the sledge again. Stone 58 is one of the heaviest, but there are a further 74 sarsens needed at the site: 9 of similar size to 58, with their 5 lintels of around 15 tons each; 30 stones for the circle of between 15 and 30 tons; and 30 more lintels of 5 or 6 tons. All of these may have come from somewhere on the Marlborough Downs, and for most of their journeys they would have been taken along the same route, carving out ruts, pulling up vegetation, wearing the ground into a swathe of mud and pools. A track would be a substantial engineering project consuming a vast amount of timber and labour, but this is in the nature of the madness that is Stonehenge. Without it, it's difficult to see how the project could have been concluded successfully while it retained momentum. Stonehenge has many mysteries. Why it was left unfinished is not one of them.

There are few new ideas to be had about Stonehenge. I think Robert Cunnington (1877–1959) was the first to suggest a sarsen track, for 'the marshy ground of the river valleys', where water-logging, he said, might still preserve the timbers. Ted Garfitt, as I noted in Chapter 4, went further. He had the empire credentials for Stonehenge-theorizing: he worked for the Malayan Forest Service, joining the Royal Indian Naval Reserve in 1941 before Japan invaded. Back in England he became an influential forestry consultant and prolific poet, but in the forests of Southeast Asia he worked with timber trackways. A colleague reported on what he called a sled-way or *panglong*, for dragging out tree boles weighing up to 7 or 8 tons and as long as 20 m (70 ft). A sled-way consisted of a pair of roundwood runners supporting cross-ties like raised railway sleepers, fixed every 50 cm (20 in.) with simple notching. Small cuttings and bridges, made by levering the track up to allow more tied runners to be pushed in underneath, helped to keep the route level, and along it would be dragged narrow sleds with hardwood runners. Poles were used to roll logs to the track and up pairs of

Timber sled-way in southern Malaysia in the 1920s, with a narrow sledge in the foreground and behind this men using levers to manoeuvre a log.

timbers onto the sleds to which they were tied. Men towed the sledges with ropes, aided by grease painted onto the centre of the sled-way, using the protruding ends of the cross-ties as footholds.[3]

By this means, said Garfitt, between two and five men could move a ton for 8 km (5 miles) in a day – from which he calculated that a 30-ton sarsen would have needed 90 men to achieve the same thing, thus reaching Stonehenge from the Marlborough Downs in four days. This might seem optimistic, given the extra challenges brought by the substantial scaling up. Experiments and other observations suggest that such a journey would more realistically occupy a minimum of 200–300 people for a few weeks (assuming a track is in place).[4] If there were 1,000 people available for labour, all the sarsens could have been delivered in 6 to 18 months.

We might double the time for added rests, feasting and rituals. My suggested sledge may be over-generous with timber, which only experiments on a grand scale could resolve, but even if we halve its weight, we have a combined load of at least 40 tons for Stone 58. But this is one of the largest stones, and overall, collecting the sarsens remains a surprisingly brief endeavour. The traditional view of dragging sarsen stones to Stonehenge is that it was a slow, dangerous and thankless challenge. If we think back to the tomb builders on Sumba, the larger stones there drew huge teams to pull sledges in celebratory events; on one occasion, it was said, three slabs, each weighing 11.5 tons, occupied 2,000 people for a week as they pulled them 5 km (3 miles) to the construction site. Having watched megaliths being moved in Madagascar, Mike Parker Pearson observed that the difficulty was not so much in finding enough people to do the work, as having to cope with too many![5]

We miss the point if we focus too strongly on engineering. For us, of course, that part will always remain a bit of a mystery as we can never be sure, but at the time they did what they had to do and were capable of doing. What would have impressed people as much, and would have lingered in memories and stories, was the spectacle: the crowds, likely to be far in excess of the numbers needed, the celebrations and sacrifices, and the ultimate achievement standing on the plain.

It's time to leave the quarry.

A sled-way from West Woods to Stonehenge may sound like a lot of wood if you think of it as something piled up in a lumber yard, especially if, as I suspect might be the case, we need more than two rails to support the huge weights. But that's not how it was. As I have noted, evidence suggests that by the time Stonehenge was built the surrounding landscape was quite open, but there remained patches of old woodland, and in the Avon valley alder and hazel grew among sedges near the water's edge. The Marlborough Downs were more wooded, as probably (here we have little data) was the Vale of Pewsey. Quality is less important than quantity, and carpentering is relatively simple. If we imagine the sled-way being constructed in sections by local people, they would have known where best to route it and where timber grew – they might well have cultivated coppiced trees. Furthermore, it seems not unlikely that large old trees would have been sought out and if necessary, or perhaps (as with stones for Stonehenge) as a deliberate choice, transported to Salisbury Plain over considerable distances.

We will need to build a temporary track to ease the sledge out of the pit and drag it to the main route, and soon we will reach the one serious obstacle: the chalk escarpment overlooking the Pewsey vale, from the top of which we can see the edge of Salisbury Plain rising the other side, and the gap made by the river to which we are heading. Immediately in front of us is a steep, dry valley that falls 50 m (165 ft) in 500 m (1,650 ft). After that the slopes are never more than gentle, but here, where the sled-way is strengthened and pegged to the ground beyond usual requirements, we will need extra precautions. Our load is too precious to launch over the edge, and instead we have to control its descent with ropes wrapped around posts at the top, fixed firmly into the ground.[6]

Once down, it is plain sailing.

We follow the wooden track around a low rise, across two of the Avon's three ditch-like feeder tributaries, bending the rails which creak and squelch into the mud. Passing the second stream we find ourselves on the west, right-hand bank of the Avon, and the sled-way continues, seeking a straighter course than the river which winds its way through marsh and meadows where swans and other waterbirds skitter among the fresh stubs of newly cleared coppice. We cross paths that rise towards houses on higher ground. People come out to watch, to cheer and swell the crowd of harnessed pullers, to offer food and water, to tease and laugh. Dogs bark, and from a distant pen a cow bellows.

It takes more effort to rise up the track past Durrington Walls, where most of the gang have made their homes in a huge village that may have housed 4,000 people. Excavations have found so many pig bones, sometimes charred as if joints were barbecued, that archaeologists have suggested large-scale feasting occurred there (chemical analysis has shown that pots, on the other hand, were mostly used for processing cattle carcasses, leading to one archaeologist proposing that cattle fat was prepared to grease sledges).[7] Quite reasonably, Mike Parker Pearson, whose team excavated these remains, suggests these were the builders of Stonehenge and their families, gathered together for their unique mission. If any reminder were needed, this emphasizes that Stonehenge was not a local project; such numbers imply considerable temporary migration into the area, and the pressures and resources to bring that about. We keep level, skirting the east end of the Cursus earthwork along a small ridge, and drop into the hollow below Stonehenge for the final haul up the timber sled-way.

And here, in the archaeology, we find something interesting. Recent geophysical surveys have revealed an unexpectedly large number – none had been visible as earthworks – of small, henge-like sites around Stonehenge, more or less circular filled ditches or levelled banks, sometimes with associated pits. Without excavation we cannot be sure what any of them actually are, but in 1980 archaeologist Julian Richards investigated the largest, which alone had then been known by its marks in crops. It's southeast of Stonehenge, the other side of the A303 highway on Coneybury Hill, and consists today of an oval-plan ditch which was originally dug out around 2750 BC. I mention this because of a curious feature across the single break in the ditch, where the archaeologists found ten narrow, more or less parallel grooves in the chalk. The causeway had been lowered, apparently by traffic, and Julian wondered whether the grooves had once held timbers laid to support a wooden floor.[8]

More recently Mike and his team excavated a few trenches closer to Stonehenge across the Avenue, finding a series of linear hollows in the earth and broken chalk that run up and down the slope parallel to the Avenue's banks and ditches on either side. It is suggested that these grooves had two origins: the deeper ones are Ice Age structures, formed long ago when the ground was seasonally thawing permafrost, and the shallower are cartwheel ruts of recent centuries. Interpretation of these is difficult, and a third option could be that some result from embedding timbers to support a sled-way at the most crucial point of the sarsens' journeys. In another trench to the northeast were four perfect parallel grooves in the chalk. If these had anything to do with a sled-way (there is no direct dating evidence for any of these features) they could tell us something about the route: all these grooves point towards the low ridge above Durrington Walls, but the alignment cuts across the end of the Cursus instead of rounding it. Back at Stonehenge, a mass of postholes across the main entrance causeway, revealed in excavations in 1922, might also have served a similar purpose, to support a timber floor to protect the ground, as sledges repeatedly made their way into the arena carrying a total of over 1,000 tons of stone.

Π

We are expected. The last time we brought a stone to the site, we approached from the south and pulled our small sledge between two pits that helped to outline a great round arena. We were contributing to a circle of megaliths, but in engineering terms at least, our stone stood alone; it could rise or fall without affecting others. As we now arrive from the northeast, things are quite different.

For a start, the arena is more tightly defined and mostly closed. The ditch that was dug to connect the pits and whose spoil was formed into parallel banks is by now five centuries old, but it remains prominent. Perhaps it has been cleared out for the occasion, dirty white chalk now emphasizing the earthwork's presence (there are indications that this did happen, though exactly when isn't clear – one of many points where new excavation is required).[9] Two gaps alone allow passage to the interior, the larger of which we face.

The power and the sanctity of the place have grown and changed. The original outer stone circle was uprooted and rearranged near the centre; the bluestone monument in the Q and R Holes and the sarsen stones around the edge have had time to gather their own authority and stories. After five centuries of cremation ceremonies, burial does not appear to continue when the new monument is built, suggesting a linked change in rituals or in the meaning of the site (archaeological evidence for funerary ceremonies becomes rare generally). It's safe to imagine that some of the most important events during those long years are entirely unknown to us. Yet nothing has happened to match what is now underway, and if we are not entirely clear why it is happening or what it will lead to, we know we are witness to something special.

All but the few outer megaliths have been taken down and moved, so that the Heelstone, until now the largest standing at the site, has renewed significance, its bulbous form a lone silhouette against the sky. If there were taboos that restricted access in the past, those seem to have been forgotten. Hundreds of people move about, digging, carrying and talking, and more watch: it is literally a building site. There are stones lying everywhere, it feels, and a din of hammering and chipping. And critically, our Stone 58, though it will rise to become one of the largest megaliths in the country and take up a key location at Stonehenge, is not a freewheeling loner subject to our whims. Every stone, here and on its way, has a particular part to play. Our job is to follow the rules.

Our immediate task is to complete the next stage of shaping. Here is where the laser survey that was touched on in Chapter 4 comes in: it shook up accepted ideas about the form and finish of the megaliths. Something that to outsiders always seems strange at famous ancient sites, whether they are Egyptian pyramids, say, or Rapa Nui statues, is to discover that academic research and recording often lag far behind public interest and debate. That this has been the case at Stonehenge is illustrated especially by an apparent lack of professional concern with the very stones: visitors could buy stereo-paired photo souvenirs in the 19th century, but archaeologists were keener to dig below the turf than to look closely at the megaliths in front of them. New 3D-imaging techniques are changing this. Work in this area began at Stonehenge as recently as 2002, with the firing up of a generator on a July evening in Mediterranean-like heat, as insects swarmed around lintels and a red sun set towards the west in a hazy sky.

The shallow Bronze Age carvings on some of the stones, mostly representing axe blades, were pecked out with hard stone hammers long after the megaliths were raised. A few show clearly in Victorian photos, yet they had apparently gone unnoticed until 1953 – you see what you are looking for – when Richard Atkinson spotted a dagger while he was preparing to record some historic graffiti on one of the trilithon uprights. A search soon revealed many more carvings, but they are difficult to see in ordinary light and they remained little known, even to archaeologists. In the 1990s I had tried to get a project going in which we would reprocess existing stereo photos taken by English Heritage, to create a 3D map of some of the carvings. It never happened, so in 2002 I was delighted to be there to witness the first laser survey at the monument, with a team that included Alistair Carty from Archaeoptics and Tom Goskar from Wessex Archaeology. It took a lot of boxes, cables and computer equipment (one visitor asked if the space rock band Hawkwind were setting up to re-live their Stonehenge festival days), and the data for a panel the size of a typical modern TV screen had to be processed over a few days back at the lab before we could see the results. It was an exciting moment: Richard Atkinson's dagger, and two newly discovered axe blades, could be thrown into high relief by manipulating light on a computer screen. The technique worked, and scanners, software and computer memory were all improving rapidly. The potential was huge.[10]

That promise was first realized a decade later when Stonehenge – all of it – was scanned in high resolution. A by-product, as we saw in Chapter 4, was the first set of measured estimates for stone weights, but the prime purpose, motivated by exhibition galleries that were soon to open at the new visitor centre, was to create a digital 3D-model so the stones could be properly scrutinized. English

Heritage commissioned the survey, which was done in 2011, and the following year Marcus Abbott, currently head of digital survey at TJC Heritage, and Hugo Anderson-Whymark, now a curator at National Museums Scotland, sat down to visualize the 850 gigabytes of data and see what they could tell us. It was a pioneering project, most notably for its scale and its attention to archaeological detail, unmatched at the time in such a context anywhere in the world. It is no exaggeration to say that the two archaeologists were over the moon with the outcome. No one had ever examined the surfaces of the stones in such detail before, and what they saw more than rewarded the effort.[11]

Imagine that a sarsen megalith is a stone axe blade. There is archaeological evidence from Neolithic Britain and elsewhere, supported by stories told by men in Papua New Guinea who were making identical blades into at least the 1960s, that the process had several distinct stages. Small gangs would venture out to the quarries, often dangerous places remote from where people lived, to look for stone. There they would test the rock and shape half-formed axeheads, just enough to be able to bring home pieces they would be confident could be made into finished tools. These would then be further worked on, as time allowed, first with relatively coarse flaking to develop the shape, then finer flaking to create smooth, gently curving surfaces, and finally grinding on stone to remove the tiniest ridges and rough edges and generate a tough outer skin.

What Marcus and Hugo found was that the sarsen megaliths had indeed proceeded through much the same journey. The images they created from the laser data, supplemented by their own 3D photogrammetric models made with photos they took at Stonehenge, allowed them to look at every stone in the round down to a resolution of 1 mm (0.04 in.), neutrally coloured to remove the distraction of the stones' variegated appearance. They could see a huge amount of evidence for dressing and shaping: while convention had it that mostly the surfaces were a mix of natural rock and weathered stone where signs of artifice had all but disappeared, they found working of some kind on almost every megalith. What's more, they could separate different types of dressing (see pls XXI–XXIII).

Some of these had already been identified in decorated stones in Neolithic tombs and, uniquely in Orkney, in building slabs, notably at the Ness of Brodgar, where Hugo has been an excavation supervisor. Archaeologists call one of those techniques pick-dressing. This involves repeated hammering with a stone to create an even, pecked surface that has been likened to orange peel; it's common at tombs in the Boyne valley in Ireland and at two places in Orkney, where, says Antonia Thomas, an Orkney archaeologist, it was applied to highlight a slab's colour and texture, revealing 'a great interest in its surface qualities'. It is, she adds, otherwise extremely rare in Britain, seen only at a tomb on Anglesey (across the sea from Ireland) and on the Stonehenge sarsens.[12]

At Stonehenge there is none of the overt decoration so common on the softer Orkney stone (engraved geometric lines and dots and, thanks to unusual preservation, coloured paints), but there is plenty of pick-dressing. Sometimes this was done over a surface worked by other techniques, and sometimes it was itself removed, so we can see the shaping process in action. Marcus and Hugo's insights allow us to identify four key stages: heavy shaping, preparation, finishing and jointing. We completed the first of these at the quarry in West Woods. Not much survives at Stonehenge to show this stage, but it is there occasionally, especially in scars on the sides of some megaliths and in a few very large hammerstones from excavations. Most of these were recovered in 1901, when Stone 56, the standing Great Trilithon megalith, was straightened. Eight heavily used hammers lay around the base of its fallen partner Stone 55, weighing between 15 and 30 kg (30–65 lb). They must have been in the stone's pit, helping to keep it fixed in place, but whether they had been used there is a moot point: it's equally possible that such large hammers were brought to the site with megaliths from the quarries for the very purpose they now serve. Our next stage, then, is preparation.

Our stone will have to come off the sledge because we need to work on both its faces, and the ground will be a firmer place; the sledge and the poles we've used for levers will be needed elsewhere. In time we will have a sledge to take the stone across the northeast causeway of the ditch ring and onto the site, but for now we are outside. In this area fine sarsen debris was excavated south of the Heelstone in the 1920s and larger fragments to the west at my dig in 1980. Most recently, during each of the first four summers of Mike Parker Pearson's project, students rummaged through mole-hills and identified a sarsen zone over 100 m (325 ft) across a little further out. Colin Richards opened a 5 m (16 ft) square trench in the middle of this, sieved the soil and found more than a quarter of a ton of stone. About two thirds of it was hard sarsen, in the form of nearly 300 small hammerstones and many hammerstone fragments, and the rest saccharoid sarsen. That the latter had been battered from a single megalith was suggested by a heavy concentration in the middle of the trench, and almost none to the side where a great slab might have been lying, shielding the ground. There is, it seems, a buried veil of dust and debris around Stonehenge, like a negative that captured the frenzied activity of stoneworkers and megalithic engineers some 4,500 years ago, lying there waiting to be printed.

The physical appearance of Stone 58 today and the details of the laser study mean we know almost exactly what we have to do. Our goal is a stone that has a smooth, flat inner face and less intensively dressed sides and back, with a fresh stone finish almost everywhere. We established the broad shape at the quarry, which will need to be reinforced now. When our stone is paired with its neighbour, the inner sides will need to be close enough to make it impossible for anyone to pass through, so they have to be straight and there can be no great protrusions; and the tops should be nearly as wide as the bases to support the massive lintel.

We will have already determined which is to be which face, as one is flat and one, which will look out, is not. As the stone stands today, this chunkier face has a step cutting across from centre right to lower left, as if a layer of rock had flowed down from above like thick mud and hardened before it hit the ground. Above this step there is a great dish in the stone, which could be a scar left by massive flaking at the quarry. In some areas we can safely remove protrusions with hammers weighing up to 5 kg (10 lb), pounding out narrow, shallow channels that run parallel to the long sides. We can use smaller hammers, up to 2 kg (5 lb), for smoothing this outer face by working from one side to the other, and we will finish with hammerstones weighing less than 1 kg (2 lb) by finely pick-dressing most of the surface, warts and all. Similarly we will smooth the sides and the inner face, sometimes working parallel to the long axis, sometimes across it, and we will finish with more fine pick-dressing. At the bottom end we need to ensure that the pick-dressed surface continues beyond what is likely to be the turf line when the stone is erect, so that the transition between fine dressing and quarry shaping is well buried. At the top, by contrast, we will leave work to do: jointing is a task for construction.

When we dress a side, using gravity to add force to our hammers, this stone of over 30 tons will have to be propped up on its opposite side, perhaps in a timber frame designed for the purpose. We will have to turn it four times: from one face to a side, to the other face, to the second side and back onto a face again. If the archaeologists are right that the debris excavated where a stone was dressed all comes from a single megalith, then in the course of preparing Stone 58 we will have got through something in the order of 1,000 hammers. They often break with intensive use, but nonetheless the figure is evocative. For at least a century the question of how Stonehenge was built has been answered with devices for bringing megaliths to the site and then erecting them. But preparing and finishing them for use – pounding away at the rock, moving stones around and bringing them into line with what had been planned – must have been a challenging and labour-intensive programme in its own right.

That is not to say it was hopeless, however. The quest to understand Neolithic sarsen workers by imagining them to be Edwardian masons who'd lost their steel tools, led archaeologists astray with the finer dressing as much as the heavy flaking and shaping at the quarries. Richard Atkinson took part in a BBC film about Stonehenge[13] in which he demonstrated the process, dropping a heavy stone ball-hammer found in excavations at the site onto a slab of sarsen, and producing puffs of white powder – from a fallen megalith at Stonehenge itself! To achieve the result whose ruin we see today, calculated Richard, 50 masons working ten hours a day, seven days a week would need to keep going for two years and nine months without stop – 'we may safely assume the absence of Union rules', he wrote in the early 1950s. This almost certainly exaggerates the time needed – and he excluded the important task of jointing the stones.

Occasional claims have been made that large sarsen boulders, when freshly excavated, can be softer and more readily crumbled than stone long exposed to the atmosphere. Victorian gunflint makers in Norfolk used to talk of 'quarry water': lumps of flint they'd laboriously mined out of the chalk behaved more favourably in their hands when it was still fresh, compared to 'drier' flint. The beautiful limestone used for Georgian buildings in the city of Bath is said to retain 'quarry sap' when new, making it easier to cut. Some of the sarsen debris I excavated in 1980 was almost the texture of hard sugar. Is that what a Neolithic mason might have confronted?

Probably not. Fire causes sarsen to crumble, says Katy Whitaker, but not water – and Edwardian masons in Buckinghamshire, who had to dig down to find their sarsen, succeeded equally with sarsens in Wiltshire that had been on the surface for millennia. In fact a looser texture would not have helped successful flaking. The idea of sugary sarsen aiding Neolithic masons is just another well-meaning attempt by recent observers to explain how Stonehenge's builders managed without steel tools. Since the first modern excavation in 1901, it has been understood that Stonehenge is an accomplished

Stone Age construction, built with a Stone Age mentality. There is a twist, however.

As we work at Stone 58, we toil in a cloud of dust – silica dust. Gunflint makers and recent sarsen workers commonly died early from silicosis. There are many opportunities for small accidents with hammers and large ones with a falling megalith. There would have been times when being part of the Stonehenge project was a source of pride and amusement, times when it was hard work, and times when it was punishing. To begin was an act of bravura folly. To complete was a show of intense determination that even now is hard to imagine.

The job done, we lever our dressed sarsen onto a sledge for its final short journey, smooth face up, and drag it through the gap in the earthwork towards the centre of the arena – perhaps along a sled-way of moveable sections, as not one of the 75 stones that will be brought in can follow precisely the same route. Pit locations will have been marked out, including the one we must use, which we will dig the same way as we excavated our Aubrey Hole, with tools of wood, bone and antler.

How the sarsens were erected and linked together is the part of the construction process that has attracted the most interest, and we have many theories and not a few experiments to draw on – the original builders' job would have been a lot easier if they'd had access to YouTube. It's easy to dismiss some of the ideas. A proposal to move megaliths by pivoting them on a pebble requires a concrete surface. Rolling 20- or 30-ton roughly shaped megaliths in which a huge amount of religious, political and labour capital has been invested would be a risk too far – as would any erection process that didn't give people almost complete control. Most theories, however, rely on timbers and ropes and a lot of hands, and many of them look feasible.

Here Herbert Stone established modern thinking, drawing on excavations at Stonehenge that had occurred as he was writing in the early 1920s. A pit to hold a megalith had a vertical side at the back, and a sloping one at the front. The incline would make it easier to slide in a long stone, and once there lying at an angle, it could be raised to vertical with sheerlegs. Ropes would be attached to what was to become the top of the stone and tied to a tall A-frame of oak poles standing the other side of the pit. Then longer ropes from the top of the timber A would allow a team of men – Stone calculated 180 for a circle upright – to pull and lift the megalith upright.

This idea of a large gang of men hauling on long ropes, their efforts amplified by the leverage of sheerlegs, lies behind almost every believable proposal made since. Richard Atkinson drew an illustration of it for his book about Stonehenge, Garfitt proposed sheerlegs for raising both uprights and lintels, and a version features in the current English Heritage guidebook. An elaborate interpretation and the most ambitious execution, using full-scale concrete replicas of all three Great Trilithon stones, was broadcast by the BBC and PBS Nova in the 1990s. Informed by an archaeologist and an engineer, the project used a heavy weight on the bottom end of the megalith (a 'pivot stone') to aid its allegedly controlled fall into the pit.[14] We can take our pick from a number of similar schemes, it seems, never knowing if our choice is what actually happened. The trouble is, except perhaps for the atypical case of the trilithons, none of them could have been possible.

There is a simple reason for this. Models, diagrams and discussions have focused on a single stone. In an experimental context, the Nova erection project is unusual for having two uprights, but like the others it was conducted in an otherwise empty field. Once the first stone was raised, however, the site was not empty. Everyone agrees that the trilithons must have been erected before the circle. Once that's done there's no scope for raising the circle using long ropes, whether you lie stones down on the inside pulling outwards (no room for the stones) or outside pulling in (no room for sheerlegs, ropes and pullers). However you try it, most of the upright stones at Stonehenge cannot have been erected in this way.

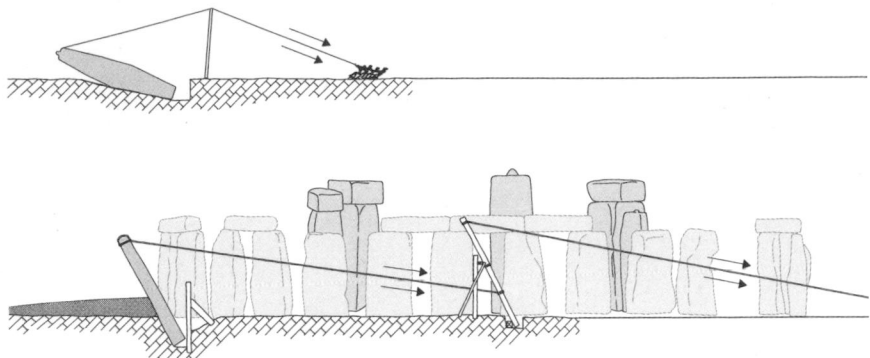

Trilithons standing in the centre leave no room for long ropes hauling stones up from the outside: upper redrawn after Garfitt, lower Richards and Whitby (scaled to size of circle stones) with surviving stones today after English Heritage. There is no evidence at the site for sheerleg pits.

John Sibbick's illustration, showing the conventional way of raising a circle stone with sheerlegs on the inside, inadvertently proves the point – there is no room. On the right a lintel is levered up on a growing timber platform.

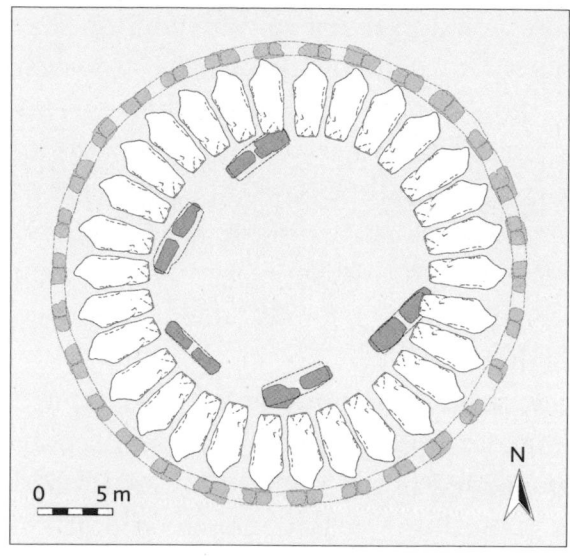

N

0   5 m

Once the trilithons are
up, there is no room
for raising circle stones
from the inside, except
at the northeast.

Which begs the question, how *were* they raised?

Let's start with the evidence from the ground. On and off between 1919 and 1964 archaeologists excavated all or part of the pits in which most of the stones still standing were placed.[15] This revealed several recurring features, though there is more variety than is usually described. The impression is that every megalith, with its distinctive shape and weight, had its own story of how it rose to become upright and be part of something bigger.

Many of the pits have one more or less sloping side of the kind described by Stone, in all but one facing outwards, appearing to confirm that that was the direction from which most of the stones were erected. This oblique side is commonly described as a ramp, and it features in all descriptions and illustrations of stone raising at Stonehenge as if it was a necessary part of the engineering – a misleading impression, as on the recorded evidence around half the stone pits do not have it.

Mixed with a pit's filling of earth and chalk rubble are many rocks, some of them used hammers, some just lumps of stone. The latter include large chunks of what early excavators described as Chilmark limestone or ragstone, which were common in five pits where the circle is best preserved to the northeast (for Stones 27, 29, 30, 1 and 6) and curiously recorded nowhere else.[16] The nearest source for these is 20 km (12 miles) to the southwest, where there is a quarry today selling 'one of Britain's finest building and masonry stones as used in Salisbury Cathedral'. Perhaps they were a gift of local people who, unable to procure a megalith, managed the next best thing; the stone's presence in the pits supports my suggestion that perhaps the really large hammers, found only in stone pits, were also brought from a distance.[17]

Following the usual pattern, there are some antler picks, though apparently never more than one in a pit. In one case the tip of an antler tine was found embedded in the chalk rock where it had broken off as the pit was being dug. One day, I hope, radiocarbon dating will be able to obtain a date from a tiny sample of this

Julian Richards (left) and Mike Parker Pearson, professor at the UCL Institute of Archaeology, examine packing stones and broken megaliths, both of which are common below the turf, from the 2008 trench in the background. Behind centre are fallen and standing stones of the southern part of the Sarsen Circle, where megaliths were of poorer quality compared to the north.

antler that will leave it largely undamaged – it would be the most reliable date from the monument. In the meantime we have two results, one from the circle and one from a trilithon, which, with dates from Durrington Walls where archaeologists think those who built Stonehenge lived, suggest construction around 2500 BC.[18]

Several pits have holes on the bottom for posts or stakes: most are against the inner edge, but in others timbers seem to have been placed more centrally, and must have been removed before the stones were vertical. Evidence of sticks placed at the back of pits as stones were being erected – often described as 'anti-friction stakes' – has also been recorded beneath some of Avebury's huge sarsen megaliths. It is a practice that was witnessed in a place we have been before, among the Naga people. In this case, the recorder was another British colonial, Stephen Dewar, who had been a tea planter in Assam in the 1920s. Typically, most of the action involved feasting, dancing and dressing up, and when the stone – weighing 8 tons and dragged to the site on a sledge by 100 people – was finally raised, Dewar made an explicit comparison with the stakes at Stonehenge and Avebury. A row of poles, he says, was set up on the far side of the hole to prevent the edge of the stone's base from jamming. Then it was levered up at the top end and supported with wooden wedges. As more chocks were slid underneath, rope was tied to the top while men with poles at the other end struggled to stop it slipping forward. With more levering and chocking the moment came when the balance was right, and men grabbed the ropes and pulled the stone erect. Throwing stone blocks into the pit to hold fast the megalith, the men and the watching crowd rapidly headed back to the village for drinks.[19]

Here is a different vision of stone erection, and one that holds the key to what I think happened at Stonehenge. The effort is focused not on long ropes and poles with people distant from the object of their attention, but on the stone itself. The distinction is more than one of engineering and organization. When stone and people come together, visually and physically the relationship changes. There is no longer an opposition between the mass of the stone and the energy of the pullers, but an intimate embrace in which ropes, timbers, people and stone are one. If we picture two images created in the 1940s, it is the difference between one drawn by Henry Moore and now in the British Museum – *Crowd Looking at a Tied-Up Object* – in which a half-megalith half-human shape wrapped in white drapery towers over a compact group of people, who look expectant, separate and vulnerable; and Joe Rosenthal's famous photo of US Marines raising a flag during the Battle of Iwo Jima. In that shot the soldiers will their flag upright with their bodies, and flag and men are in symbiotic composition though one of the men is not touching the flag. There is nothing romantic about the scene: the battle is in progress, and three of the six, and a photographer who was with Rosenthal on the expedition, will soon be dead. But the image melded nation, individuals, object and hope, and generations later it continues to work hard, as much in parody as in honour. That is what Stonehenge is becoming as we prepare to raise Stone 58, a monument bigger than its parts that will live on in the re-invention.

We are pushing rather than pulling, and to do that we might look to help from mounds, timbers and ropes placed under the stone. The trilithon on Tonga, according to the memory of 'an old chieftain' who in 1920 had said the lintel symbolized the bond between two royal brothers represented by the uprights, was raised with an earth mound built while the stones lay flat on the ground. It was heaped against a rough timber retaining wall parallel to the pit edges, and the stones hauled up on rails using ropes, levers and wedges and tipped over the edge.[20] Thor Heyerdahl used a mound to raise a statue on Rapa Nui, but here, with stones rather than earth, a dozen men built the pile under the slowly rising figure as they levered it up.

Were we to build mounds at Stonehenge, you might think they would have to be of the Tongan type, earth and soft chalk piled up before the stones were moved. Herbert Stone thought this is how the lintels were raised, dragged up embankments which reached to the top of the standing uprights, as he demonstrated with models at public talks. This fails, however, because there is no evidence for earthworks of such size – either the material they were made of, or the holes in the ground that would have been dug to obtain it. To raise an upright exclusively this way would require a huge mound. With timber, however, we can create a Heyerdahl-type pile, slowly accumulating as the stone above rises.

In fact we already have evidence that something of this sort was used in Neolithic Britain and Ireland, in the construction of dolmens. Though commonly thought to have been encased in mounds themselves, as we see them today these are exposed tomb chambers composed of closely spaced megaliths usually supporting a single, large horizontal slab known as a capstone. Kit's Coty is a small example. There are some famous ones in the west of Britain, such as Trethevy Quoit in Cornwall and Pentre Ifan in Pembrokeshire. Capstones can weigh considerably more than any of the Stonehenge megaliths. In northwest France that at La Bajoulière near Angers weighs 100 tons, and at Brownshill in southeast Ireland is a monster estimated to weigh 160 tons.

Colin Richards and his archaeological colleague Vicki Cummings have been thinking about these giants.[21] They argue that the engineering achievement was half the point, and that the stones were never hidden away beneath mounds, but hoisted as awe-inspiring displays (as we might say of Stonehenge, which only a few have imagined was ever buried). They have found signs of surface dressing on the flat undersides of some capstones, such as those at the Goward dolmen in Northern Ireland (50 tons) and Garn Turne in Pembrokeshire (80 tons, the UK's largest). Their excavation at Garn Turne unearthed hammerstones and rhyolite debris from the shaping, which occurred around 3700 BC, a millennium before the bluestones in Wiltshire were dressed.

As to how such a great rock was raised into the air, Colin and Vicki are convinced it was moved like Heyerdahl's statue, but working at both ends – alternately lifting with levers and propping up with stones until the right height was achieved, when the megaliths could be inserted underneath and the stone pile removed. It's difficult to think of any other way of doing it. And hey presto, we're back in Sumba.

The tombs which Ron Adams describes are a form of dolmen, in which standing slabs support a large capstone – ranging from 2 to 27 tons – to create a closed burial chamber. In one place, says Ron, the stone is laid beside the tomb, and different parts are lifted with vines as small logs are wedged underneath. These steadily build into a scaffold that reaches the height of the walls, when the stone is pulled across. At another location, a capstone is positioned before the walls are raised. Here a wooden structure of three or four layers of horizontal logs is built, tied together, with a ramp up which the stone is pulled on a sledge. Stone supporting pillars are then erected, the timbers removed and the capstone drops into place. The dolmen itself is then built underneath this stone table,

Sliding a capstone from a timber scaffold onto uprights for a tomb in West Sumba.

first the walls and then the inner capstone, which is pulled up a log ramp with ropes or vines.

So on this small Indonesian island, at the same time at two locations a couple of days' walk apart, one might witness two different ways of raising a stone: seesawing it up beneath a slowly growing pile of logs and wedges, or pulling it up a pre-constructed ramp. All of this – Tonga, Assam, Sumba and Neolithic Wales – can help us imagine what happened at Stonehenge. As large as the monument is and with so many gangs at work, we should not expect every lift to follow exactly the same procedure. But we can use Heyerdahl's experiment on Rapa Nui in particular as a guide.[22] Easter Island has figured little in the archaeology of Salisbury Plain. No surprise, you might think: but some of the statues match Stonehenge's sarsen megaliths for size (Heyerdahl estimated his weighed 30 tons – similar to Stone 58), and, like no other standing stones in Europe, they had 'hats', stone drums balanced on top like Stonehenge's lintels, weighing as much as 12 tons (compared to lintel 158's 16 tons, and typical circle lintels of 5.5 tons).

What strikes you most about the statue raising, is the slow, gentle way it was done. At first Heyerdahl could barely see anything move. As three or four men hung on the end of each of three large poles squeezed under one side at the top of the head, the leader lay on his stomach pushing small stones underneath. By day's end the figure had risen 1 m (3 ft). The next day ten men worked with two poles. The team moved to the other side of the head, subtly rolling it to allow more stones to be placed beneath. Then back to the first side, and across again and back, until on the ninth day the statue lay on a wedge-shaped pile of stones rising to nearly 3.5 m (12 ft). By now the men could no longer reach the poles, and relied on trailing ropes to manoeuvre them. Other ropes tied to the top of the head were there not to pull it upright, but to keep it in on the stone ramp and be ready should it slip.

After more than two weeks of this, with controlling ropes at back and front, 'the last cautious jerks with a wooden pole began'. Now,

Rapa Nui islanders raised a statue for Thor Heyerdahl in the 1950s by slowly piling material under it as they created space using levers – a model for raising sarsens at Stonehenge.

finally, the statue visibly moved, rebalancing in a cloud of dust and falling stones and coming to rest in an upright position (the statues stand on stone platforms, not in pits). It had taken 18 days.

Remarkably, a strikingly similar image was presented by a group of archaeologists who took time out for an experiment at a Neolithic henge monument at Mount Pleasant, Dorset. It was 1971, and they had excavated long stretches of a narrow, deep trench that had originally been dug around 2500 BC; a tall oak palisade had once encircled the hilltop. They obtained a telegraph pole, and raised it into the trench without the use of ropes, simply by gathering close, and pushing and pulling while using the spoilheap as a readymade ramp on which they could stand and pivot the timber. They might almost have been re-enacting the flag raising at Iwo Jima.

All we need to do at Stonehenge is substitute timbers for Heyerdahl's rocks. We slide our stone off its sledge onto a carpentered frame lying on the ground, so that its base is over the pit and its top away to the northwest. We are going to raise the far end, so we will need to anchor its base with posts placed vertically in the pit to stop it sliding forward. Then, slowly and softly, we use levers to rock the great stone from side to side on its frame, aided by the irregular shape of its back. At first we force small wooden wedges underneath its top, then gradually add more until it becomes possible to insert complete logs. Bit by bit, in almost imperceptibly small increments, the top of Stone 58 rises on a growing timber scaffold, its parts held together by tying and the weight of their burden.

After a week, perhaps, with a larger gang than Heyerdahl's, the stone will be ready for the last, watchful push, as short ropes on one side topple it upright and on the others strain to prevent it from falling over. For the first time working with a sense of urgency, we remove timbers from the pit and allow the stone to rise free. We adjust it from all sides to a true vertical, rocking it as necessary on its pointed base, aligning its smooth inner face and positioning its

In 1971 archaeologists raised a telegraph pole in a deep Neolithic palisade trench they had excavated at Mount Pleasant, Dorset. Using their spoil heap as a ramp, they eased the pole into place without ropes.

centre precisely according to the plan. When we are satisfied we pack the pit with waiting boulders – even this is no casual task, with every fragment needing to be fitted carefully to ensure no future slippage. We take apart the scaffolding, and the first part of our challenge is complete. If it happens to rain, dirt will wash off the stone which will sparkle when the sun shines, the freshly dressed almost white surfaces contrasting with the darker brown and grey of what remains of the boulder's forest skin. It's time to celebrate. Stone 58 is a megalith.

Π

One megalith does not a circle make, and Stonehenge is no ordinary monument: as I noted earlier, there are rules. The evidence for planning and design lies in the structure. The layout is simple and symmetric. The largest ten sarsens, of which ours is one, are to stand in pairs around a horseshoe plan whose end opens to face the midsummer sunrise. Five heavy lintels will emphasize the twinning and create trilithons, which will noticeably increase in height from the northeast to the southwest, to the Great Trilithon at the back.

This arrangement will stand in the centre of a perfect circle of 30 stones. As the megaliths vary in shape and width, they maintain their regular spacing by having uneven gaps between them, the only exception being Stones 30 and 1, on the solstice axis: here a wider gap is created by moving the stones apart a little, closer to their neighbours. Like the trilithon uprights, these stones are also connected by lintels, which will form a continuous horizontal ring some 4 m (13 ft) up in the air; the tops of the uprights will need to be level with each other. Lintels on the trilithons will have flat fronts, and backs swelling to match the arc of the horseshoe, while both sides of circle lintels will be dressed to follow the ring's curvature. If we can't tell whether the 56 stones of the original Aubrey ring embodied a meaningful quantity, it's easier to think that the numbers are deliberate here. The maths is simple. Five trilithons make 10 uprights and 15 stones, which are, respectively, a third and half the number of stones in the circle.

We have already noted that today Stone 58 is similar to its partner, 57, and the other surviving upright pairs in the Horseshoe are also loosely matched. The inner faces of the trilithon uprights are smoother than the outer, a feature that holds true for uprights in the circle as well.[23] Many of the latter are now badly damaged or missing, but enough survive to show that stones to the northeast – those we see today as we approach up the Avenue or look through as we stand in the centre with our back to the Great Trilithon – were from the start more substantial than those to the southwest, behind the Great Trilithon. This difference caused much debate in the past about whether the circle had originally ever been complete, and recent geophysical surveys had failed to find enough hidden pits that might have held missing sarsens at what feels like the back of the monument. However, the laser survey of the stones identi- fied joints on what does remain to leave the existence of only one megalith in doubt, and in 2013 a pit for that one showed up in the grass, when a hot dry July parched the turf and left distinct brown patches above ancient pits in the chalk.[24]

There is something strident and confident about the trilithons to suggest they command the numbers, and it's tempting to wonder if the uprights represented particular people – leaders or communities – and the lintels connections or alliances. By this reading, for example, the paired megaliths, which tend to have one stone more dressed and smoothed compared to its rougher, less 'polished' companion, might be a chief and a partner or child. Different groups, perhaps, would have been responsible for different parts of the monument, so that, for example, the larger circle stones to the northeast might have been the gift of those with the power to command more labour or access to better quarries, in contrast to the diminutive stones to the southwest, which spoke of less favoured people; yet everyone was shown to belong to the wider whole by the connecting lintels.

All of this – the smoother faces looking in, the matching sizes and surfaces of particular stones, the curving of the lintels, the joints and even perhaps the differences in quality of the circle stones from one side to another and the colours we noted in Chapter 3 – will have been planned, and may have affected decisions at the quarries as well as at the site where the monument is to be raised. So too the layout of horseshoe and circle, the latter 30 m (98 ft) across between the stone's inner faces (very close to a third of the diameter of the old Aubrey circle, whose circuit is memorialized in the Station Stones), will have been agreed in advance. The sheer size of the trilithon uprights means they will have to be erected before the circle: it would be impossible to get them through gaps between standing circle stones,[25] and the latter would get in the way of mechanisms required to raise them. Yet the circle will have to be marked out before the inner stones are raised and themselves interfere with ropes and survey lines – further confirmation of a coherent plan.

As well as our stone, 39 other slabs need to be prepared and finished for the uprights – 9 larger ones for the horseshoe and

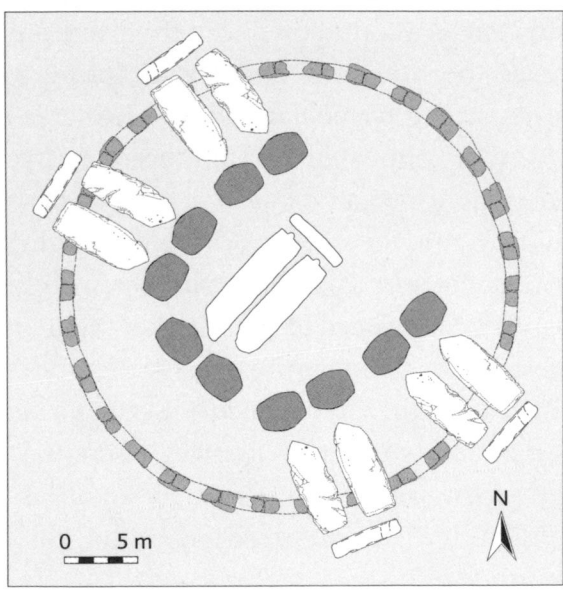

Schematic diagram of stones for the five sarsen trilithons on the ground ready for erection. The background plan shows to scale the completed Sarsen Circle (lintels dotted): trilithons must be raised before the circle.

30 smaller for the circle. The final forms are determined partly by the original nature of the sarsen boulder, partly by the quarry work, which left a few very large flake scars too deep to remove and in every case created a unique shape, and partly by decisions about the intensity and style of preparation and finish. Two stones, however, demand more attention, to be smoothed and precisely fashioned like no others: 55 and 56, the Great Trilithon.

Stone 55 fell and broke in two before written history and is weathered and battered, but what we can see suggests it was treated the same way as its partner. Stone 56's faces and sides are all even to a degree you'd think impossible with sarsen, and are almost entirely finished with fine pick-dressing. Seen from the front as it now stands (that is, from the inside of the horseshoe, looking southwest), its left side is almost dead straight along its full height of 6.6 m (21½ ft). Its right, outer side is lightly curved, swelling outwards by 25 cm (10 in.). It looks as if Stone 55 was its mirror image, so when new they would have risen together with a narrow gap of just 40 cm (16 in.) between them like a gunsight – through which, in a clear sky, the red globe of the setting midwinter sun would have burned as it disappeared below the horizon. The gently curving outer edges might have given the impression of a wide, smooth and slightly rounded single giant slab, echoing the sun's disc. Stone 56 also swells slightly seen from the side – curving at the front, straight as a rule at the back. Interestingly, there are patches of undressed stone near the ground on both faces. This exceptionally thin stone must have begun as a very unusual natural slab (perhaps it had a previous life as a significant thing at its original location) and it seems likely that a great deal of stone had to be removed to give it its tall, narrow shape.

Back to our stone, we now need to repeat our task with its companion, Stone 57. As we do so, Stone 58 may settle a little. It seems likely that we will see all ten of the trilithon uprights erected, adjusted, allowed to settle and if necessary readjusted, before we embark on our next challenge: fitting the lintel.

It's worth taking a moment to step back, and reflect on what we are about to do. Standing stones, single, in rows or in circles, are a distinctive feature of Neolithic and Bronze Age northern Europe – well over a thousand rings are known in Britain and Ireland alone. They occur mostly where suitable material is available, which means stone that breaks naturally into megalith-like blocks; dragging bluestones all the way to Salisbury Plain was an unmatched project, but the choice of source outcrops followed this standard pattern. The stones are usually left entirely in their natural shapes. As we saw, there are instances in Wales and Ireland of large ones being dressed to flatten a face, and at various places in northwest Europe – notably in Brittany and Ireland, but also occasionally in mainland Britain – we can see elaborate, shallow designs hammered out in rings, lines and dots. Stonehenge does not have such decorations (the dagger and axe blades came later), though some of the outlying megaliths – the two Station Stones and the Heelstone – were treated to some relatively superficial abrasion.[26] But the intense shaping and jointing in the centre are quite unique. Was this an idea that came out of the blue?

Certainly it was once thought so. Over the past century, however, excavations have revealed a growing number of timber structures – in the form of their postholes in the ground – of comparable scale to Stonehenge, and broadly of the same era, which once boasted many great posts arranged in concentric rings. Opinions have varied on their appearance, but the evidence is today usually read as indicating free-standing posts, perhaps sometimes joined by lintels, and possibly carved or adorned with hangings. That was how its discoverer, archaeologist Maud Cunnington (1869–1951), envisaged the first to be found, making an explicit comparison with Stonehenge by naming it Woodhenge – it's just 3 km (2 miles) to the northeast of the stones; it had six oval post-rings. Woodhenge is immediately beside the henge at Durrington Walls, and two more were found there. The largest known, at Stanton Drew in Somerset, 55 km (35 miles) to the northwest, sported four or five hundred posts in nine circles, the outer one about 100 m (330 ft) across; interestingly, the whole affair is surrounded by a ring of undressed megaliths, the largest perfect stone circle in the UK.[27]

It doesn't seem too great a leap to imagine such timber monuments as having partly inspired the Stonehenge we are building: tongue and groove joints connecting the stone lintels, and mortises and tenons that bond lintels and uprights, are more at home in carpentry than masonry. In this light, Stonehenge is an idea more commonly expressed in soft, perishable timber, made in the hardest, most enduring material then known. And its architects and engineers probably drew on experience of acquiring, shaping and building with massive timbers. As far as we know, this was the only time the two technologies were brought together in this way.

As before, logic and the evidence of the stones leave little doubt as to what we have to do next.

When positioned, the lintels at Stonehenge have cups on their undersides and uprights have studs on their tops. The studs have to fit into the cups, the surest way of achieving which is to carve them together to match each other.[28] We have left this until now, because the process is tied up with achieving a precise level for our stone with its partner, at the exact desired height, as will be the case separately with the other four trilithons – and also the entire circle. One way to do this would be to dress stones close to the height needed, and then to erect them so their tops settled in the right place by bedding their bases at exactly the right depth. Excavation has shown that there is even greater variety in the sarsen megaliths below ground than there is above; there is no consistency in their lengths. Realizing perfect height during the erection of stones weighing at least 20 or 30 tons would be an extreme and probably insuperable challenge. The only alternative is to do it once they are upright.

We would still need to raise Stone 58 to close to its intended height, but we leave the finer adjustment to after it has settled by removing stone from the top. That it was done this way is clear

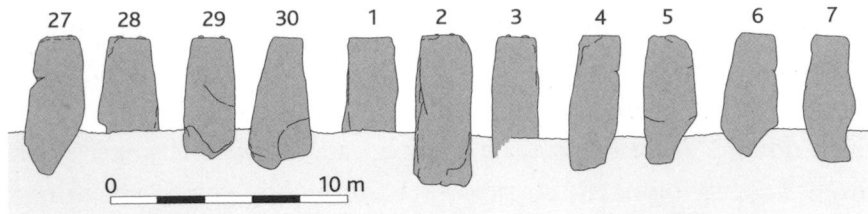

27   28   29   30   1   2   3   4   5   6   7

0   10 m

The most complete line of Sarsen Circle stones, showing stone below ground where excavated. The tops are perfectly levelled (here some have moved slightly).

from the surviving, visible tenons. They are finely made, arguably the most finished and symmetric elements of the monument, looking like upturned bowls. They could only have been shaped by hammering from above on upright stones.

We need ladders, then, or perhaps more likely scaffolding, to allow us to work at the top of Stone 58, wielding hard sarsen hammers weighing between 500 g and 2 kg (1–5 lb). The laser survey revealed

Stone 56

Stone 60

2 m

Sarsen Horseshoe stones with visible tenons seen from the inner sides, as recorded by laser scanning. Stone 56 would have had to have been at least 40 cm (16 in.) taller before the tenon was dressed, and Stone 60 20 cm (8 in.) taller, adding around a ton of sarsen to each stone.

that construction dressing, the jointing work, left a coarser finish than the finer pick-dressed stone that it sometimes bashed away; these surfaces were not expected to be seen in the completed monument. So as we create our tenon, we are simultaneously lowering the top of the stone on which the lintel will rest. In fact the latter will come first: we will leave a block from which we will later mould the tenon, but the critical task is to remove stone to get that perfect height and level. By the end we will have pecked away about a ton of sarsen.

A curious feature of several of the stone tops is a raised edge around a slightly lower inner surface – Richard Atkinson likened the effect to a tea tray. This appears to have been designed to strengthen the joints, with lintels appropriately dressed by removing stone along the edges of their undersides, allowing them to sink into the dished tops, as seen from the ground creating a seamless join. In addition, it might have transpired in some cases that the right level was achieved for the top of the stone too soon – leaving a weak stump of a tenon. The only way to address that would be to remove more stone around the tenon while leaving the rest of the top alone.

Top of sarsen
Stone 22 during
restoration in
1958, showing
two tenons
inside a shallow
dished area.

We are not yet done. Now that we have tenons on the tops of Stones 57 and 58, with their precise positions and distance apart fixed, we can make mortises in the lintel to match. The lintel itself will have been shaped already, and will lie on the ground downside up. We can transfer the tenons' locations with a marked rod, and then hammer and grind out the mortises. It's critical to get this right, and sometimes it went wrong.

The lintel for the Great Trilithon, Stone 156, has mortises on both faces, top and bottom. The pairs are the same distance apart and both sets could apparently have functioned. However, one is slightly deeper than the other, and it seems likely that the abandoned set was started on the wrong face. Both pairs reflect apparently asymmetric positioning of the tenons, but in different directions: the best fit of the abandoned mortises would have had the lintel's curved side facing inwards rather than out. The stone is now on the ground and very weathered, but if it was like its better preserved fellows 152 and 154, it would have had a top and a bottom, widening as the sides rose – not narrowing. One of the lintels in the circle has two sets of mortises on its underside,

Lintel 154, partly hidden by Stone 56 with its prominent tenon, is one of the best preserved. Note how the sides flare outwards.

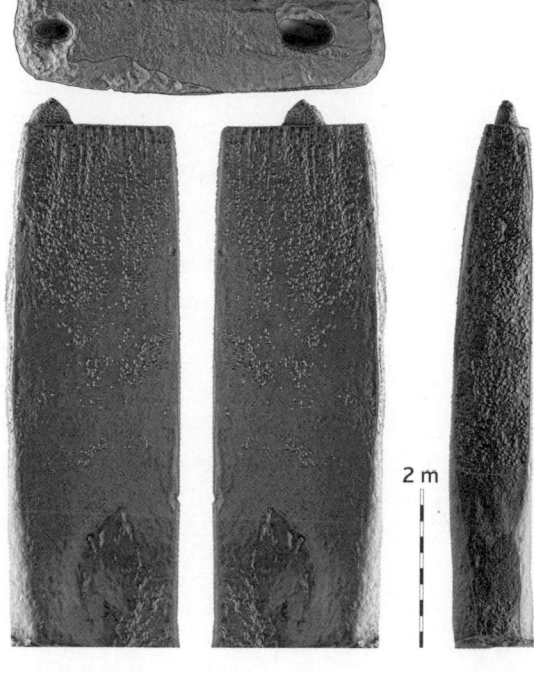

2 m

The Great Trilithon completed, using a mirror image of Stone 56 for Stone 55 (far left, with appropriately positioned tenon), as recorded by laser scanning.

and here it appears that the first was wrongly located.[29] In one curious case, the mortise in Stone 154 resting on Stone 54, there is a gap between the tenon and the surrounding lintel big enough for jackdaws to climb in – as John Aubrey noted in the 17th century, 'Several of the high stones of Stonehenge are honycombed so deep that the Stares doe make their nests in the holes.' Here a natural hollow in the sarsen seems to have contributed to a large mortise hole, to no loss: the lintel has never fallen since it was first raised.

So with mortises in our lintel, all that remains is to get it into position. Realistic ideas about how to do this fall into two camps. First is the timber ramp, ranging from a huge scaffolding construction for the Nova film, up which a concrete lintel tied to a sledge was hauled along three great wooden rails, to two oak poles and a few levers. The latter were successfully applied to another full-scale concrete replica trilithon by ten men led by Pavel Pavel, in Strakonice, Czechoslovakia (now the Czech Republic), just after the revolution in 1991. Though the experiments were successful,

Sarsen trilithon Stones 51 (left) 52 (right) and lintel 152 from the inside (looking southwest). Jackdaws have nested in a natural hole that was extended to make a mortise in the lintel.

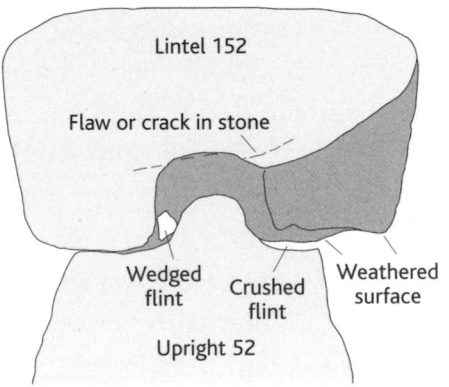

Lintel 152

Flaw or crack in stone

Wedged flint   Crushed flint   Weathered surface

Upright 52

Section showing a great mismatch between the tenon on Stone 52 and mortise in Stone 152. The lintel appears to have crushed loose flints on top of the upright. Based on an unpublished measured drawing by Robert Newall, unknown date.

in both there were moments when things could have gone fatally wrong (at one point Pavel's lintel fell off). Any such ramp has to be supported at its top end, either with large posts (no appropriate pits have been excavated at Stonehenge) or by resting it on the upright stones, at the very least risking minor movement to megaliths so painfully positioned. The other option seems to me the more likely – not least because we have already employed it to erect the uprights.

We will raise our lintel, then, as if it were a capstone. We place it close to Stones 57 and 58, mortises facing down, and lever it onto oak logs. Then bit by bit, as we did with one end of the uprights, we rock it with levers from side to side and end to end, every time inserting more wedges and poles as it slowly rises. These timbers will need to be substantial, so that for stability the rising tower extends at least 1–2 m (3–6 ft) beyond the stone on all sides. This is the method favoured by Richard Atkinson (and endorsed by George Gauld, an engineer who worked on hydroelectric projects in South India), and is illustrated in English Heritage's guidebook, though as we've seen in Assam and Indonesia, there is no need to square the logs as indicated there. Eventually the lintel will reach a height where its base is above the top of the two tenons. At this point the raft can be extended over the megaliths, the force acting vertically, and the lintel slid across. We check the match, and where necessary hammer off any surplus stone – a difficult task, but one that the very close fit of lintels and uprights suggests was probably done, often removing a thin skin of sarsen across the whole of the lintel's base where it makes contact with an upright. Then we remove the raft, and gently lower the stone into place with levers. At long last, Stone 58 is doing what it was designed to do as part of the emerging Stonehenge.

We can see that, with space for workers and timbers around the great lintels, we could, at most, erect two megaliths at once, one on each side of the Horseshoe. Allowing two weeks for each stone, we would need a minimum of twelve weeks just to raise the trilithon uprights: four for a trilithon on each side, four more for the other two and four for the Great Trilithon in the centre. With a week, say, to dress down the tenons on top and another week to carve out the lintels' mortises (which technically could all be done at the same time), creating these trilithons requires at the very least fourteen weeks – in practice probably considerably longer.

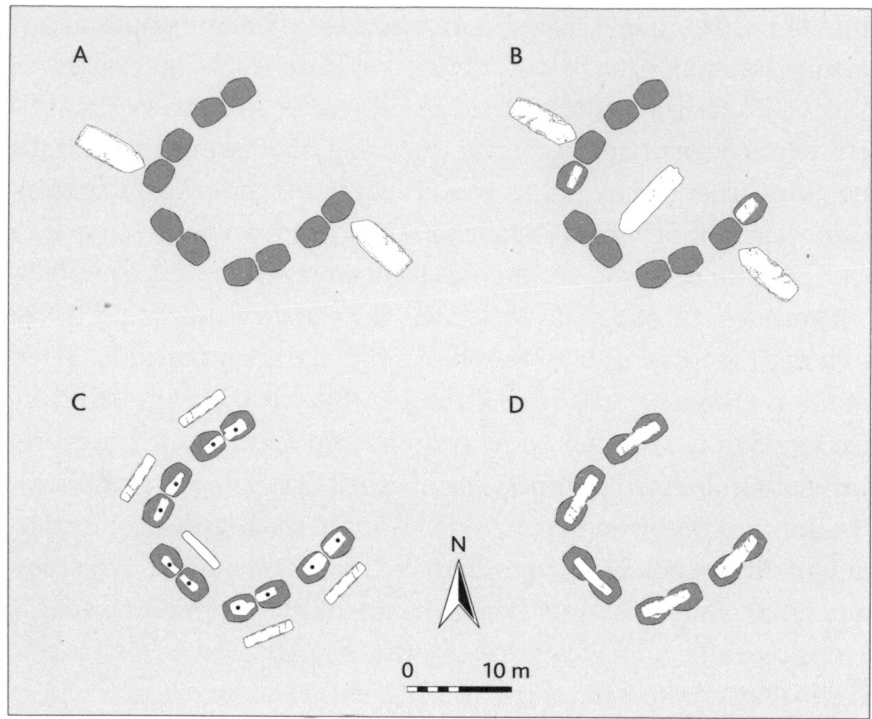

Space needed for timber and gangs means that at the most urgent, only two trilithons can be raised at once apart from the Great Trilithon, leading to a minimum of six raising stages, each taking perhaps two weeks (A, B). When uprights have settled, the tops of the stones are dressed down to the right levels, leaving a tenon on each one (C); matching mortises are carved in the lintels before they are raised and positioned on the uprights (D).

How long the whole project took would have been partly a matter of work time in this sense of practical engineering, but there would have been two other opposing forces. On the one hand, rest needs, ceremonies, socializing and demands on people to attend to other tasks – not to mention random factors such as severe weather, disease outbreaks or food shortages – would have substantially extended the process. On the other, allowing things to move too slowly would bring a serious risk of failure, as individuals needed to return home, and the challenge of keeping a workforce on site stretched resources and management control or social pressure to succeed. If Mike Parker Pearson is right that a large settlement was created at Durrington Walls to house workers, then the focus was on getting the job done: a thousand men could deliver many separate gangs simultaneously, and feeding them would put severe pressure on otherwise small, gardening communities which would be hard to sustain. It may have been no more than a year, then, when the next major task was faced in a single season: raising the Sarsen Circle.

If Stonehenge is a design conjured by master builders with experience of creating similar structures in timber, this familiarity is no more apparent than in the circle's lintels, which served as a ring-beam bringing strength to the entire edifice. Today there are just nine lintels at Stonehenge doing their proper job, resting horizontally on the top of standing sarsens. Remains of a few others lie about on the ground, most notably the Great Trilithon's, the only other one that is more or less complete. There is as we have seen no reason to doubt the former presence of a complete set of thirty-five, but only six survive from the circle – one in five – to show what they looked like. Some of them are badly weathered.

I have emphasized how much the standing stones vary in shape and finish. What we can see of the lintels suggests that they were more standardized – trilithon and circle lintels constituting two types – but qualification is needed. For over a century guidebooks and academic texts have shown diagrams of circle lintels connected to each other with tongues and grooves and to uprights with mortises and tenons, all perfectly shaped for immaculate fits. This would have been astonishingly hard to achieve, and such as it is the evidence suggests the actual joints are not so well matched. They are almost impossible to see (we'd have to lift the lintels to do that properly) and were largely inaccessible to the laser study. This difficulty shows when one archaeologist describes a tongue on the end of a lintel where another sees a groove. Two lintels are said to have tongues at each end, but there is disagreement about which two. If they are representative, there would have been ten lintels with two tongues, requiring ten with two grooves – not a feature seen in any reconstruction illustrations.

Such is the delicacy and precision required in shaping and jointing the circle lintels, I suggest it's likely the ring was created before the uprights were raised, much as a medieval timber-framed building would first have had its structure carved, jointed and fitted, before being taken apart and reassembled on site as the house was built – a practice also likely to have been familiar to Neolithic carpenters. The circle itself would already have been marked out – Richard Atkinson suggested with buried wooden stakes – and would now need to be made visible. At a little distance around this would be placed the 30 lintels, roughed out for their final dressing. With a team working on every other stone, at its most urgent, 15 lintels would be moved to their exact intended locations. The same size of hammerstone as we used on the top of Stone 58 would then be employed to finish the surfaces, flat at top and bottom, long sides curved to match the circle, and ends jointed with a tongue or a groove. When this was done, the other 15 stones would be brought in and shaped the same way, this time with greater precision at the ends which would need to be fitted

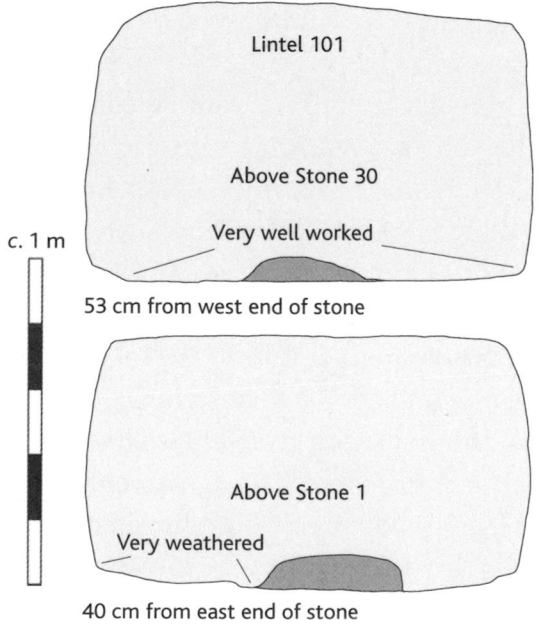

Lintel 101

Above Stone 30

Very well worked

c. 1 m

53 cm from west end of stone

Above Stone 1

Very weathered

40 cm from east end of stone

Sections through the two mortise holes in Sarsen Circle lintel 101. Based on an unpublished measured drawing by Robert Newall, unknown date.

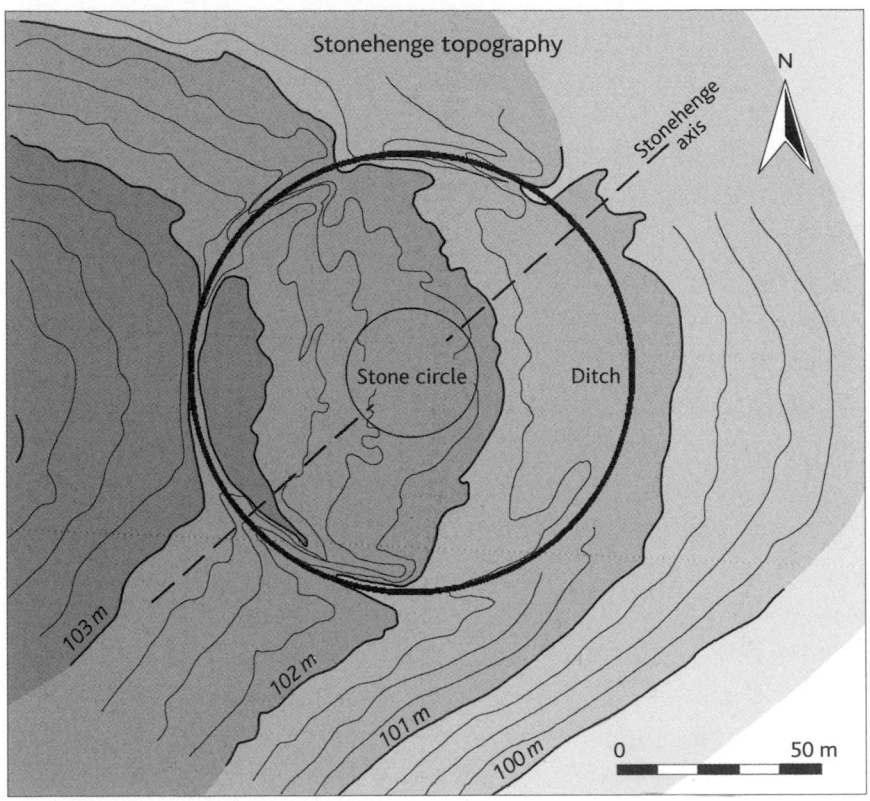

Stonehenge is on the end of a low spur falling to the east, so that within the stone circle the ground rises to the west by about 30 cm (1 ft).

to the first set. They would then all be moved back away from the circle to make room for the uprights.

Now the pits would be dug, megaliths raised in the same way we raised Stone 58, tops levelled and tenons carved – two to each stone in the circle – and mortises hollowed out at the end of each lintel. Lintels would be levered and seesawed up and fitted to the uprights. One of the remarkable features of Stonehenge is that the site is not perfectly level: on average, across the Sarsen Circle it falls around 30 cm (1 ft) from west to east. This may not sound a lot, but the tops of the circle's stones are, as far as we can tell, exactly levelled. The increase in height among the trilithons, from northeast to the Great Trilithon at the southwest, was achieved not by making the stones gradually taller, but, because the ground is uneven, by paying close attention to the level of the tops, as I found out when we built our polystyrene 'foamhenge'. The experimental field was flat, and I presented the modellers with measurements as taken from the actual megaliths. The result was that while the Great Trilithon was taller, the others were all the same height (much to the annoyance of Julian Richards!) – two trilithons, whose stones measured the same from turf to top at Stonehenge itself, rose to different heights because of the topography. Not only does this highlight the skill of the builders, but it also makes it almost certain, as Richard Atkinson recognized, that they had some unknown mechanism for establishing a horizontal level.

In theory the entire circle could have been built in a second season, 1,000 men offering 15 teams of 60 or 70, with enough space between every other megalith for them to work side by side. By comparison to all this, the final tasks are simplicity itself. They involve the bluestones.

We last encountered these in at least two structures on Salisbury Plain, on site at Bluehenge, in the Q and R Holes (56 stones, if we assume a literal rearrangement of the earlier Aubrey circle, though there might then already have been some in the centre as well, whose traces are currently unseen), and in a ring at West Amesbury (around 25 stones). So the estimated final total of some 80 or 90 bluestones could have been achieved by bringing all these together – if that had not happened earlier, for as we saw in the last chapter, details of the second Bluehenge are obscure.

As we contemplate the fresh, towering sarsens, all that is required is to bring the smaller stones to the centre of the site, dig their pits and raise them up. We select the best pillars to form a Bluestone Oval to stand inside the Sarsen Horseshoe. The Altar Stone goes in front of the Great Trilithon, standing or flat on the ground (which of these is not clear). All the others, 60 or 70 of them, are squeezed together into a ring that runs just inside the Sarsen Circle. Before long – how long is a guess – the Oval will be rearranged into a

Bluestone Horseshoe of 19 stones. The whole monument will then be ready to start its journey of decay and destruction leading to what we see today.[30]

As with the sarsen megaliths, Marcus Abbott and Hugo Anderson-Whymark's interpretation of the laser survey casts interesting light here. Many of the bluestones are now missing or reduced to stumps, but a striking pattern exists among those still there. First, all 14 surviving uprights in the Horseshoe are dolerite, and all are more or less finely dressed into slightly rounded and tapering pillars with rectangular sections and sharp corners. By contrast, the stones in the Bluestone Circle display varied lithologies, shapes and sizes, and only three of them appear to be dressed.

This seems to echo concerns visible in the sarsen arrangement. The fine pillars of the Bluestone Horseshoe stand close to the inner, better finished faces of stones in the Sarsen Horseshoe, and some of the bluestones are themselves dressed more intensively on their inner sides. Again, such as it survives, the assembly of the Bluestone Circle reflects a feature of the Sarsen Circle. As we saw, the latter's most impressive arc is on the northeast side, framing the solstice axis, and it is here that are found the larger Bluestone Circle stones: although undressed, the two either side of the axis (Stones 31 and 49) are separated by a wider than usual gap, and are today the largest standing in the circle.

There seems no reason to doubt that this arrangement was deliberate. That's not the end of the story, however, for hiding in the present bluestone structures is another, older one.

The three carved stones in the outer circle are dolerite, like all those in the inner horseshoe. That might be just a curiosity, but one looks like a horseshoe pillar (Stone 45), and two of them are lintels (36, 150), with pairs of mortise holes now redundant on what would have been their vertical faces (both are now fallen, see pl. xx). The first of the lintels is among the finest examples of dressed stone at the site, a superbly finished block that, unlike sarsen lintels, is higher than it is wide and tapers towards the top with gently swelling faces.[31]

These unexpected oddities imply the existence of bluestone uprights with tenons on top, and that is indeed the case – or was. Four of the horseshoe stones (numbers 67, 69, 70 and 72) have subtle indications that they once had tenons that have been removed. Two other stones, now a little distance apart, seem to have been carved to fit into each other, with a tongue (Stone 66) and a groove (Stone 68, the better preserved of the pair and 'exceedingly finely pick-dressed' all over) the length of one side.

What does this mean? At the very least – and it's not impossible that this was in fact the total of such features – we have three formerly paired uprights, two of them supporting lintels and one consisting of two stones jointed to effect a wider slab; the three stones now standing reach around 2.5 m (8 ft) high. Which begs the question, where were they before?

Sadly, fitting these carved bluestones to their original holes in the ground is for us a hopeless task. No pits are known separated by the right gaps for uprights to hold the two lintels, whose

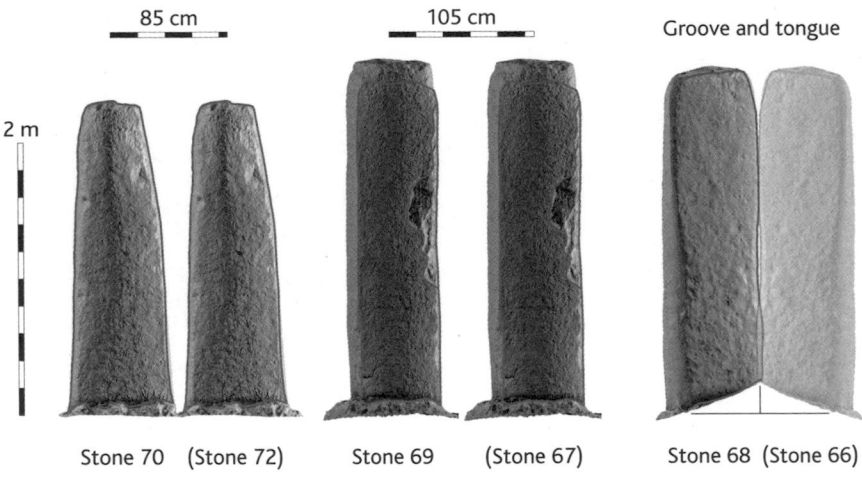

85 cm   105 cm   Groove and tongue

2 m

Stone 70   (Stone 72)   Stone 69   (Stone 67)   Stone 68 (Stone 66)

Eight bluestones at Stonehenge have redundant carved joints. Four had tenons on top (mostly removed). Stone 68 has a groove the length of one side, Stone 66 (broken) has an apparently matching ridge. They are shown here as three hypothetical upright pairs (Stones 72 and 67 are broken), two spaced to fit mortise holes of two former lintels (now mostly underground and not fully recorded). Stone 68 is leaning, and has been straightened. All spotted dolerite.

mortises are 85 and 105 cm (2 ft 9 in. and 3 ft 5 in.) apart. That is too small to bridge the paired stones in the Q and R Holes or the stones in the circle at West Amesbury, all of which were typically around 1.5 m (5 ft) centre to centre. They might have been carved for the Bluestone Oval, though what we know of that area makes it unlikely. One possibility, suggested by Mike Parker Pearson and Colin Richards, is that all the carved dolerite stones at Stonehenge had once been in the West Amesbury circle. If that was the case, perhaps these three groups stood in the centre, or perhaps they formed a kind of gateway feature on the southwest, river side of the ring, which has not been excavated.

So the possibility is raised that the concept of a stone trilithon, or at least of stone carving, was originally created somewhere other than Stonehenge, over the hill down by the Avon, or even in Pembrokeshire, with a rock type more amenable to fine dressing than sarsen. I noted earlier that one face of a capstone on a Welsh dolmen appears to have been hammered smooth a good millennium before the carved Stonehenge was built. Garn Turne, where that happened, is 15 km (10 miles) southwest of the dolerite quarry at Carn Goedog. The idea of shaping megaliths could have begun in an area rich with igneous rocks (some of which were used to make axe blades), first from a desire to flatten surfaces then developing into a more three-dimensional approach to boulders which were already megalith like. That mentality could then have been carried east with bluestones, and ultimately transferred to sarsen, at the same time as a local tradition emerged of building large with timber-inspired stone jointing.

Thinking back to Bluehenge, you might notice a curious thing. The arrangement of bluestones inside Stonehenge, the circle within the Sarsen Circle and the northeast-facing horseshoe within the Sarsen Horseshoe, mirrors the earlier structures – the Aubrey circle, and the U-shape in the centre, then facing northwest. There is a strong sense that the highly engineered, brutal and overwhelming sarsens are there to honour and protect the old bluestones (the

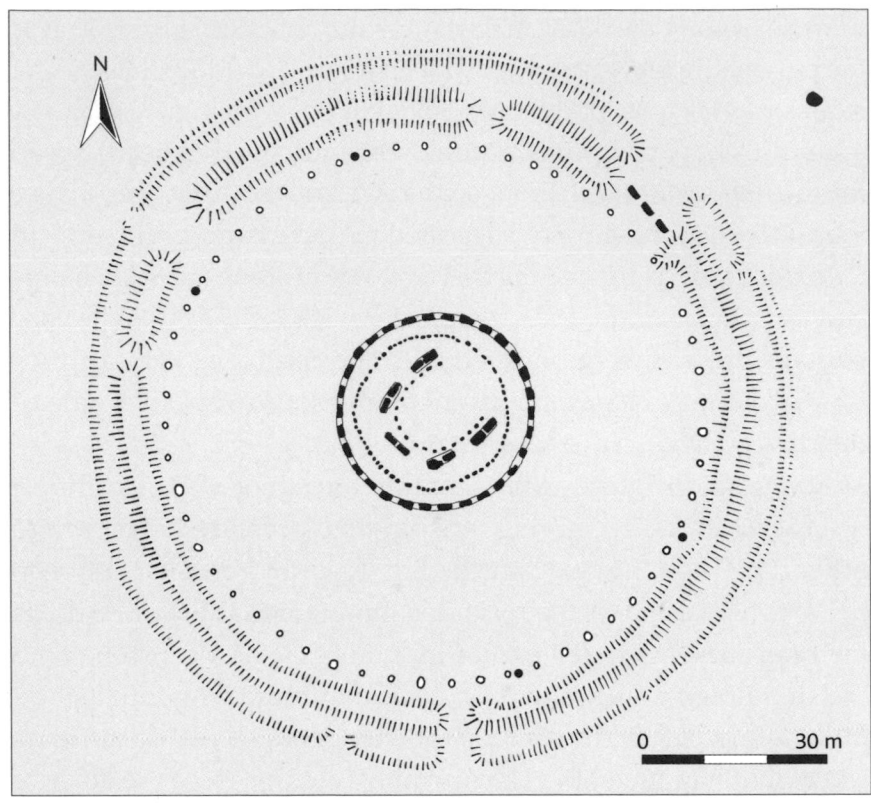

Stonehenge complete: the Sarsen Horseshoe and Sarsen Circle surround similar arrangements of bluestones.

taller of which, in the half light of dusk, can feel uncannily like giant hooded human figures) and their associated burials and memories. In the process, the whole has been yoked to the sun, rising at midsummer through the widened gap in the Sarsen Circle and over the distant Heelstone to the northeast, and apparently more importantly, setting through the Great Trilithon at midwinter to the southwest (might even the pink and orange sarsens have embodied the sun, and the inner bluestones – pale sparks in the fresh blue dolerite looking like stars in a night sky – the moon?). Something was happening. It wasn't local, but drew people from across at least southern England and Wales. It was new – the sheer scale, the engineering, the sun – and it looked back. It was urgent.

It is done.

There would have been a huge tidying up operation – perhaps larger construction timbers, with all their associations, themselves became part of arrangements like the post rings at Woodhenge. Workers needed to return home. Communities had to get back together, to address interrupted lives. At Stonehenge new rituals and stories needed to be conjured and rehearsed. But as rain washed the stones clean, turf regrew and seasons passed, the great megalithic mass rose arrogantly against the sky, as if framing the memory of its creation for eternity.

For a moment, surely, they thought it was all over.

But it wasn't then. It isn't now.

CHAPTER 7

AFTERLIFE

It would be over 4,000 years before anything was seen at Stonehenge to match what happened when it was built. When that came, in 1958, the raising of five sarsen stones – the trilithon that included Stone 58 and two other stones in the circle – naturally drew much attention. A quarter of the monument was fenced off, and became submerged beneath mobile cranes, trailers and scaffolding, huts for offices, stores and 'dormitory and ablutions', and a diesel-powered electricity generator. Despite the intrusions, thanks to a BBC film about Stonehenge in 1954, a book by Richard Atkinson in 1956 and media coverage of the engineering itself – a special viewing platform was provided for press photographers – there were many more visitors that year than usual.

When the Ministry of Works announced the project in February, Sir Mortimer Wheeler (1890–1976), a leading archaeologist and a public figure (he'd been on the cover of *TV Mirror* in 1954 as personality of the year), reflected on events in *The Times* of London. There was no fence when he first saw the stones, he wrote, and no car park: just towering sarsens 'in a drear and gusty scene'. Times had changed.[1]

Sir Mortimer could see 'angry readers groping for their pens' at the mention of the word 'restoration', but, he pleaded, they should desist. The only stones that were to be re-erected had fallen relatively recently in Stonehenge-time (the trilithon in January 1797, and the other two in December 1900); the monument would otherwise be left untouched. This had been much discussed, with the conclusion that Stonehenge should remain more or less as it looked when the first proper depictions were made in the late 17th century. Recent excavations added support to the policy, explained Wheeler, by suggesting that 'a single and deliberate act' accounted for most of the missing and fallen stones, probably perpetrated by the conquering Roman army 'during their ferocious campaign against Druidism'. The destruction was part of the Stonehenge story, and worth preserving.

Not everyone agreed, of course, and many reached for their pens. 'Stonehenge', proposed one reader, 'is a symbol of British independence. That some stones were thrown down by a foreign invader is the more reason for putting them back.' The use of concrete would turn the monument into a fake, wrote another. Hugh Molson (1903–91), the minister responsible for Stonehenge, commented that he was long used to be being told what to do, and he'd make up his own mind after taking expert advice. And then *The Times* published a letter from Richard Atkinson.

The idea that the Romans had destroyed Stonehenge, he said, was his. But Mortimer Wheeler and the Ministry had over-egged it. The evidence was circumstantial, and it was quite possible that stones had simply fallen over and decayed naturally. But even if

Stones 57 and 58 on the ground in 1956, with their broken lintel on the right. Both uprights have shaped pointed bases, to the left.

Raising Stone 58 with a steel cradle in 1958. The base of the stone is to the left, and when raised into the air the cradle was pivoted to bring the stone into an upright position.

Raising the repaired lintel for Stones 57 and 58 into position in 1958.

there had been intentional damage, the only reason for associating it with Romans was a scatter of their pottery. Other potential culprits were available.

There was a moment when I wondered if Richard was in fact right about the Romans. In 1999 I found a long-lost human skeleton that had been excavated at Stonehenge over 70 years before – we all thought it had been destroyed in the London Blitz, until I tracked it down to a bomb-proof basement in the Natural History Museum. We'd assumed it was probably Neolithic, but when we were able to see the bones we found the man had been beheaded with a sword. Could he have been a Druid, murdered as an example to native insurrectionists? In only a few months, however, radiocarbon dating disproved the notion: he was Anglo-Saxon, probably executed and buried for a forgotten crime.[2]

Nonetheless, all of this makes an important point about what happened to Stonehenge after the building stopped. Up to that moment, we have a pretty good idea of what was going on with the structures. Arguments will continue about which parts were raised when, and there will always be gaps in our understanding, but we can set out a broad narrative, as I have done, with reasonable confidence. Afterwards, however, we struggle. Until very recently, few archaeologists had taken much interest in Stonehenge's afterlife; what information there is has not been well recorded, and still less sought. I'd like to continue by explaining what happened when and why, but instead, I will offer a series of snapshots. It is a tale of loss: far too many stones are missing to be explained by simple deterioration. We know more about recent changes, so I will start in the present and work backwards, eliminating events as we go until we are left with what might have happened in prehistoric times.

You may be surprised at the scale of damage, removal and restoration. The Ministry of Works claimed to reinstate a few megaliths to a timeless monument, and probably believed that that was what it was doing. The grass was cut to look more like a carpet than a living thing, and discreet signs cautioned visitors not to write their names on the stones, which had 'stood here for over three thousand years'. Until very recently, there was brief mention of any modern works in the guidebooks. It was, however, all a conceit.

Indeed, it became easy to turn it into a conspiracy. In 2001, Brian Edwards, then a history student in Bristol, criticized English Heritage for hiding restorations from the public, failing to tell us that 'virtually every stone [had been] re-erected, straightened or embedded in concrete': 'It has been as if Stonehenge had been historically cleansed,' he said.[3] Soon a Russian website, backed by photos of the engineering works, claimed Stonehenge had actually been *built* in the 20th century.

The mistake – and it's one that many people still make – had been to picture Stonehenge as an ancient landscape, as if somehow walking in it is to experience the Neolithic world. It's not: it's a 21st-century place, with old things in it to be sure, but it's alive. The stone circle didn't die in 2000 BC: it continued endlessly to be and to change, to be puzzled over and re-imagined, to look different as stones fell or were pushed and as the use of surrounding land changed. Even when English Heritage (or its predecessors in government departments) saw the monument as a 17th-century fossil, the world around it moved on. Visitors brought new experiences; archaeological understanding grew; changing management led to wild flowers growing around the stones, and more lichens on them.

There is a story of 20th-century works that has yet to be fully told. The notion that almost every stone has been rearranged is, fortunately, an exaggeration – only around half of them were moved.[4] That is still a lot of messing about, and when we look at a plan we can see that it's mostly fallen or small stones that have not been touched. We will start our journey backwards in time not from 1958, but from 1964, when another stone in the Sarsen Circle was raised and set in concrete. It had fallen only the year before. The public reason given for the collapse of Stone 23 was that this

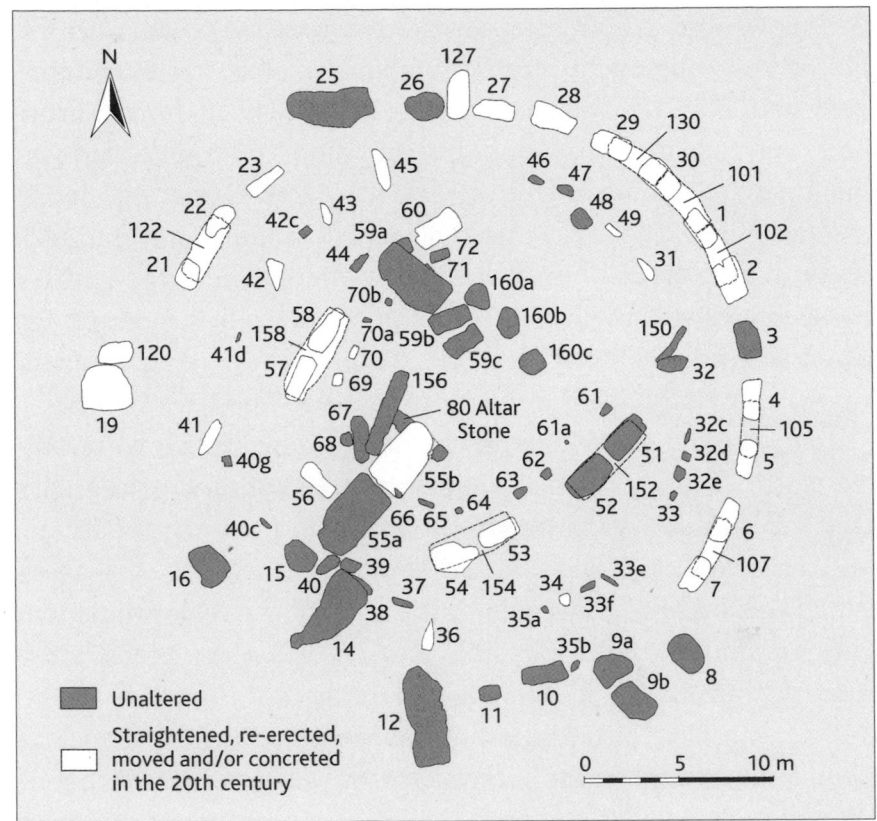

N

127
25 26 27 28
29 130
23 45 46 47 30 101
22 43 48 1
122 42c 60 49
21 42 59a 72 31 102
44 71 2
70b 160a
58 70a 59b 160b 150 3
120 158 70 59c 160c 32
41d 57 69 156
19 41 67 80 Altar 61 4
68 Stone 61a 32c 105
40g 62 51 32d 5
56 55b 63 152 32e
40c 66 65 64 52 33 6
55a 53 107
16 15 39 37 54 154 34 33e 7
40 33f
38 35a
14 36 35b 9a
10 9b 8
12 11

Unaltered

Straightened, re-erected,
moved and/or concreted
in the 20th century

0   5   10 m

Provisional plan of stones at Stonehenge moved since 1901.

16-ton sarsen blew over. The more complete story was that it had been hit five years before when Stone 22, weighing 18 tons, swung out of control as it was being moved by a crane. With all the kit and men assembled in 1964 to re-erect Stone 23, it seemed sensible to the Ministry to continue elsewhere, and Stones 27 and 28 were straightened and concreted, fallen lintel 127 was lifted out of the way so archaeologists could have a look before it was put back, and concrete was poured into the foundations of the trilithon stones 53 and 54. It may be at this time that Stone 34, a stump of a bluestone that had as much chance of falling over as a parked car, was pulled up and put back into a bed of cement – with no archaeological investigation.[5]

This was the culmination of the project that began with the idea of restoring the five recently fallen sarsens in 1958, and that grew until more than two dozen megaliths had been moved. There had been calls for such rebuilding and more for many years – in one case as a tribute to Queen Victoria on her Golden Jubilee in 1887, and there'd been the first of several doomed attempts to seek re-erection of the trilithon immediately after it fell in 1797 – but all had been resisted by the site's then private owners. Under public ownership and state supervision, Stonehenge was dug over and ripped apart, and tidied up as if nothing had happened.

In 1999 an international row erupted over the British Museum's treatment of the Parthenon sculptures in its collection: unauthorized cleaning of the marbles in the late 1930s with copper chisels and carborundum, it was said, had brutally damaged their surfaces. When this had been revealed at the time of the restoration, two curators and all the responsible workmen lost their jobs. More recently the museum has apologized for the works and a cover-up, and non-invasive surface analysis has identified surviving ancient paint and toolmarks – the harm was less severe than some claimed. What happened at Stonehenge in the 1950s and 1960s was worse. Apart from physical damage to stones from rough handling and accidents, the irreversible destruction of unique archaeological deposits in the ground around them, essential to understanding the monument's story, is even now difficult to credit.

It may be that some of the stones attended to in the 20th century would otherwise have tumbled, but we'll never know. All that is certain is that Stone 23 was, effectively, knocked down. There was an earlier restoration programme, however, that undoubtedly did prevent the collapse of some of Stonehenge's most prominent megaliths. Soon after Sir Cecil Chubb (1876–1934) had given Stonehenge to the nation in 1918, having bought it at auction only three years before, the Office of Works – predecessor of the Ministry of Works, which took over in 1940 – conducted a thorough structural survey. It was decided to 'repair' those parts in danger of falling, while avoiding anything cosmetic, and work began late in 1919. By then decades of argument about restoration had borne no fruit beyond the raising to vertical in 1901 of the Great Trilithon's Stone 56, which had been leaning inwards as long as anyone had been recording the monument. There was also a bit of carpentry, designed to stop visitors being struck by falling stones. A timber gallows (as it was referred to by objectors, though they might equally have called it a trilithon, for such it resembled) had been erected in 1881 under the lintel spanning Stones 6 and 7. It was gone by 1902, when long larch poles were placed against the same pair of uprights, and also to prop up Stones 29, 30, 1 and 2. They feature prominently in photos and postcards of the time.

There seems little doubt that these poles had a job to do, and it was this group of leaning stones – 29, 30, 1, 2, 6 and 7 – which the Office of Works set to making safe, winching them out of the ground and placing them back straight and in concrete. It was the excuse archaeologists needed to excavate, and once William Hawley had attended to remains put at risk by the engineering, he

Early in the 20th century timbers supported up to six stones and their lintels in the Sarsen Circle thought to be in danger of falling. Stones 2 and 3, third and second from the left, have been chained together (photo taken 1919).

Sarsen lintel 101 being repositioned in 1920, when Stones 1 and 30, behind, with six other uprights and three other lintels, were straightened and set in concrete.

expanded his work, overseen by the Society of Antiquaries, and over the next few years dug through half the site. What interests me now, however, is the falling stones. If we include those 'saved' by the Office of Works, nine sarsen uprights and six lintels fell or probably would have done between 1797 and, say, 1950: fifteen stones over a century and a half (if they had all fallen at this rate from the start, the monument would have gone by 1500 BC). Without intervention, Stonehenge today would look very different, with as few as two lintels in place – none in the circle – and little but a pile of rocks to help us visualize how it had once been. An engineering win. Shame about the archaeology.

Moving back a century or so, there is another tale of alterations to the monument whose fuller telling has become possible only thanks to the laser survey. Anecdotes about damage to the stones had been common, especially since visitors started to arrive at Stonehenge in significant numbers after the creation of the first nearby maintained roads in the 18th century. None of us knew, however, how much of it had actually gone on.

There was plenty of talk.[6] Seventeenth-century travellers recorded stories of local people healing wounds with 'scrapings' from the stones, and pieces dropped or built into wells were said to keep the water pure. John Aubrey claimed that a large stone had been taken to Amesbury for a bridge. In the 1720s William Stukeley objected to visitors 'breaking pieces off with great hammers'. An anonymous letter-writer to *The Times* related how, in 1871, their solitude was disturbed by 'a constant chipping of stone', and there were said to be hammers for hire in Amesbury for the purpose. Others justified taking something home for the purposes of scientific inquiry. Nevil Maskelyne (1823–1911), who published the first, pioneering geological study of Stonehenge in 1878, could speak 'only with indignation and contempt' of anyone knocking off fragments 'in a mere spirit of relic-hunting': but his own 'little flakes... will be found to have served to add something, I trust, to the more intelligent kind of interest shown in Stonehenge'.

On the other hand, it was common for complaints about visitors, typically delivered by more privileged men, to turn out, on examination, to be exaggerated. In 1756 one Benjamin Martin fretted that 45 minutes of hard labour with a hammer gave him 'but one Ounce and half' of stone. A century before, the diarist John Evelyn (1620–1706) had fared even worse, finding the stones 'so exceeding hard, that all my strength with a hammer, could not breake a fragment', and in 1876 'Druid' (as they signed themselves in *The Times*) overheard 'a party of ladies and two gentlemen (?)' bemoan the ineffectiveness of their carpenter's hammer. When a Victorian shepherd sold what he described as chips off the megaliths to unfortunate visitors who'd arrived without their own hammers, the defence that he'd actually found the fragments out in the fields and that his crime was fabulation not vandalism, was probably valid.

Sir Edmund Antrobus, 3rd Baronet (1818–1899), the site's owner in 1871, defended the public 'for the very little damage done' (though somewhat spoiling his point, in his letter to *The Times*, by claiming that the only recent signs of vandalism were on the corners of two fallen stones, broken by 'an individual of the mechanic class [who] brought a large sledgehammer'). The oft-repeated (including by me) story about hired hammers, however, is now thought to be a rural myth, and John Aubrey's bridge stone has yet to be found.

There was known to be graffiti, too (see pl. XXVI). There was an elaborate inscription that looked tantalizingly like the signature of Lucas de Heere (1534–84), a Flemish refugee and artist of the first good view of Stonehenge, but almost certainly wasn't. And there was an 'I WREN' which might or might not have been the mark of Sir Christopher Wren (1632–1723), the great architect who was born not far from Stonehenge (as it happens, near the Chilmark quarries). But none of this hammering and engraving had attracted much modern attention beyond curiosity. What we hadn't appreciated, was that it had radically affected the way Stonehenge looks to us today.

Analysing the laser survey, Marcus Abbott and Hugo Anderson-Whymark identified 44 prominent instances of graffiti – but these are 'the tip of the iceberg', and many hundreds more are there but hard to read. They found a John Louis de Ferre, whose name matches the abbreviated oldest, probably 17th-century inscription, but he was born in London in 1802 so, at best, must be a descendant rather than the culprit. There are eight dated carvings, ranging from 1721 to 1866, the latter a carefully chiselled H. Bridger of Chi Sux, presumably Chichester in Sussex, where the name was common, and conceivably representing a Harriett Bridger, who was buried in the city in 1873 aged 24. The date range neatly encompasses most of the era of complaints: clearly there was something to write home about. Though the graffiti are superficially troubling, however, it was the souvenir collectors who really made their mark.

With various forms of Neolithic stone dressing identified, Marcus and Hugo were able to do something that had been impossible before: distinguish work that was *not* prehistoric. One stone offered a unique insight: 158, the lintel supported by Stones 57 and 58. Two other lintels in the Trilithon Horseshoe display fine working: 154, the only sarsen at Stonehenge that can match the dressed perfection of Stone 56, with sharp angles between sides and top and bottom and fine, rounded vertical corners, and 152, a lintel with similar indications but only where the surfaces have survived deep weathering. Today 158 is unlike those two, its edges scarred and irregular, its form rounded and pitted. What might account for that difference?

William Stukeley drew the trilithon in the 1720s, showing a sharp angle between the lintel's base and sides. Lintels 152 and 154 have always remained out of reach to casual visitors, but between 1797, when Stones 57 and 58 fell, and 1958 when they were raised back into the air again, lintel 158 was on the ground and accessible to anyone with a hammer. The laser data showed that its edges and corners had been bashed away through the Neolithic surfaces. All that missing stone can only have been removed between January 1797 and May 1901, when the monument was permanently fenced and provided with a guardian. The transformation occurred within a century (see pl. xxv).

Marcus and Hugo found more than 50 areas of such hammering on 40 stones or stone fragments. Almost all the sarsen damage was to fallen stones ('convenient seat[s] while one hammered', they note laconically), and sometimes it was dramatic, where 'very little of the original faces survive. To the untrained eye, these stones are now little more than amorphous lumps.' Standing bluestones, on the other hand, had suffered chipping along their edges, effectively hiding the extent to which the pillars were originally finely and sharply dressed (see pl. xxvii). It may be we are seeing two effects: the legacy of casual curiosity and superstition, attracted more to the large megaliths on the ground where you could wield a sledge-hammer with apparent impunity, and of self-justifying geological inquiry directed at the mysterious foreign stones.

It was a waste. Much of the debris will have been discarded and now lies useless in the soil. Rob Ixer has tracked down a handful of old geological samples, not all of which can with total confidence be assigned to Stonehenge, let alone individual megaliths, and the sarsen souvenirs have vanished like sand in the desert. But that era of unrestrained tourism, that began slowly in the 16th century and reached a climax in the 19th, changed Stonehenge more than two millennia of weathering had done. It dulled the monument, blunting its sharp edges. Inigo Jones, the architect we met in Chapter 1, was criticized by some for imagining it, in 1725, as a regularly sculpted Roman building. There's no doubt that the stones had their distinctive characters from the first, with bulging irregularities and varying thicknesses. But it would have been in the corners and angles that carving was most manifest, and these were the areas easiest to knock off. If you have the opportunity to look closely at the stones, you will notice that as they disappear beneath the turf their corners are often crisper and better finished there than anywhere else. Jones's angular vision may not have been as much a complete fantasy as we have all assumed.

We're not finished yet. John Wood, the other prominent early modern architect drawn to Stonehenge, conducted the first detailed survey of the stones, still one of the best. Remarkably, though done in 1740, it is almost identical to a modern plan. The major difference is with Stone 14, one of those lesser sarsens on the southwest of the circle, which Wood shows standing. Another plan drawn 30 years later, which in most respects looks as if it is traced off Wood's, shows the stone fallen inwards, and you can follow its gradual decline through later depictions, until it is all but flat in the first photos.[7] But it's still there, as are all the other stones. Tourists took chips home with them it seems, but none carted off entire megaliths.

Which begs the question, who did? Today you can see a total of 84 megaliths at Stonehenge (some are in two or three pieces, amounting to 91 separate blocks in all). Our best calculation, however, is that there were almost exactly twice that number of

An edge on Stone 69, a spotted dolerite pillar in the Bluestone Horseshoe (BU1), shows damage from hammering except close to the ground, where the original sharp angle is preserved.

megaliths in the original monument – something between 163 and 173. The missing half, which includes two Station Stones and a large number of bluestones, must have gone walkabout before 1740. What happened to it?

There is, in fact, some evidence for large chunks of stone having been taken away. I earlier mentioned the Boles stone, a lump of spotted dolerite weighing more than half a ton and now in The Salisbury Museum; recent study has shown it to have been pared with metal tools, and it was almost certainly taken from Stonehenge.[8] We don't know when that happened, but we do know that around 1865 a 25-kg (55-lb) mass was broken off Stone 38, a dacite megalith in the Bluestone Circle, 'apparently by means of a sledge hammer'. The laser survey revealed that the strange sarsen Stone 11, standing but only half the height it should be, at some time had its upper part removed. And the angular foot of the Slaughter Stone is crossed by a line of six small rectangular pits, as if perforated with a view to tearing off a piece. The weathered holes were chiselled out with steel tools for wedges to hammer and split the rock, and someone had clearly planned to take home a souvenir of more than usual size but for some reason abandoned the attempt.

How representative these incidents are is hard to know, but we might think, in view of the extensive evidence for graffiti and lesser damages in the laser survey, that such determined destruction was in fact not uncommon in recent centuries. The brutality of the practice was vividly brought home to me in 2008.

That summer Tim Darvill and Geoff Wainwright excavated among the stones. They hoped to find a previously undisturbed Q or R Hole.[9] It was 'quite easily the most complex little trench that

Tim Darvill (far left), archaeology professor at Bournemouth University, with Geoff Wainwright excavating at Stonehenge in 2008. In the ground to Wainwright's left is the stump of Stone 35a; the small stone beside the buckets on the far left is Stone 35b, thought to be part of the same megalith (BU1).

I have ever worked in', commented Geoff (though as director of excavations at Durrington Walls in the 1960s, for long the largest in the area, he might have said it was almost the *only* little trench he had dug). Its complexity was due to what they deemed to be disturbances in the ground that were Roman in age, or more recent, and which had made finding their target much harder than they had anticipated. The earth was full of small pieces apparently broken off bluestone and sarsen megaliths, and they found two small iron wedges, which might have been used for such a purpose. Near one corner of the trench was Stone 35a, a stub worn smooth by generations of feet that is normally just visible when the grass is newly cut. Now it was revealed in its greater glory below ground.

It was a shocking sight (see pl. xxvIII). At one time it must have been an impressive component of the Bluestone Circle, around 1 m (3 ft) wide with a height that can only be guessed. Now it was a fissured apology, the stump that its attackers abandoned after taking the greater part. The smooth brown side of the quarried stone contrasted with the rippled dark blue of freshly broken rock, spattered with white crystals like snowflakes against a night sky, that presented a jagged surface across the thickness of the former megalith. This had not been taken apart with wedges, but savaged with heavy hammers. A small tap now, it seemed, and it might shatter into bits.

When was this done? Why? The largest ancient pit that Tim and Geoff found had a Roman coin and pottery in it, along with a collection of animal bones that reads most un-prehistoric (including horse, hare and rabbit). When all the records of 20th-century Stonehenge excavations were analysed, a scatter of Roman debris was identified – nearly 2,000 small and abraded pottery sherds, 20 coins spanning the full range of 4 centuries of occupation, and 3 bronze brooches.[10] While that is insufficient to indicate that Roman people built anything or lived close by, it's enough to suggest the sort of interest that in the 19th century bequeathed glass bottles, picnic scraps and horse droppings. Did that concern embrace destruction?

Was Richard Atkinson's initial hunch right? Perhaps Stone 35a was smashed up and taken down into the valleys for a Roman building, though to date no such stone has been found in excavations. One wonders, though, if that were the case, why the great stump was left – and why, if appearances are correct, it was taken out and put back? Perhaps, as Tim and Geoff thought, there really was something 'ritual or ceremonial' going on in Roman times?

There is another possibility that takes us yet further back into the past. Stonehenge could first have been despoiled not long after the last megalith was put in place.

As with this whole saga, proof is elusive. There's a suggestion that Stones 8 and 9, sarsens in the circle, fell within four centuries of their erection. The standing monument is surrounded by rings of filled pits; two of these circuits have been partly excavated and are known as Y and Z Holes. The rings seem to divert around the two sarsens. These mysterious pits need more study, but what evidence we have suggests they were dug between around 1900 and 1800 BC, implying the two stones fell – or were pushed – before then.

Could the stone debris we excavated in 1980, noted in Chapter 2, derive not from shaping megaliths as I'd originally proposed, but, as I suggested more recently, from breaking them up?[11] The single, admittedly technically poor, radiocarbon date (2200–1300 BC) is too recent for construction, but is compatible with some very small Beaker-style pottery sherds we found with the rubble. We now know from ancient DNA (aDNA) studies that that distinctive pottery, along with much else new in the way of lifestyle, religion and economy, first appeared in Britain at a time of substantial immigration and population change that began around 2400 BC.[12]

By the time the Stonehenge we would recognize today was built, people had been living continuously in Britain for 9,000 years. For most of that huge span they had done so as hunter-gatherers. As the climate warmed after the Ice Age, they experienced dramatic changes to their world, grassland becoming forest and large areas disappearing under rising seas, which after 3,500 years – around

6000 BC – definitively separated Britain from the rest of the continent. It was people, however, who brought it all to an end.

From 4000 BC continental farmers got into their boats and crossed the North Sea and the Channel to make new lives, bringing with them a new culture. They explored the unfamiliar landscapes with different eyes, looking for soils to grow crops, browse for cattle, pigs and goats, and timber for large, carpentered houses. They dug mines and climbed mountains in search of stone for tools, and sought out clays for pots, all made with alien technologies. Strange too were their beliefs, reflected in great burial mounds and other monuments not seen in any form until then. We know they looked different (aDNA shows the hunter-gatherers were dark skinned, the farmers lighter), they must have spoken different languages, and aDNA confirms that all these changes were driven by immigration. Archaeological evidence seems to show the old way of life coming to a sudden end.

If Stonehenge was built within a generation either side of 2500 BC (see Chapter 6 and Appendix), it was created by descendants of these aboriginal farmers, who bore only a small amount of the hunter-gatherers' genome. Yet they too encountered transformative migrants. Again, new continental people with different beliefs and technologies, and this time the first metallurgy skills, almost immediately came to dominate their world as it is now visible to us from excavations – Beaker pottery being one of the signs.

The people responsible for Stonehenge made pottery that we call Grooved Ware. There is very little Grooved Ware from Stonehenge itself: given the large quantities at contemporary Durrington Walls, this must reflect what was happening among the stones – and what was not acceptable. By contrast, Tim Darvill and Geoff Wainwright found a lot of Beaker pottery in their Stonehenge trench, and around 1 kg (2 lb) of sherds survives from earlier excavations.[13] The new migrants were there. Could they have broken up bluestones? The latest aDNA research, backed by data from burials around Stonehenge, suggests a better way of phrasing the question: could bluestones have been destroyed at a time of change – which the aDNA suggests spanned some four centuries – when migrants and their descendants were living side by side with a continuing indigenous Neolithic population?[14]

Certainly megaliths were smashed in one incident, two or three days' walk from Stonehenge to the southwest. There, at Mount Pleasant in Dorset, is another great Neolithic henge complex, where, in 1970, I first met Geoff Wainwright. I was studying A-level archaeology at school, and I was among the volunteers on another of his large excavations. We found the remains of sarsen stones that had been raised within large, concentric rings of oak posts, around the time Stonehenge was built. The stones had later been broken up and were mostly in burnt fragments, in a ditch around the former structure, with only chips and a single jagged stump remaining in the original pits.

That was not in fact how Geoff saw it: he thought the debris derived from the stones' shaping. However, apart from leaving the broken stump unexplained, this missed the fact that the fragments were mixed with heaps of charcoal and Beaker pottery, not the Grooved Ware found elsewhere on the site and assumed to have been made by the people who originally raised the uprights (among the debris were a few sarsen hammerstones, surely used to break up megaliths and suggesting that some of the hammers at Stonehenge might too have been so used). It seemed to me that Beaker users had smashed the monument, and I linked that event to a once unfashionable idea of population change.[15] We now have aDNA data to support the latter, and also a new dating project to confirm that the megaliths at Mount Pleasant were broken up at the very time that the first Beaker migrations had reached Wessex, around 2300 BC.[16]

Interestingly, this date is similar to that given by the skeleton of a man buried at Stonehenge, a unique occurrence (by then, burying people wasn't part of the monument's story): locally born, he had died by being shot at from close range with arrows, tipped with the distinctive flint barbs made by people who also made Beakers.[17] Meanwhile, across the River Avon and 4.5 km (3 miles) to the southeast of Stonehenge, another man was buried with these distinctive arrows. But this time they were his proud possessions, rather than the cause of his death – along with a haul of treasures that make his grave one of the richest of its kind in Europe. We know him as the Amesbury Archer. Isotopes in his bones suggest he was born in central Europe, and his Beaker pots (an exceptional five) would have looked at home on the continent. Broken pottery of the same style lay with the smashed megaliths in Dorset. There are too many as yet unanswerable questions here, but the hint of interesting times in the world of Wessex henges is strong.

An important insight from the new radiocarbon dates for Mount Pleasant is that events that the old history suggested had occurred over some six centuries, emerge, under the glare of new high-precision dating and sophisticated statistics, to have played out in three or four generations – within a span of living memory. We've seen how modern analysis of elements of Stonehenge has moved that way too, from Richard Atkinson's more than a decade to drag sarsens to the site, for example, to, as proposed here, as little as six months.

At the same time radiocarbon dating has extended the duration of the Neolithic era as a whole. In my version of Stonehenge history (see Appendix), we see what Richard envisaged as five centuries has become over a millennium. There must have been occasions, perhaps covering generations, when little happened in the way of engineering: but who are we to say that at such times there weren't significant events or changes affecting lives and beliefs? As it is, we can identify four quite different archaeological periods when the Stonehenge site was active. In excavations across Britain, the Middle and Late Neolithic, the Copper Age and the Early Bronze Age each have a host of distinctive attributes, from styles of artefacts to traditions in technology, eating, housing and funerary rites. It seem likely that during these times Stonehenge would have carried different meanings and opportunities, even beyond those we can tentatively identify – such as the 'solar dance' I proposed in Chapter 5, suggesting that bluestones and early sarsens mapped alternative cosmologies in a symbolic joining of disparate peoples.

So the first seven centuries of activity – what I refer to as the Bluehenge era – had surely bequeathed a hallowed and much-storied site, when it was suddenly transformed with massive engineering that drew in thousands of people. Even then the distant new practices associated with Beaker users were changing continental Europe: they were late to cross to Britain. Was the sarsen Stonehenge an act of wasteful bombast by powers that felt threatened? Did Beaker users, when they eventually came, find an exhausted economy and a Stonehenge already beginning to fall down? Or did land-hungry immigrants encounter a competitive society with values which were a challenge that had to be confronted? Did the new settlers re-invent ancient monuments they came across, ascribing them to their own ancestors as they put down new roots (as later happened with Anglo-Saxon migrants investing in prehistoric burial mounds)? Or, again, did two communities change and eventually merge their ways and beliefs as they accommodated each other over generations? Might this have been when bluestones were first broken up?

Somebody did it. It's not just chips from geological hammers or a battered Stone 35a. The ground at Stonehenge is full of bluestone debris. About 1 km (0.6 miles) to the northwest, as we saw in Chapter 2, are more such fragments; finds include a flint hammer weighing about 1 kg (2.2 lb). These are traditionally ascribed to the shaping of megaliths for a missing stone circle, but fieldwork has failed to find the ring and we may instead be seeing more signs of breakage, perhaps, even, of Stonehenge megaliths. Many of these have disappeared, to the extent that our perception of the monument today is far off how it would have looked at its prime.

This was brought home to me when we built foamhenge for TV in 2005. I designed a full-scale Bluestone Circle based on the excavated evidence for stone pits, and the model-makers copied surviving stones to complete the set. The effect was quite unexpected: there were so many stones so close together, it was almost as if a circular wall had been raised around the trilithons and the Bluestone Horseshoe. On the one hand, removing fallen stones revealed a large and highly theatrical enclosed space in the centre. On the other, the Bluestone Circle wrapped around it like a physical and visual barrier, itself hidden behind by the larger Sarsen Circle.

Above ground at Stonehenge today there are 27 dolerite megaliths, and just 4 of other igneous rocks. Non-dolerite debris dominates excavated collections, however, and the great majority of those pieces find no matching stones. Richard Bevins and Rob Ixer reasonably argue that this supports the idea that the debris comes from broken up megaliths. But why were so many andesite and rhyolite stones destroyed, while dolerite ones mostly survive? An obvious explanation would be that dolerite is harder, though the state of 35a shows that at some point it could be smashed if the will was there. Whatever the reason, the result is striking. Today we see a substantially complete Bluestone Horseshoe, where all the stones were dolerite. The Bluestone Circle, however, is no longer a barrier: it's not even a circle, but a straggle of small and battered stones with many gaps. The effect of the destruction was to expose a once private place containing Stonehenge's most defining megaliths for all to see.

Stonehenge was unique in its scale and ambition, but there were circular monuments of various forms across Neolithic Britain. It's common for these to have attracted the interest, in later centuries, of people who used Beaker pottery, and often they changed things. What they seem to have been up to, however, was largely adaptation, not ruination, perhaps hand in hand with older local communities; religious and ritual sites important to earlier generations continued in use, but with altered structures, and, we may guess, ceremonies and meanings. Wrecking bluestones at Stonehenge might look to us like vandalism. Maybe to people at the time it was the opposite – an old monument became more accessible, and less exclusive. And if that was the case, it was but the start of a long journey of modification and re-invention, touched by awe.

We might individually bemoan change as we so often do in many areas of life. Few archaeologists today can be happy with the way the site was treated in the 20th century, even if we benefit from the new knowledge that came with the pact. It's a shame so many visitors took souvenirs that survive only in the voids left behind. But fraught conversations between past and future, mystery and understanding, and permanence and mutability, are what Stonehenge is for. As it did thousands of years ago, today the monument draws people together from afar in a common mission to reflect and be challenged, to strive to appreciate different cultures, to escape the present, to marvel at antiquity and to ponder the future. As long as science and archaeology continue, as Stonehenge gets older our understanding of the world in which it began will grow.

Those are some of the reasons why I think Stonehenge is a very special place. I hope you do too.

APPENDIX: A BRIEF HISTORY OF STONEHENGE

This story of the principal remains at Stonehenge unburdens the text of detail and makes for easier reference. The version I adopt in the book is given first below, followed by the current 'official' history, with brief explanations. I make a key division, between Bluehenge, a focus for cremation burial and so named because its truly distinctive features are Welsh bluestones (Chapter 5), and Stonehenge, the monument whose ruins we see today (Chapters 6, 7). Remains we can still identify, at least partly, are <u>underlined</u>.

BLUEHENGE

From 3200 BC (Middle Neolithic)

87 m (285 ft) wide circle of undressed bluestones standing
    in 56 Aubrey Holes.
110 m (360 ft) wide ring of pits.
<u>Sarsen Heelstone</u> (in its natural site?).
Cremation burial starts, ultimately of hundreds of people.

From 3000 BC (Late Neolithic)

Pit ring joined up to form continuous <u>ditch with bank on either
    side, and entrances at northeast and south.</u>
Aubrey bluestones moved into Q and R Holes.
<u>Station Stones and Heelstone (erected?).</u>
Cremation burial continues until...

STONEHENGE

From 2500 BC (Copper Age)

<u>Five sarsen trilithons and 30 m (98 ft) wide Sarsen Circle.</u>
<u>Heelstone, Slaughter Stone.</u>
Stones from West Amesbury ring brought to site, and with stones
    from Q and R Holes arranged into outer <u>Bluestone Circle</u> and
    inner Bluestone Oval.

Oval later rearranged to make <u>Bluestone Horseshoe</u>.
<u>Avenue</u> from Stonehenge to the River Avon.
<u>Durrington Walls</u> village, large circular timber structure and
*   henge around 2475 BC.*
The body of a man, killed by arrows, is buried in the Stonehenge
*   ditch near the northeast entrance around 2275 BC.*

From 2200 BC (Early Bronze Age)

Y and Z Holes, rings of pits around the <u>Sarsen Circle</u>.
<u>Dagger and axe blade carvings</u> on sarsen stones.
Collapse and breakage of stones begins.

Not only, in this story, was Stonehenge a busy and changing monument for at least a millennium, but also that long era crossed two UK-wide cultural boundaries, between the Middle and Late Neolithic (3000 BC) and the Late Neolithic and Copper Age (2500 BC). These ages are marked by different artefact styles (notably of flint arrowheads and pottery) and latterly the rare appearance of the first metals, copper and gold.

This greatly simplifies a large and complex set of data. It is often impossible to know exactly what stood in now empty pits, when they were dug, or when stones were erected; there are few or no useful radiocarbon dates for most of the arrangements. Except for the major sarsen structures (dated by just two samples at around 2550 BC), whose engineering implies a single plan and building event, we do not know the extent to which megalithic arrangements were designed and then briefly executed, or grew and changed over what could be generations. The key reasons for the differences between this history and the widely accepted version (which follows below) are:

From 3200 BC: Animal bones dated to around 3350–3150 BC are usually assumed to have been ancient relics buried in the ditch dug in 2950 BC. Here these are presumed to have been buried fresh in pits which were later combined in the continuous ditch.

From 3000 BC: 20th-century histories put the Q and R Holes before the sarsen structures, on evidence that one of them had been dug through when a pit for a sarsen stone was dug. This relationship has recently been rejected, but for unconvincing reasons.

From 2500 BC: We must assume all standing bluestones were removed before the Sarsen Circle and trilithons could be erected for logistical reasons. Stones formerly in the Q and R Holes and in the ring by the Avon were then re-erected in the centre, where now there is a dense muddle of empty pits below the ground. The Stage 3 'bluestone circle' (see below), a tentative suggestion based on five sockets on the west, is here expanded into a hypothetical, only partly discernible separate Oval with the addition of two sockets on the east found by Richard Atkinson and Stuart Piggott in 1964, and five on the northeast which Atkinson proposed as an arc, whose removal converted an Oval into the Horseshoe (as below).

Y and Z Holes (two pit rings which parched grass has recently revealed may be accompanied by at least one more) are on irregular arcs apparently set out around the standing Sarsen Circle. One pit is dated, but radiocarbon samples were obtained from complete antlers (not picks) that could have been buried long after the pits were dug: they might have been part of the Copper Age monument. Their function is unknown.

STANDARD HISTORY (Parker Pearson *et al.* 2020)

Stage 1 – between around 3000 and 2800 BC

Bluestones in Aubrey Holes.
Ring ditch.
Heelstone, Stone 97.
Curated animal remains at southern entrance.
Cremation burials.

Stage 2 – between around 2600 and 2400 BC

Sarsen Circle and sarsen trilithons.
Bluestones in Q and R Holes, some dressed.
Station Stones.
Slaughter Stone.

Stage 3 – between around 2300 and 2200 BC

West Amesbury ring to site, 10 m (33 ft) wide bluestone circle added.
Avenue.

Stage 4 – between around 2100 and 2000 BC

Bluestones rearranged into outer Circle and inner Oval.
Six stones later removed from Oval to make Horseshoe.

Stage 5 – around 1900 to 1500 BC

Y and Z Holes.

HOW TO SEE STONEHENGE

Stonehenge makes a good day out, and more if you have time. World Heritage Site designation covers 2,600 hectares (6,500 acres), some of which is private, but much of the landscape is in National Trust ownership and the stones themselves are owned by the state and managed by English Heritage. You can walk freely across much of the downland, for which the large-scale English Heritage Stonehenge and Avebury walking map is invaluable. For example, from the north you can cross from the slight earthworks at Durrington Walls and Woodhenge (where the sites of Neolithic timber posts are marked by concrete stumps), past the Cuckoo Stone, through groups of Bronze Age barrows (good picnic site), along part of the Cursus and up the Avenue to face the stone circle. Or from the south, the proposed route for bluestones moving up Lake Bottom, on private land, is a public bridleway which can be walked from the hamlet of Lake, diverting up Normanton Down and leading to one of the best views of Stonehenge from a ridge with important Bronze Age barrows. Footpath signs direct you from Amesbury to the east, a walk that offers less often seen views of the World Heritage Site, mostly from beside a dual carriageway road.

To get close to the stone circle – fenced in since 1901 – you need to pass through the English Heritage visitor centre 2.4 km (1.5 miles) west of the stones (the official guidebook by Julian Richards is excellent), and advance booking is advised. For the Woodhenge and Amesbury walks you can obtain tickets first at the centre (where there are exhibitions, toilets, a café and a shop), or continue walking to collect them before returning to the stones. The route to the stones from the Lake walk is blocked by the A303 road, which has no safe crossing points; you have to return whence you came or look for alternative rights of way within the southern half of the World Heritage Site. You can also walk among the stones, for one of the world's great heritage experiences, as one of up to 30 people outside opening hours in early morning or late afternoon. Book well ahead with English Heritage (look for 'Stone Circle Experience').

For help with visiting, see English Heritage (www.english-heritage.org.uk/visit/places/stonehenge/plan-your-visit) for museum and monument, and the National Trust (www.nationaltrust.org.uk/stonehenge-landscape) for surrounding countryside. The Salisbury Museum and the Wiltshire Museum in Devizes hold important Stonehenge collections, and have displays about the stones and surrounding archaeological sites.

NOTES

PREFACE

1 A high sum, perhaps, compared to the real thing which last sold for £6,600, but that did not include 87 hectares of cattle ranch and 'a stunning award winning home'.

2 Stone 1924. There are many articles and pamphlets on the topic, mostly not by archaeologists. Among the few texts that are, the best are Richards & Whitby 1997 and, perceptively written by one who saw parts of megaliths during reconstruction work hidden to the rest of us, Chapter 4 in Atkinson 1979 (a slightly updated edition of a book first published in 1956, halfway through its author's excavation of 40 trenches at and around Stonehenge). A more recent contender is *Stonehenge: A Novel of 2000 BC*, in which Bernard Cornwell describes moving, carving and raising the stones in vivid detail. Since it was published in 1999, however, almost everything we then understood about the archaeology of Stonehenge has been revised or over-turned.

CHAPTER 1

1 In that part of the landscape, little has changed since Naipaul wrote his book in the 1980s.

2 Everything I describe in what follows can be seen by any visitor, but not necessarily on one visit; some planning is required. See the 'How to see Stonehenge' section opposite.

3 See Stukeley 1740, and Burl & Mortimer 2005.

4 Everything has its number: Altar Stone (80), Station Stones (91–94, clockwise from west), Slaughter Stone (95) and Heelstone (96). Petrie's scheme, working clockwise from the northeast, allocated 1–30 (uprights) and 101–130 (lintels) to the Sarsen Circle, in this case taking into account presumed missing stones; 31–49 to the Bluestone Circle; 51–60 (uprights) and 152–160 (lintels, evenly numbered) to the trilithons; and 61–72 to the Bluestone Horseshoe. More than one stone assumed to be broken parts of the same megalith are distinguished by a letter (e.g. 9a/b). Since this scheme was drawn up, several broken stumps have been discovered underground. These are labelled by taking the nearest existing number and adding a letter, e.g. three stumps between Stones 32 and 33 are known as Stones 32c, 32d and 32e (32a and b are stone pits with no stone). Such discoveries were left in place and are now mostly buried.

5 Though this is Stonehenge's tallest megalith and was often

described by early observers as the tallest in the UK, there are three taller, all in Yorkshire. A lone giant in the churchyard at Rudston rises nearly 8 m (26 ft) above the ground, and two of three stones in a row near Boroughbridge (the Devil's Arrows) are said to be 6.8 and 6.7 m (22 ft 4 in. and 22 ft) high; the third is a paltry 5.5 m (18 ft). These pale beside two in Brittany: the tallest standing megalith, the Menhir de Champ-Dolent, which is 9.75 m (32 ft) high, and the Grand Menhir Brisé, which fell and broke into four in antiquity, and would have towered an astonishing 20 m (65 ft).

CHAPTER 2

1   Some geological terms have changed over the past century; I use modern British equivalents throughout.

2   You can actually see 34 bluestones, but since Petrie's survey it has been assumed that 2 small boulders in the grass, numbered 35a and 35b, are parts of a single megalith. Excavation in 1959 showed that 71 and 72 also appear to be parts of one stone, making the visible *megalith* count 32. 'They think it an ominous thing to count the true Number of the Stones,' wrote Daniel Defoe touring Britain in the 1720s, 'and whoever do so, shall certainly die after it!', proclaiming there to be 140, thus breaking 'the magical Spell,

which has so long perplexed the Vulgar!' I would not be so confident.

3   Stone 1924.

4   Burl 2006, chapter 7.

5   Pitts 2001, 198–204. The Salisbury Museum has two blocks of spotted dolerite, the Boles stone and another, smaller piece, that we *know* was taken from Stonehenge over a century ago.

6   *The Stonehenge Bluestones*, by B. John (Newport: Greencroft Books, 2018).

7   As told to me by Richard Bevins. See R. Thorpe *et al.*, *Proceedings of the Prehistoric Society* 57 (1991), 103–57.

8   *Proceedings of the Prehistoric Society* 48 (1982), 75–132; Pitts 2001, 144ff.

9   See R. Ixer & R. E. Bevins in *British Archaeology* 138 (2014), 50–55, and for a more recent and technical summary with references to other studies, R. Ixer & R. E. Bevins, *Wiltshire Archaeological and Natural History Magazine* 114 (2021), 1–17.

10 The spots were originally crystals (known as phenocrysts) of feldspar, later altered by saussuritization, when hot fluids around 400°C flush through an igneous body. At this stage the plagioclase feldspar was replaced by a mass of very fine-grained crystals of secondary minerals. The dolerite was later affected by heat of around 250–300°C, which created further

secondary minerals in the background rock. R. Bevins *et al.*, *Journal of Archaeological Science: Reports* 36 (2021).

11 *Archaeological Journal* 104 (1947), 18. Marcus or Jack Stone co-directed excavations at Stonehenge until his untimely death. Sadly both he and Herbert Stone had died before I came on the scene, or the three of us might have written a memorably co-authored article about the place.

12 *A Tour in Quest of Genealogy, Through Several Parts of Wales, Somersetshire, and Wiltshire, in a Series of Letters to a Friend in Dublin,* by R. Fenton (London: Sherwood, Neely and Jones, 1811).

CHAPTER 3

1 Tim Daw, a Wiltshire farmer who once worked at Stonehenge, has said he grew up with people calling the stones 'Saracens', and his daughter pronounces both 'sarsen' and 'Saracen' as 'sarsen' (see www.sarsen.org).

2 *Diary of the Marches of the Royal Army during the Great Civil War; Kept by Richard Symonds,* ed. C. E. Long (London: The Camden Society, 1859), 151.

3 K. Whitaker, in *Mining and Quarrying in Neolithic Europe: A Social Perspective,* ed. A. Teather, P. Topping & J. Baczkowski (Oxford: Oxbow Books, 2019).

4 N. E. King, *Wiltshire Archaeological and Natural History Magazine* 63 (1968), 83–93.

5 In 1904 Ralph Vaughan Williams, an English composer, collected a classic folk song in Sussex which opens, 'As I walked over Salisbury Plain'. It ends with the singer's lover being hung for robbing a mail coach.

6 McOmish *et al.* 2002, 151–52.

7 Bowden *et al.* 2015, 40–41.

8 D. J. Nash *et al.*, *PLoS ONE* 16/8 (2021), e0254760.

9 D. J. Nash *et al.*, *Science Advances* 6 (2020).

10 Field *et al.* 2015, 129.

CHAPTER 4

1 Stone 1924, 101.

2 I saw the Ferriby boats in Humber museum as a student, in the form of a wondrous record created by Ted Wright and his brother: rolls of linoleum flooring on which they had outlined planks retrieved from the muds of the Humber estuary, the first one in 1937. The timbers went to the National Maritime Museum in London, where much was lost after they were first left outside in a harsh winter, and later their conservation tank was thrown out because of the smell. On the plus side, the lost property office retrieved Wright's records when they were left on a London Underground train.

3 'There are almost as many fragments of "Stonehenge bluestones" lying along the proposed transport route

between the Preseli Hills and Salisbury Plain', wrote Rob Ixer to *Current Archaeology* in 1997, 'as pieces of the True Cross.'

4 R. Adams, in *Megaliths Societies Landscapes*, ed. J. Müller, M. Hinz & M. Wunderlich (Bonn: Institut für Ur- und Frühgeschichte der CAU Kiel, 2019), 1113–32. Adams's 2007 doctoral thesis, referenced in this article, is a mine of information.

5 See Abbott & Anderson-Whymark 2012. Stone (1924) estimated, for example, that the average upright in the Sarsen Circle weighed 26 tons, a figure repeated up to today; here it is 20 (or 21 if the stubby Stone 11 is excluded). Average weights for parts of Stonehenge calculated by Harris (2019) are similar to mine (e.g. 20.4 tons for sarsens). A project is needed, in which sub-surface surveying would play a part, to definitively weigh Stonehenge.

6 Across 16 cases moving stones for 500 m (1,500 ft), the correlation between stone weights and person days works out at 0.7.

7 See https://youtu.be/ XrPmb3Fkhkc, with Indonesian commentary. I'm grateful to Ron Adams for translating for me; he suggests the presence of Tourist Board cameras would themselves have added to the event's prestige. You can avoid the animals by stopping at around 11 minutes.

8 A recent study concluded that cattle were not intensively used for traction in Britain until Roman times, though no bones older than 800 BC were examined: R. Thomas *et al.*, *International Journal of Paleopathology* 33 (2021), 84–93. At Arbon-Bleiche 3, Switzerland, a village that burnt down in 3370 BC, bone pathologies have been interpreted as indicating draught cattle, and a charred wooden object as a yoke: A. Grabundžija *et al.*, *Antiquity* 95 (2021), 627–47.

9 B. Harris, *Oxford Journal of Archaeology* 37 (2018), 267–81.

10 *Stonehenge Live*, Channel 5/ National Geographic.

11 *Building Stonehenge: A Radical New Theory*, by G. Pipes (Derby: Birchwood Publishers, 2009).

12 J. E. Garfitt, *Antiquity* 53 (1979), 190–94.

13 *Antiquity* 3 (1929), 324–38. William Gowland, an engineer who worked for the Japanese government and in 1901 excavated at Stonehenge, claimed that stones of 20 tons were carried in north India: *Archaeologia* 58 (1902), 74.

14 *Naga Path*, by U. G. V. Bower (London: John Murray, 1950).

15 The cord was not directly carbon dated, and no longer survives. A piece of wooden bucket, like the cord preserved in water at the bottom of the well, was dated to around 3400 BC – older than Stonehenge. Other bucket fragments gave dates 2,000 years younger, but though

archaeologists choose this younger age for well construction, there is no apparent scientific reason for rejecting the older date. The well is a remarkable find that deserves to be better known, and is less so partly because of the late excavator's determination to argue that it was a ritual shaft with no practical purpose. As well as ropes and buckets, finds included remains of grass cropped by grazing sheep, sheep dung and two aborted lambs. *Wilsford Shaft: Excavations 1960–2*, by P. Ashbee, M. Bell & E. Proudfoot (London: English Heritage, 1989).

CHAPTER 5

1 T. Darvill & G. Wainwright, *Antiquity* 88 (2014), 1099–114. R. Bevins, N. Pearce & R. Ixer, *Journal of Archaeological Science: Reports* 38 (2021).

2 C. Osenton, *Antiquity* 75 (2001), 293–98; Harris 2019.

3 *A Walk through Wales, in August 1797* (Bath: R. Crutwell, 1798).

4 G. J. Barclay & K. Brophy, *Archaeological Journal* 177 (2020). See also R. Madgwick *et al.*, *Archaeological Journal* 178 (2021).

5 J. H. Hutton, *Journal of the Royal Anthropological Institute of Great Britain and Ireland* 52 (1922), 242–49.

6 These pits with a stone at either end were unique, until in 2004 an excavation at Catterick in North Yorkshire uncovered the foundations of two concentric palisade rings, in which around 2400 BC paired timbers were set in similar elongated pits.

7 Parker Pearson *et al.* 2020, Chapter 5 (where the circle is named Bluestonehenge).

8 *Antiquity* 95 (2021), 85–103. This paper is more cautious than the film. The idea of a 'second-hand Stonehenge' is not new. Finding bluestone chips near the Cursus, Marcus Stone suggested a 'very early Bluestonehenge' had been dismantled there, or (echoing Herbert Stone) in Wales, and re-used at Stonehenge: *Stonehenge in the Light of Modern Research* (Salisbury, *c.* 1955), 9–11. Bernard Cornwell adopted this idea in his *Stonehenge: A Novel of 2000 BC*, where what is in effect the traditional Q and R Hole monument is found standing in Pembrokeshire and moved, stone by stone, to Stonehenge.

CHAPTER 6

1 *Science* 133 (1961), 1216–22.

2 Weight estimates for green oak calculated as for the timber circles at Durrington. See *Durrington Walls: Excavations 1966–1968*, by G. J. Wainwright & I. H. Longworth (London: Society of Antiquaries, 1971).

3 Cunnington 1935, 48–49. D. B. Arnot, *Empire Forestry Journal* 8 (1929), 233–37.

4 Harris 2019; Richards & Whitby 1997.

5 Parker Pearson 2012, 267.

6   There are holes carved out of the bedrock high at the statue quarry on Rapa Nui that seem to have served this purpose.

7   L.-M. Shillito, *Antiquity* 93 (2019), 1052–60. Richards & Whitby (1997) successfully greased a sledge for their concrete trilithon. E. Wright *et al.* suggest a pig-killing peak in autumn and winter (September–February): *Journal of Archaeological Science* 52 (2014), 497–514.

8   Richards 1990.

9   *Antiquity* 83 (2009), 23–39.

10 The project gave me my first cover story as editor of *British Archaeology* (73, 2003).

11 Abbott & Anderson-Whymark 2012. Imaging has already moved on: new scans will reveal more.

12 A. Thomas, in *The Ness of Brodgar: As it Stands*, ed. N. Card, M. Edmonds & A. Mitchell (Kirkwall: The Orcadian, 2020).

13 *Stonehenge*, which you can see at www.bbc.co.uk/programmes/ p0181bfw.

14 J. E. Garfitt, *Antiquity* 54 (1980), 142–44; Richards & Whitby 1997.

15 But fortunately not all: excavation and recording standards were far below what would be expected today, and a few remain for future research, as well as several pits from which stones have fallen.

16 For Chilmark stone in the pit for Stone 27 see the Ancient Monuments Board for England's report for 1964, Appendix A.

17 This stone was presumably not used to build Stonehenge because large pieces would have required quarrying from solid rock (as opposed to using natural slabs or boulders, in the raw or dressed), a practice not seen in Britain until Roman times.

18 Two good samples from old excavations, both around 2550 BC (and two others rejected), are a poor basis for dating Stonehenge. Otherwise, pending new excavation at the monument and accepting that the great village at Durrington Walls housed its builders, our best guide to when the sarsens were raised would be Durrington's settlement, henge and timber structure known as the South Circle (phase 2), all of which are radiocarbon dated to around 2475 BC. See Appendix, and Parker Pearson 2012.

19 S. Dewar, *Folklore* 77 (1966), 264–69.

20 *Archaeology of Tonga*, by W. C. McKern (Honolulu: Bernice P. Bishop Museum, 1929); the mound's size is not given, but one suspects it was significantly lower than the height of the stones. See also G. Clark & C. Reepmeyer, *Antiquity* 88 (2014), 1244–60. Trilithon symbolism offers endless possibilities. As I write, a new town is being built in Georgia, 'Designed for the film and creative industries... where

makers, thinkers and dreamers feel at home.' It is called Trilith: 'the three pillars' of 'storytelling, purpose-built places and emerging technology' (www.trilith.com).

21 Cummings & Richards 2021.

22 *Aku-Aku: The Secret of Easter Island*, by T. Heyerdahl (London: George Allen & Unwin, 1958), 142–49; Harris 2019, 103–9 and 217–31.

23 It has been suggested that outer faces were less well finished because that work could be done only once stones were standing: 'their backs (facing outwards) are either unmodified or have been dressed to about head-height only. When the sarsens lay in the dressing zone, the stone-dressers would have been unable to get at the stones' undersides' (Parker Pearson 2012, 251–52). The laser survey, however, showed that all upright circle and trilithon sarsens (bar Stones 28 and 29) are dressed the full heights of both faces (Abbott & Anderson-Whymark 2012).

24 *British Archaeology* 132 (2013), 6. These same marks had appeared in a dry summer in 1933 and can be seen in photos taken by the artist Paul Nash (and now in the collection of Tate Britain), but their significance was not realized at the time.

25 The widest gap in the circle is between Stones 1 and 30, around 1.4 m (4 ft 7 in.). If they could somehow be manoeuvred on their sides, the only upright trilithon stones thinner than this above ground are 56 (1 m or 3 ft 3 in.), 53 and 57 (both 1.2 m or 3 ft 11 in.). The average thickest point of the others is 1.6 m (5 ft 3 in.).

26 It is always said the Heelstone is undressed, but there is a small area of surface smoothing close to the ground on the southwest side, missed in the laser scanning because it was hidden by grass at the time.

27 Many ring plans are oval, egg-shaped or irregular. At 113 m (370 ft) across, Stanton Drew's circle leads Waun Mawn, the Ring of Brodgar in Orkney and two rings in Avebury, Wiltshire, all a little over 100 m (330 ft) (Avebury's largest, outer ring, and the UK's largest, around 330 m or 1,080 ft wide, follows an irregular ditch circuit). Stanton Drew, Brodgar and the Aubrey ring at Stonehenge (87 m or 285 ft) are enclosed by circular ditches and banks.

28 A recent press story suggested Stonehenge was built like Lego, but stones and bricks are different. In the latter studs fit with micro-precision into gaps between tubes and grip fast. In the former, a lintel's cup rests loosely over a stone's stud, and there is no hold other than friction and gravity.

29 Stone 122 (Atkinson 1979, 208).

30 This is a slightly simplified version of the standard history, which is based on poorly

understood archaeology. See Appendix.

31 It is one of the oddities of Stonehenge that this stone was immediately reburied after excavation in 1954. We have only a few snapshots to show us part of its form.

CHAPTER 7

1 *The Times*, 26 February 1958; Wheeler was Chairman of the board that advised the government about ancient monuments. An open Stonehenge is still remembered by many visitors today. Born in 1890, Wheeler had a right to the claim, but the site was fenced with a ticket gate in 1901 and a car park added in 1935: modern recollections reflect childhood priorities.

2 *Wiltshire Archaeological and Natural History Magazine* 95 (2002), 131–46.

3 *New Scientist*, 9 January 2001.

4 Some 45 stones (54%) have apparently not been moved and 39 have, counting fragments of a single stone as one (one half of Stone 55 has not been moved, for example, the other has, putting it among the 39). Barber (2014) provides an excellent history of Stonehenge restorations.

5 Information from Tim Darvill, who tells me the Ministry was so proud of these works that it filmed them in action.

6 Barber 2014; Chippindale 2004.

7 A decade or so before Wood's survey, Stukeley shows Stone 14 leaning against a bluestone. Stone 32, in the Bluestone Circle and now lying across part of Stone 150, is also shown standing by Wood and fallen by John Smith in his 1771 plan.

8 Parker Pearson *et al.* 2020, 174.

9 T. Darvill & G. Wainwright, *Antiquaries Journal* 89 (2009), 1–19.

10 Cleal *et al.* 1995, 431–35.

11 *Wiltshire Archaeological and Natural History Magazine* 106 (2013), 13–14.

12 See my *Digging up Britain* (London: Thames & Hudson, 2019), Chapter 6.

13 Wainwright's excavations at Durrington Walls recovered 80 times as much Grooved Ware as Beaker pottery, while at Stonehenge the pattern is reversed: Beaker sherds exceed Grooved Ware by 20 times.

14 T. Booth *et al.*, *Cambridge Archaeological Journal* 31 (2021), 1–22.

15 Pitts 2001, 255, 292–93.

16 S. Greaney *et al.*, *Proceedings of the Prehistoric Society* 86 (2020), 1–38.

17 The man's aDNA has not been sampled.

FURTHER READING

Abbott, M. and H. Anderson-Whymark, 2012. *Stonehenge Laser Scan: Archaeological Analysis Report*. Swindon: English Heritage.

Atkinson, R. J. C., 1979. *Stonehenge* (2nd ed.). Harmondsworth: Penguin.

Barber, M., 2014. *'Restoring' Stonehenge 1881–1939*. Portsmouth: English Heritage.

Bowden, M., S. Soutar, D. Field and M. Barber, 2015. *The Stonehenge Landscape: Analysing the Stonehenge World Heritage Site*. Swindon: Historic England.

Burl, A., 2006. *Stonehenge: A New History of the World's Greatest Stone Circle*. London: Constable & Robinson.

Burl, A. and N. Mortimer (eds), 2005. *Stukeley's 'Stonehenge': An Unpublished Manuscript 1721–1724*. New Haven and London: Yale University Press.

Cleal, R., K. Walker and R. Montague, 1995. *Stonehenge in its Landscape: Twentieth-century Excavations*. London: English Heritage.

Chippindale, C., 2012. *Stonehenge Complete* (4th ed.). London: Thames & Hudson.

Cummings, V. and C. Richards, 2021. *Monuments in the Making: Raising the Great Dolmens in Early Neolithic Northern Europe*. Oxford: Windgather Press.

Cunnington, R. H., 1935. *Stonehenge and its Date*. London: Methuen & Co.

Darvill, T., 2006. *Stonehenge: The Biography of a Landscape*. Stroud: Tempus Publishing.

Field, D., H. Anderson-Whymark, N. Linford, M. Barber, M. Bowden, P. Linford and P. Topping, 2015. 'Analytical surveys of Stonehenge and its environs, 2009–2013: Part 2 – the stones.' *Proceedings of the Prehistoric Society* 81, 125–48.

Field, D. and T. Pearson, 2010. *Stonehenge, Amesbury, Wiltshire: Archaeological Survey Report*. Swindon: English Heritage.

Harris, B., 2019. 'Landscapes of Labour: A Quantitative Study of Earth-Moving and Stone-Shifting in Prehistoric Northern Wessex'. PhD thesis, UCL.

Hill, R., 2008. *Stonehenge*. London: Profile Books.

Johnson, A., 2008. *Solving Stonehenge: The New Key to an Ancient Enigma*. London: Thames & Hudson.

Long, W., 1876. *Stonehenge and its Barrows*. Devizes: Wiltshire Archaeological and Natural History Society.

McOmish, D., D. Field and G. Brown, 2002. *The Field Archaeology of the Salisbury Plain Training Area*. Swindon: English Heritage.

Parker Pearson, M., 2012. *Stonehenge: Exploring the Greatest Stone Age Mystery*. London and New York: Simon & Schuster.

Parker Pearson, M., J. Pollard, C. Richards, J. Thomas, C. Tilley and K. Welham, 2020. *Stonehenge for the Ancestors. Part 1: Landscape and Monuments*. Leiden: Sidestone Press (free access at www.sidestone.com/books/stonehenge-for-the-ancestors-part-1).

Pitts, M., 2001. *Hengeworld* (2nd ed.). London: Arrow Books.

Pryor, F., 2016. *Stonehenge: The Story of a Sacred Landscape*. London: Head of Zeus.

Richards, J., 1990. *The Stonehenge Environs Project*. London: English Heritage.

Richards, J., 2017. *Stonehenge: The Story So Far* (2nd ed.). Swindon: Historic England.

Richards, J. and M. Whitby, 1997. 'The engineering of Stonehenge.' *Proceedings of the British Academy* 92, 231–56.

Stone, E. H., 1924. *The Stones of Stonehenge: A Full Description of the Structure and of its Outworks*. London: Robert Scott.

Stukeley, W., 1740. *Stonehenge: A Temple Restor'd to the British Druids*. London: W. Innys and R. Manby.

A valuable resource for Stonehenge spotters is *The Stones of Stonehenge* (www.stonesofstonehenge.org.uk), a website by Simon Banton that has a page of photos of every megalith. For introductions to the Neolithic in Britain see:

Miles, D., 2016. *The Tale of the Axe: How the Neolithic Revolution Transformed Britain*. London: Thames & Hudson.

Ray, K. and J. Thomas, 2018. *Neolithic Britain: The Transformation of Social Worlds*. Oxford: Oxford University Press.

ACKNOWLEDGMENTS

Like Stonehenge, from a personal perspective at least, this book has been long in the making. I was at school when I first visited the site, bought the official guide I still have and, as we all did then, climbed over fallen stones – though my main memory is hearing football goals announced over the tannoy during a military display at nearby Larkhill: it was the day of the World Cup final in 1966. I didn't know it then, but Richard Atkinson had finished his major run of Stonehenge excavations two years before. Later, Chris Potter taught me A-level archaeology at Ardingly College (my first sight of Wiltshire's other great stone circle, at Avebury, was through the window of Chris's Sunbeam Alpine sports car). I was inspired then, reading Richard's book about Stonehenge, to think it would be fun to be an archaeologist. My colleagues and I entered Stonehenge archaeology at the closing of one era and the opening of another.

My first excavation there, in 1979, came about by accident rather than design. But from that moment, with the realization that behind its public facade lay a world of untested assumptions and under-researched stories, the monument's intellectual challenges have never lost their fascination for me. So first I'd like to thank the archaeologists and scientists who have shared their journeys of discovery, and done so much to improve our understanding of Stonehenge and its times. When I last wrote about it in a book (*Hengeworld*, first published in 2000), I drew on a substantial monograph which had recently appeared and which presented, mostly as revelations, a full analysis of all the 20th-century excavations at Stonehenge. At the time one of its editors, Ros Cleal, told me that archaeologists never address the question visitors always ask: how was it built? She was right, and this is my attempt at an answer.

I have tried this now (academics will recognize it as more of a giant research proposal than a construction manual) because we are approaching a second watershed, with the near culmination of decades of new projects. These include excavations at and around the stones and at stone sources in Wales (2009–21), comprehensive research into bluestone characteristics and origins (2010–21), detailed discussions of Stonehenge history and chronology (2012–20), the first comprehensive study of the megaliths' shape and surface finish (2012), and the first large geological study of the sarsens (2020–21). There is more to come – work continues on both bluestones and sarsen, reports on other excavations are anticipated, and there is plenty to inspire new research – but the published information is more than enough to support a new book.

My special debts to Tim Darvill and Mike Parker Pearson, Marcus Abbott and Hugo Anderson-Whymark, Richard Bevins and Rob Ixer, and Dave Nash and Katy Whitaker, will be clear from the text. I first met Tim and Mike when we were students (Mike was a volunteer at my 1979 dig, and I joined him in 2008 when we re-excavated an Aubrey Hole), and we have enjoyed many shared discussions and site visits. Marcus and Hugo's heroic work on the megalithic laser study has been inspirational, and it was good to share a Stonehenge visit with them. More than anything, perhaps, it is Richard and Rob's research (bluestones), and most recently that of Dave Nash and Katy Whitaker (sarsen), that has made this book even possible: we can get nowhere with Stonehenge if we don't understand its raw materials. Martyn Barber's pioneering research into the site's recent history is important, as are Ron Adams and Barney Harris's studies of contemporary and experimental megalith moving; I thank Ron for supplying photos from his fieldwork. In this context, I will be ever grateful to Pauline Hubner, the book's picture researcher, for unwittingly leading me to Ursula Graham Bower's under-appreciated work in Assam. I would also like to thank Susan Greaney, Heather Sebire and their colleagues at English Heritage, who battle for the interests of Stonehenge in the face of little public understanding of the challenges they face, and always welcome researchers at the stones.

My editor at Thames & Hudson, Ben Hayes, has always been supportive and seemed always to be there, as the book grew from my initial idea of 40,000 words and no illustrations (it'll be done in three months, I assured my family) to what you see now. Ben Plumridge was the perfect copy editor, noting my omissions and inconsistencies, of which any survivors are of course my responsibility. It is, again, a pleasure to work with Thames & Hudson, who somehow maintain traditional values while around them publishing is in turmoil.

My wife and daughter have known my Stonehenge interest as long as they have known me, and I owe them both huge thanks for their patience and for their insistence that not everyone shares my obsessions. If this book can be enjoyed by anyone not entirely smitten by Stonehenge, much of that will be due to Nicky's editing and Mia's questioning. Thank you all.

SOURCES OF ILLUSTRATIONS

Laser-scanned megalith data from Abbott & Anderson Whymark 2012/ Historic England/ArcHeritage 180 (below), 183, 192

Photo © David Abram **I**

Photo © Ron Adams 170, **XVII**

Alamy Stock Photo PA Images 62

Photo Arthur ApSimon/Mike Pitts 40

From D. B. Arnot, *Empire Forestry Journal*, Vol. 8, No. 2 (December, 1929), pp. 233–237 150

Image © Ashmolean Museum, University of Oxford: Alan Sorrell, Blue Stones Being Transported by Raft (714) 82

Photo courtesy Dave Buckley 173

Photo English Heritage/Sam Frost 67

Photo © Christine Faulkner 41

Photo © Jason Hilton 42

Historic England 181, 197, 198 (above and below), 203, 204

The Kon-Tiki Museum, Oslo, courtesy Thor Heyerdahl Archives, photo Erling Schjerven 172

Collection Nationaal Museum van Wereldculturen, Netherlands: Photo Ludwig Borutta, *c.* 1915 (Coll. No. TM-10000952) 97 (above); Photo J. Borutta, *c.* 1915 (Coll. no. A169-24) 97 (below)

Photo © Pitt Rivers Museum, University of Oxford 100, 101, 113

Photo © Mike Pitts 2, 29, 31, 37, 44, 64, 68, 72, 83 (above), 83 (below), 95, 98 (above), 99, 105, 107, 108, 109, 110, 166, 182, 184 (above), 209, 210, **III, IV, V, VII, VIII, IX, X, XI, XII, XIII, XIV, XV, XVIII, XIX, XX, XXI, XXII, XXIII, XXV** (above right and left), **XXVI, XXVII, XXVIII**

By Mike Pitts 32, 48, 55, 87, 115, 116, 122, 146, 148, 164 (above), 165, 176, 184 (below), 186, 188, 201; adapted from Cleal *et al.* 1995 10, 124, 130, 131, 194; contours after Field & Pearson 2010 189; sarsen data after N. E. King 1968 58; redrawn from Office of Works records 180; data from Parker Pearson *et al.* 2020 134

Courtesy Project Wildscape, photo Henry Chapman 98 (below)

The Salisbury Museum **XXIV**

Science Photo Library/© John Sibbick 164 (below)

Photo © Adam Stanford 74, 118

Photo © Tara Steimer-Herbet **XVI**

Wellcome Collection, London 13, **XXV** (above left)

Photo © Wessex Archaeology 128

Young Gallery Salisbury: Edgar Barclay Collection **VI**

INDEX

For Mia and Nicky

Frontispiece: Stonehenge from the northeast, approaching up the Avenue earthwork.

Quotation from Sir Antony Gormley on p. 6 from interview with Mike Pitts (2021).

First published in the United Kingdom in 2022 by
Thames & Hudson Ltd, 181A High Holborn, London WC1V 7QX

First published in the United States of America in 2022 by
Thames & Hudson Inc., 500 Fifth Avenue, New York, New York 10110

British Library Cataloguing-in-Publication Data
A catalogue record for this book is available from the British Library

Library of Congress Control Number 2021943303

ISBN 978-0-500-02419-5

Printed and bound in Slovenia by DZS-Grafik d.o.o.

MIX
Paper from
responsible sources
FSC® C112556
FSC
www.fsc.org

Be the first to know about our new releases,
exclusive content and author events by visiting
thamesandhudson.com
thamesandhudsonusa.com
thamesandhudson.com.au